ACADEMY AWARD–WINNING ACTRESS TURNED BESTSELLING AUTHOR SHIRLEY MACLAINE DAZZLES US WITH THE SUBJECT SHE KNOWS MOST INTIMATELY—HOLLYWOOD. IN THE MEMOIR THAT MADE HEADLINES, SHE TALKS ABOUT . . .

**Her wildly unconventional marriage to Steve Parker**

"As soon as [we met], I knew my life was to take a new course. . . . Our connection had the shock of destiny to it. . . . There was nothing I could have done to alter or avoid the experience we were intended to have together."

**Her friendship with the Clan—especially Frank Sinatra**

"I was comfortable and friendly being around the guys in the group because I was perceived by most of them as a mascot. I was the only woman they allowed in the house, but that was because there had been a kind of communal decision made that I wasn't really a girl—I was a pal, maybe even one of the boys."

**The movie she made with Dean Martin and Jerry Lewis**

"Dean, not Jerry, was the funny one to me. His humor was subtle, spontaneous—a result of the moment. Jerry's was brilliant, but usually premeditated."

**Please turn the page for more. . . .**

P9-DOE-195

**Her love affair with Robert Mitchum**
"He saw himself as a common stiff, born to be lonely. . . . I willingly fell into the role of rescuer, saving him from himself."

**Her take on Hollywood lives**
"I don't know many really happy people in Hollywood. There is always that *look* lurking behind the eyes of the accomplished. It's the look of 'lostness.' . . . Any one of them would be nostalgic for the days of struggle."

**Her Oscar-winning film, *Terms of Endearment***
"I began the scene—I was on the telephone with Emma while Jack slept. Suddenly, under the covers, I felt a tongue on my ankle. It went up my leg and then it stopped. . . . I realized it was Debra under the covers."

**And much, much more . . .**

# My Lucky Stars

## A HOLLYWOOD MEMOIR

## Shirley MacLaine

Bantam Books

New York   Toronto   London   Sydney   Auckland

MY LUCKY STARS

A Bantam Book

PUBLISHING HISTORY
Bantam hardcover edition published June 1995
Bantam paperback edition / December 1996

ISBN 0-553-57233-4

Published simultaneously in the United States and Canada

Bantam Books are published by Bantam Books, a division of Bantam Doubleday Dell Publishing Group, Inc. Its trademark, consisting of the words "Bantam Books" and the portrayal of a rooster, is Registered in U.S. Patent and Trademark Office and in other countries. Marca Registrada. Bantam Books, 1540 Broadway, New York, New York 10036.

PRINTED IN THE UNITED STATES OF AMERICA

OPM     0 9 8 7 6 5 4 3 2 1

FOR SACHI
With all my love

AND TO PETER
For being there

BY SHIRLEY MACLAINE

"Don't Fall Off the Mountain"
You Can Get There from Here
Out on a Limb
Dancing in the Light
It's All in the Playing
Going Within
Dance While You Can

The great mystery is not that we should have been thrown down here at random between the profusion of matter and that of the stars; it is that from our very prison we should draw, from our own selves, images powerful enough to deny our nothingness.

André Malraux
*La Condition Humaine*
("Man's Fate")

# Contents

# The Films of
# Shirley MacLaine

The Trouble with Harry (1955)
Artists and Models (1955)
Around the World in Eighty Days (1956)
The Sheepman (1958)
The Matchmaker (1958)
Hot Spell (1958)
Some Came Running (1959)
Ask Any Girl (1959)
Career (1959)
Ocean's Eleven (1960)
Can-Can (1960)
The Apartment (1960)
All in a Night's Work (1961)
Two Loves (1961)
The Children's Hour (1962)
My Geisha (1962)
Two for the Seesaw (1962)
Irma La Douce (1963)
What a Way to Go! (1964)
The Yellow Rolls-Royce (UK) (1964)
John Goldfarb Please Come Home (1965)
Gambit (1966)

Woman Times Seven (1967)
The Bliss of Mrs. Blossom (UK) (1968)
Sweet Charity (1969)
Two Mules for Sister Sara (1970)
Desperate Characters (1971)
The Possession of Joel Delaney (1972)
The Year of the Woman (documentary, 1973)
The Other Half of the Sky (documentary, 1975)
The Turning Point (1977)
Being There (1979)
A Change of Seasons (1980)
Loving Couples (1980)
Terms of Endearment (1983)
Cannonball Run II (1984)
Madame Sousatzka (1988)
Steel Magnolias (1989)
Waiting for the Light (1990)
Postcards from the Edge (1990)
Defending Your Life (1991)
Used People (1992)
Wrestling Ernest Hemingway (1993)
Guarding Tess (1994)
Mrs. Winterbourne (1996)
Evening Star (1996)

# Preface
# STAR FALLOUT

*W*e live in a world of images. They bombard us twenty-four hours a day. If not in the newspapers or on our television screens, then most certainly in our heads. The birthplace of many of those images is Hollywood, where artists create the illusion of infinite possibilities. Hollywood dangles golden fruit on branches that are out of reach for so many, yet it also inspires hope and optimism.

The image of Hollywood itself is that of a universe of stars, a great factory of power with rotating constellations of success and failure, with times and tides of creative fulfillment as well as of humiliation. Now, as I sit and reflect on myself and on the reality of what happened during my years in Hollywood, I want to go behind the image that I was part of, that I drew to myself. The reality of Hollywood is that every person creates his or her own image, and in the process can so easily be exalted or ruined, held aloft in the light or burned out by his or her own luminosity.

Once I hit the golden shores of the American Dream, no matter where I went or what I did, Hollywood was the place I always returned to. It was the place that made me feel I could walk on water—if I knew where the sand bars were. It taught me discernment. It glistened in the dark like a tinsel township that sailed so fast and used so much of my fuel, I often felt I was struggling toward a future that was already the past. It has all been so swift, yet so slow—slow in the struggle to achieve perfection, fast when it really went wrong . . . but always so en-lightening . . . so meant-to-be.

Hollywood was the land where I did any damn thing I wanted because, more than any place on earth, it offered me the opportunity to create my own reality: the reality of success; the reality of failure. It taught me that success was always temporary, and failure, a lesson about self. It taught me that winning and losing were essentially the same and the secret was to treat each with equal detach-ment. I ventured out in the real world, collected experi-ences, cultural artifacts, friends from faraway places with strange-sounding names, and returned to Hollywood a deeper, more knowledgeable person who sometimes tried to incorporate what I had learned on the screen. Hollywood was the place where I utilized anything I thought I was, and explored so much of what I was afraid I was not.

Hollywood was a playground, with emotions, people, audiences, and costars as my playmates. Whatever I could paint with my characters on celluloid I felt I could identify in life, and vice versa.

When I was younger and in the thick of the experi-ence, Hollywood didn't seem so cosmically miraculous to me. It was play, definitely, but it was also hard work. I was learning. I was struggling to stay afloat, to understand what was happening to me. I had fun and I had depression, oh yes, but I didn't take the time to revel completely in the fullness of either. I was too busy regarding myself—keeping an eye on the future and looking over my shoulder at the past—to understand the miracle of the breathtaking creativity around me. Now, in retrospect, how I wish I had appreciated the real reason for Hollywood's magic . . . the creative people. The extraordinary individuality of those talented human beings who surrounded me at every level, some of whom I had loved and admired since childhood. I wish I had lived more in the moments of their laughter, their love, and their turmoil. I wish so much now that I had seized the moments then to fully appreciate them.

Only now as I write this do I realize how much I missed of their true meaning. It is a cliché that youth is wasted on the young, but a true one. We think so much about ourselves, not realizing that we are truly mirrored in the people around us.

So as I recollect my feelings and celebrate, with tardiness, part of my forty years in Hollywood, I am curious, even surprised, as I wander around in my memory, at the people whom I feel the need to dwell upon, to understand, and resolve my feelings for. All observations are clues to oneself, and I realize now how important it is to take myself seriously in observing others. Why do *these* people emerge from my memories as leading players in my play? Because they set me on my course and they taught me many things. When I was a young girl in Hollywood, they were the people destiny provided as my guides. And later, as the years passed, these people were my mirrors. I feel profoundly lucky to have known them. I want to thank these stars who were lucky for me, who enriched and troubled my life, who brightened my days and my nights. These people who were so generous with the expression of their hopes and fears and joys and even neuroses, because now I see that they served as reflections for some of my own problems. I celebrate all of them, these children of creative genius who came to light up and reflect the world. These people who struggled with themselves and persevered, demonstrating the need all of us have to know ourselves better. These people who were responsible for showing me how to love and be more understanding.

# My Lucky Stars

# 1

# THE QUESTION

Not long ago I was having lunch in New York with a friend when he asked me a question that set me to thinking deeply.

"How did you manage," he said, "after so many years in the minefields of Hollywood, to retain the capacity to have your feelings hurt?"

The question stunned me. I couldn't answer.

My friend pressed on. "I want to know," he said, "why you haven't become one of those well-functioning *thing* people? The ones with shrewd dead eyes who no longer live behind their faces; the ones who operate successfully but can't feel pain anymore. One of those people who got what they wanted from Hollywood, but never knew what they wanted from themselves. How come that didn't happen to you?"

I sat in silence. I couldn't reply. Why was it good that

I could still have my feelings hurt? It was awful. It made me angry and sometimes cruel. I couldn't simply be hurt and leave it at that. So why was that praiseworthy? I became confused, left the restaurant, and went back to my hotel. For a long time I sat by the window and gazed out at Central Park. I had begun my career in New York. I was from the East Coast, yet Hollywood was now my home. In every way. And it had been for more than forty years. I did my first picture when I was twenty. But was my friend right? Was I really not jaded, dead-eyed, and shrewd? There was so much neither he nor anyone really knew. I had been naive to the point of denial. Was that because I never really allowed Hollywood to hurt me? Had I encased myself in a pleasant bubble of light while denying the darkness outside? Had I chosen to be unaware of the chunks Hollywood and some of the people around me had bitten from my heart because to acknowledge the truth would extinguish my enthusiasm?

My mind spun.

Another friend had accused me once of being relentlessly optimistic. My daughter had said I trusted too much, purposefully ignoring other people's demons and my own as well. Now, as I stared out the window, I understood what she had meant. I had denied so much in my personal life, but that was what had allowed me to go on. Yet I was fully aware that most people in Hollywood were motivated by their own internal demons. The kings and queens of power held on to those demons as an identification. Neurosis was a protective coverlet a great deal of the time, and provided the impulse for their ambition. They were quick to reject before suffering rejection from others. No, I knew Hollywood could be a torture chamber of rejection. It could shred you, bleed you, tinker with your sanity, leave you torn and tattered along the highway of the misbegotten. And now, as I thought about my friend's question, I remembered all the times people had said to me, "How come you keep popping back up again?" Was my longevity the result of having experienced Hollywood at arm's length? Or had I taken pain and turned it into something else? I never wanted to adopt a mask. I feared that my face would grow into it.

A mask was too confining anyway. I wanted, I *needed* to be free . . . free of any image I would create. Free of dependency upon it, free of committing myself completely to it or to anything else for that matter . . . there it was . . . I wanted to be free of the long-term soul-searing pain that only comes from committing completely to something. So as snow began to fall on the park and my mind whirled backward in time, I thought, My friend is only partially right about me. Yes, I can still be hurt by Hollywood, but no, not deeply because I never honestly committed myself to the requirements of the town in the first place.

Instead I think I regarded Hollywood as a game. A game of expression, a game of humor, of love, of power, money, and fame. A game of created illusion where pain itself would be a choice. To me Hollywood was a place to learn, a test site for my identity, a new land where I could experience anything and evolve from it. But the game that I played exacted a high personal price. From the moment I came to Hollywood, I knew I would never be from Richmond, Virginia, again.

People in Hollywood are usually sophisticated in wading through certain shoals of human behavior, inept and maladroit in others. Human behavior is, after all, our business, our work, our survival: The more we understand its underbelly, the better we can play our parts. But more to the point, the more we understand *ourselves,* the better we are at our work. This is not an easy task because we so often enjoy playing other people in order to avoid who we are. Most of us have had therapy and, for the last ten years, have begun to understand that we are spiritual as well as physical and mental beings. This helps. We are becoming more and more conversant with the "Karma" of our behavior. Therefore, with our growing spiritual sophistication we understand the profound necessity to take complete responsibility for our words and actions. Well, maybe not *complete,* because we are also possessed of insecurities, envy, and jealousy; within our own creative community, we are often suspicious of each other. Therefore, even among friends, guarding the safety of one's own heart and position is paramount. Often we feel reluctant not only to allow our hearts to be opened and examined, but also reluctant to see others put themselves in the same position. We know that sharing that kind of intimacy can lead to the agony of feeling used—and of using. Yet it becomes excruciatingly clear, all too soon, in this land of *reel* life, that if we can know and understand the murky depths of our coworkers, we have a fallback position for our own ultimate survival. Knowledge of self . . . *numero uno.* Knowledge of others a close second.

People in show business call everyone else "civilians." That's because we think no one else is hip enough to understand the depth of emotion in any given situation. We are an insecure yet arrogant breed. We can't believe that any other line of work so challenges the human heart, its terrors and demons, or indeed its joys and scaled heights of ecstasy. So within our community—our social lives, our relationships, our problems with our children, our attempts to sustain friendship, even the way we conduct meetings, script conferences, and character-development talks—Hollywood people tend to revel in the belief that we are more free and more open and more explorative about ourselves in relation to our own product (ourselves) than, say, a CEO at General Motors or a guy selling baby food or tract houses. *And* we know that even with all our explorations of self and others we tend to manipulate what we find to suit our own individual needs. Sometimes we don't even know we're doing it, but we are. Manipulation is often our livelihood, our technique of choice in order to succeed at being noticed, acknowledged, and loved. Like Oscar Wilde's definition of a cynic, we sometimes know the price of everything and the value of nothing.

From the time I was six, movies have been important to me. I'm not sure why. I would sit for hours in the movie house, becoming the characters who shone down from the screen. I loved the feeling of being totally immersed in the story, the relationships, the drama.

Perhaps the reason was as simple as wanting to get out of the house. Or perhaps early on I had the feeling that there was, as Walt Whitman wrote, "a multitude of humanity within me," and I enjoyed identifying with the multitude on the screen.

My brother, Warren, and I went to the movies every Saturday and stayed for as long as we could sit there. And sometimes sitting in the movie house wasn't enough. Sometimes we would go "behind" the movie house and listen to the dialogue of pictures that were particularly horror-filled, like *Frankenstein Meets the Wolfman* or the torture scenes from *The Purple Heart*. Perhaps, symbolically, we viewed these films from behind so that we could surprise-attack anything that frightened us. Perhaps we needed the option of recreating the truth the way we wanted it to be.

This business of rewriting the truth, of creating the reality we desired, is of course at the bottom of everything. I think I was interested in Hollywood so early because I knew that every day of my life I was doing what they were doing every day of their lives up there on the screen. "Acting"—we were all acting. Only the movie actors knew how to do it best. Acting in relationships, acting within families, acting in jobs. It seemed to me that we were all acting out our lives according to what was in our own best interests. I know I learned very early to act my life according to how much in or out of control I was in any given situation. If I wanted something from my father, I would put my little feet together pigeon-toe style, tilt my head, and smile. I got what I wanted every time. If I wanted a boyfriend, I'd charm then withdraw, or even use my vulnerability to seem helpless and needy so that he could define a role for himself in our relationship. I acted my life very often according to my need to be loved. Not so different from how Hollywood works.

In my particular family, we were very aware, very early, that we needed to learn how to act in order to get attention. After all, Mother was a teacher of dramatics and a reader of poetry and an actress herself in little-theater work. And Dad was a musician, a teacher, and an actor of supremely high standing in the living room. They both had personalities like very subtle vaudevillians; therefore, finding out "how it was done" became a high priority very early in our lives. How else could we compete with them for attention?

That must be true of every child, basically. But I think Hollywood's luminaries begin to practice the art of being loved at a very young age. I can't say that I wasn't loved as a child—not at all. I remember feeling temperamental, though, and ignored. I used to scream and yell and bite the back of my hand until it bled before I could get a rise out of my mother. She existed in her own world of forbearance, exuding patience and tolerance almost to the point of paralysis, it seemed. She was Canadian and not at all demonstrative with her feelings. So as I erupted from time to time in order to arouse her passion, I saw that it required ever increasing levels of drama on my part to elicit a response. This was frustrating, to say the least, until finally she quietly consulted the pediatrician, who simply recommended she turn the hose on me to calm me down. I never felt any of *her* come through that water though. Of course, I wanted a demonstration of love, but I would have settled for some passionate anger from her, or hysterical frustration; even sadism would have sent a tidbit of emotional spontaneity traveling through those harsh droplets of water. But there was nothing, just a forceful spray that was sometimes cold, but not much else. Just the advice from the doctor once removed.

My dad internalized most of his tumultuous emotions and suppressed them with liquor. There were some dramas with him though. Every now and then he'd come home drunk, set something on fire, leave again until the wee hours, then return and sleep till noon. But at least he was more broad stroked in his emotions. I knew what he was feeling. He'd curse at the communists and bemoan the "niggers" who ruined his lawn and often I'd see him reduced to tears in front of the television set at two o'clock in the morning while they played "The Star-spangled Banner."

But for the most part, my childhood was painfully regular (which is to say, probably dysfunctional), a breeding ground for the emotional terrain of show business.

People in Hollywood understand that the need to be loved and to have attention paid is fundamental in their lives. We have not put these childish demands aside and "grown up." Instead we've made a business out of it. A business and an art. What an impossible combination. We have forever banished ourselves from being regular. Regular people decided to grow up, or they found a safe place, like a corporation, where they still had an external structure, a mother and a father, so to some extent they *never* had to grow up. In either case, they became "civilians." We reflections of the silver screen remained in the ranks of those who are emotionally needy, forever dedicated to getting attention, to being loved however and whenever we desire. We make "pretend" real and have from the beginning.

In my case I pretended that I was Rita Hayworth. God how I loved her long red, wavy hair, and her dancing, and her tempestuous ways. I had long, wavy red hair like she did. And I was a dancer too. It wasn't such a stretch. I wanted to be alluring and vulnerable like Rita, because even though she could be difficult and was sometimes battered and bruised, she ended up being loved.

I adored Eleanor Powell's tap dancing because my father said she was the best at it. And if I learned to whirl and tap dance too, then he would love me.

I loved Fred Astaire because he could do anything with props and I was forever juggling something when I played.

All of these stars accomplished what I longed to do. And somehow, way back then, I knew there was a science to it, a well-schooled glorification of oneself—playing in the right light, having beautifully coiffed hair, teeth that sparkled, and shoes that clicked on the pavement. The science of perfection. The gods and goddesses were perfect even in their dishevelment. They were perfect in their anguish. They were perfect in their reactions to their traumas. It wasn't like my life, which was okay and pleasant enough, but was somehow only lived and not observed and celebrated.

So, when I first came to Hollywood, still in my teens, and shook hands with my beloved Clark Gable, and noticed that the cuffs on his shirts were frayed; or when I turned around to meet my idol, Alan Ladd, and had to lower my eyes two feet in order to see his face because he was so short; or when I met my favorite, Doris Day, and saw that her eyes were really too close together and her freckles were more prominent than the ones I hated on my own face, I began to realize that the queens and kings of my illusions were only people just like me.

I had sat mesmerized by these people for so many years. That they were actually human beings was a swift shock to my system, almost beyond my comprehension.

In the absence of spontaneously expressed feelings in our family home, I had erected fantasy perfection for my idols. They were not supposed to be regular. They were not supposed to feel, or hurt, or cry—not for real. They were perfect. So the expectations I had visited upon them were not fair. Also I came to see that they suffered from Hollywood's most common psychological sickness . . . *undeservability*. We devote our lives and energy to being noticed and then suffer from feeling we don't deserve it because we believe we can't truly deliver what is expected of us.

I remember the environment of being a new star in Hollywood, full of my own anxieties about undeserved attention. I had devoted my life and energy to being noticed, only to find that I was afraid I wouldn't live up to what was expected of me. I didn't want to be served, so much. I didn't want the assistants to bring me lunch or the wardrobe girls to shop for me. I was not comfortable that the state of my well-being attracted so much attention. Whether that was because I had come from

the world of ballet, where everything was a private institutionalized struggle, or whether it was because I had
worked so long on Broadway, where sweat and discipline
were rewarded more by direct praise than by attention
and pampering, or whether it was because I, personally,
insisted on remaining free from being enclosed in a
prison of privilege, I didn't feel like being singled out
and put on a pedestal. The height was too rarefied for
breathing, the fall, when it came, too far. But as everything in our lives relates to childhood conditioning, I
think I found myself in a position of finally garnering
attention, and as my mother cast a weary but demanding
look in my direction, I found that I feared I had wasted
her time with my insistent temperament. I was afraid I
basically had nothing to say.

I remember the class distinctions of the old days. On a
set the makeup people, the hair people, the costume
people stayed to themselves and rarely associated with
"star" people. I was continually crossing over those
lines, usually to be admonished by a production manager
or an assistant director who, for some reason, didn't like
it. So I'd go back to my trailer confused. I needed to ask
inhabitants of the real-people world about their lives.
The real people were the ones I identified with. The
stars were idols who possessed secrets of perfection I
knew nothing about.

And I didn't like it when the real people fell silent at a
producer's approach. Early on I perceived a subtle fear
in their faces, a kind of blank-eyed expression of concern
that the higher-ups, "above the line"—the director,
writers, actors—might not be happy with something. It
was the kind of subtle fear I had as an unrecognized
child. The better part of valor would be to have no
opinion rather than risk disagreement, because disagreement meant time, and time was money, and it was

therefore all so wearisome. So unless a real person was willing to go to the mat and be fired out of principle, those production people usually swallowed their differences and "went along." That didn't mean they refrained from airing their feelings among themselves. Sometimes I overheard what they really thought of me or others, only to have to deal with their hypocrisy later on. A set at any given time could be so golden-threaded in its web of subtle deceit that Pinocchio would have felt right at home. But their personal service to a star was out of the fabled French courts, and most of the time I think they meant it. Of course they were expected to serve us, but they genuinely seemed to love and enjoy us lords and ladies of the silver screen. I, in the meantime, felt caught in the conflict between being real and being reel.

The real people could often be quite insistent about what they thought we should look like. Sometimes I felt they were changing my face, my hair, the contours of my body, just because they needed to pull a power trip. If I refused a suggestion, they'd say "fine"—and sigh with deep distaste. They'd then go to the above-the-line "reel" people and protest, with discretion of course, that I had no concept of what was right for the screen.

That was when my survival instincts surfaced. It didn't matter to me what either set of jokers thought. I was going to do it my way. I became aware early on that rebellion and refusal were good attributes. Otherwise, I'd get lost in the conflict of other people's perception of me. The muddled hierarchy of the gods and goddesses, of the people above and below the line, and just the whole business of contrived fantasy made me restless and impatient.

It was a very difficult experience to come from the staccato-paced, hardworking world of ballet and Broadway to the elongated time frame of a Hollywood set, with all its waiting around while your every need—emotional, cosmetic, physical, or even sexual—was attended to in detail. I was taught to come prepared completely. I was a disciplined personality because of my background. My dancing/ballet days informed my value system.

For example, the first day of my first film, *The Trouble with Harry,* for Hitchcock, I had learned the entire script. My lines and everyone else's. I didn't realize that wasn't necessary. When the soundman asked me how far I wanted to go in the first scene, I said, "All of it." He proceeded to lay out fifteen pages of script around his sound equipment. They made a lot of noise.

Hitch walked on the set and just laughed. He was used to filming a few lines at a time. I was schooled to be ready for anything and everything.

Therefore, I can see today with so much more clarity why some young stars who make it quickly, without having any previous training relating to personal discipline and struggle, find themselves behaving with temperamental arrogance born out of self-loathing because they are paid more tribute than they feel they're worth.

We feel we're commissioned with the task of being the expressers and caretakers and emulators of human emotions when we're not even sure of what we ourselves feel. We try to identify with characters we would like to be because we're not sure of who we are, or we play characters we're glad we've escaped from being, and in the end we've turned ourselves inside out in our subservience to what Rodgers and Hammerstein called the "Big, Black Giant." We know that our very souls are being judged by that collective, unseen, observing power in the darkness out there. That silent dark giant plagues our nights and shadows our days as we go through the trials of satisfying its hunger, its needs, its desires, and its prurient interests.

That Big, Black Giant is our lord and master and we never know how it will react. It is the parent from whom we never received approval. It is the jury we will testify before for the rest of our days.

We're desperate to be noticed by them, we hunger to be acknowledged by them, yet the more they notice us, the more we feel invaded. The more we're acknowledged, the less we feel we deserve it. The more we're loved, the harder it is for us to accept it. The more they trust us, the more we distrust ourselves. This dance between those of us who create movies and those whom we long to please becomes a mirroring. We are them. They are us. They see themselves in us. We try to become what we see in them, until the mirroring of our common emotions becomes clear. Our secrets are exposed and we are One. The collective parent and the needy child continue the dance together.

Perhaps because I don't want to dwell on the pain, the memories of my Hollywood come as quick and intensely flashed pictures in my brain, like a Braverman documentary telling the story of forty years in ten seconds. The DeMille gate at Paramount, the Tudor style buildings that housed the makeup and hairdressing departments, where early morning confidences were kept under wraps as we secretly quelled our fears before the nine o'clock ready-on-the-set deadline. My darling Frank Westmore, my makeup man for so many years, used to wrestle me into the chair because, out of a flippant anxiety, I couldn't sit still. He said he'd make me look great because he'd learned everything he knew from making up a monkey's ass. I never let him have more than twenty minutes to do his job well. I just couldn't sit still. I still can't. And although I knew it was important to stay in my key light on the set, I didn't really care that much. What a delightful unconcern when you're young. With age you are careful where you sit in a restaurant!

Frank Westmore used to tell me that would happen. Then he'd say, "Just keep movin', baby, they'll never notice what you look like."

Now, as I think about Frank, I'll never forgive myself for not taking more time to visit him in the hospital when he had his first heart attack during our location shoot for *My Geisha* in Japan. Should I have demanded time off to fulfill a humane obligation even though it would cost the production thousands of dollars to wait for me? It's a dilemma I never solved in all my years in the movie business. I was schooled to be a professional regardless of what tragedy might occur. Even when my mother and father died, I worked straight through the feelings. I couldn't bear to hold up production. It wouldn't have been disciplined. It would have been indulgent, self-centered. . . . Was that really it, or did I not feel deserving of such acknowledged sorrow? Or again, did I use the work ethic to avoid the sorrow I felt?

The day my dad died I was scheduled to do thirty-five satellite interviews on television for a new movie. I flew back to Virginia to be with Mother, stayed six hours, and flew home to California.

The next day I fulfilled an obligation to conduct a seminar on metaphysics. I remember how I stopped and asked myself if I was doing the right thing.

I could hear my dad say, "Of course you are, monkey." I remembered how impressed he had been to hear that Mary Martin went on in *South Pacific* even though her father had died that day.

"The show must go on," he said to me that day. I wondered why he said that.

Now I understood that my success was vital to him

because he had wanted show business for himself, but really didn't have the courage to pursue it. He said his mother had taught him how to fear too well. So he found himself unable to dare. It was up to Warren and me to fulfill his dreams for him. This was the clear implication that I discerned early on in my life. It was an intense motivation for my driving need to express myself. I was doing it for him.

I cried later, when I had time. I returned to Virginia for the funeral and stayed with Mother as long as I could. It was harder to leave her. I could feel her settling into my presence with her, as though I would be her new companion now that she was alone. She would wait to have her breakfast with me, asking me questions as though it were a school day and I mustn't miss the bus. Nothing should stand in the way of my objectives in life.

Always, always she was there as a support and a reminder that I would "be somebody." Of course she was talking about herself. She wanted to "be somebody," so I took on her fantasy as well as my father's. I would have the acting career she had forfeited for motherhood.

When she died I was making *Guarding Tess*. We were shooting on location in Baltimore. I remember saying good-bye to her in California, where she lived with me. She had had some problems that required hospitalization and was not completely well when I had to leave her. In the hospital she had talked about dying and I tried to decide whether this was different from the other times. For a few days she had an angelic expression that brought tears to my eyes. She spoke of seeing beautiful light all around her. She said she saw my heart and her heart and everyone else's hearts beating together like one huge heart. She said there was light at the center of the earth and people lived there. She said every human being needed to understand that life should be more loving.

She spoke of seeing God in and around everything. She described love and light and God in much the same way that my dad had done when he lay dying in the hospital. So, I thought this was probably her time.

Then she came home, bouncing back the way she always did. It was wonderfully mischievous of her.

Leaning over her chair on the day I left her, I thought I'd be humorous about the emptiness I was feeling.

"Listen," I said, "do you think you can wait and not die till I come back from shooting my movie?"

"Your movie?" she said, perking up, though her eyes were unable to focus. "Where are you going to shoot your movie?" she asked.

"Baltimore," I answered.

As though she knew something I didn't know, she smiled and shrugged and said, "Baltimore? Oh, okay."

That was all, but in that "Oh, okay" I heard something I didn't understand.

The morning she died I woke up with a start. Then the phone rang. It was Mother's nurse in California who said, "Your mom just took her last breath." Suddenly I felt Mother next to me in my rented house in Baltimore. The TV suddenly switched on to static. I pulled myself out of bed. Then I heard her talk to me in my head. She wanted me to drive to our old house in Virginia. I blindly got dressed, called the assistant director, told him I wouldn't be in that day, and got in the car. My mind was tumbling so fast. I remembered her expression when she said Baltimore. Then I realized—Mom and Dad had met in Baltimore. They had married in Baltimore. She taught dramatics there at Maryland College. Dad had attended Johns Hopkins University in Baltimore. He died at Johns Hopkins Hospital in Baltimore. And now I felt her next to me as I drove from this city of firsts for her, realizing this was the only way she could come back and die here. Because I was going to be in Baltimore, she had computed her decision to leave at the same time.

I should have recognized that light in her eye, I said to myself. I should have remembered that "Oh, okay" never meant yes with her. Yet if I had stayed in California with her, perhaps it would have prevented her from squaring the circle of her life.

I got in my rented car and went to our old house in Virginia. It looked the same. I sat in the car for a while and I felt Mother speak to me in my mind. Not in words, but in feelings. She urged me to go into the house to a drawer in an old cabinet and retrieve a letter. It was a drawer I had not known about. I opened it and found a letter she had written to me twenty-five years before. I couldn't tell if it was a letter she had never mailed or a copy of one she had mailed. I opened it with real trepidation and read it.

The letter had to do with my daughter and my husband. Mother was warning me about certain things. I broke down and cried. Had I understood that letter twenty-five years before, it would have altered the course of my life.

I was eighteen years old and working in the chorus of a Broadway musical when I met my husband, Steve Parker. It happened after the show one night as I sat with some girlfriends in the restaurant bar across the street from the stage door. As soon as Steve walked in and sat down, I knew my life was to take a new course. Yes, he was handsome, almost overly charming, intelligent, and had azure eyes of a depth and perception that touched me immediately. But more than that, our connection had the shock of destiny to it. I have looked back many times at what happened between us—the things the letter warned me about—and I still conclude that it was meant to be and there was nothing I could have done to alter or avoid the experience we were intended to have together.

Now I cried as I walked through the house feeling Mother and her wisdom in every room. Feeling how right she had been about so many things and how wrong I had been in not listening to her more. She slowly guided me through the house as though she was taking one last walk with me. This was the person who had given me life and now she was proceeding to another level of her own. It was the last time I would see the place as we had lived in it, and I felt we were doing it together.

I stopped in the living room with the white sofa and the red pillows—she loved that color combination. I sat down on it the way she used to. I crossed my legs as she used to. I felt that I was her. I thought about how much she had wanted to be a recognized actress. How much she had lived through me. I thought of her soft, measured voice reading me poetry. Why didn't she pursue her dream? I wondered. Then I felt her say, "Because I wanted to be a mother more."

It seemed so simple as I sat there on her sofa, reflecting on who she really was and might have been. Then I felt her tell me to go back to work, not to hold up production, not to keep people waiting. Again, the show had to go on. Warren and I might have believed we were not from a show-business family, but now in retrospect, because we have both lived out the unfulfilled fantasies of our parents, I think we had a greater inspirational motivation than the Barrymores or the Redgraves. And Mother and Daddy were just as theatrical in real life. They often seemed to perform their relationship, as though, in the absence of a real audience, they made our household the stage.

I sat for hours in the living room sobbing, feeling and

remembering some of their dramas, which even transcended earthly reality! I went into the bedroom where Mother said Daddy had visited her soon after he passed on. She said she smelled his pipe and saw his face quite clearly. It wasn't entirely comforting, she said, because she wanted to be free of him and felt that even after death he was observing her. I went to the underwear drawer where she claimed he had placed a hidden valentine in between his socks for her. Valentine's Day had been their special day, so she was never really certain whether the valentine was placed there before or *after* his death. She was perfectly prepared to accept this "after death" theatricality as proof that she would never be free of him. I walked away from the underwear drawer thinking that Mother had her theories of life after death and I had mine. One last time I passed through all the rooms and out of the house. I knew I'd never return. I didn't think she would either. And she didn't. For a theatrical life-after-death gesture she followed me back to Baltimore.

This is what happened.

When I returned to Baltimore that night, I lay in bed watching the swan outside my window, because it reminded me of her.

The house I was renting had an alarm system, but I didn't know that and therefore hadn't turned it on. Suddenly the alarm went off. I didn't know what to do. I certainly didn't know how to turn it off. Then I heard Mother in my head again. "The switch is in the closet in the guest room," she said. I got up, went to the guest room, opened the closet, and there it was. I turned it off and got back into bed. I turned on the TV set. I couldn't get a single station without static. Then the light in the living room, where I had placed the letter and other treasures retrieved from Mother's belongings, began to dim slowly and come on again full force. When I walked into the room I could feel Mother. Once more the light dimmed and came back again full force.

She had always claimed to have an electromagnetic field that prevented her from wearing regular watches. They speeded up on her, she said.

Now I actually felt she was using her force field to communicate with me. It was her way of saying, "I'm still here."

That night was full of theatrical bells and whistles, lights and static. She exhibited all the special effects she longed for in her own life. As a matter of fact, by morning I was so amused at her antics that I nearly went outside and got the hose so I could turn the water on *her* and come full circle.

I feel that I came to a real resolution in my relationship with my mother. It took nearly sixty years. She was my stage mother, my insistent inspiration, the person whom I acted for, and in the end the one who released me from her own dreams. I would be an actress for myself now, and she could move on to another level of understanding.

# 2

# BREAKING LOOSE
# TO FLY

When I first came to Hollywood it was difficult for me to rehearse a scene full out because I didn't want to take up the crew's time and I was embarrassed and shy when the lights weren't on me. The lights gave me permission, somehow, to indulge myself in the emotional requirements of the scene because the parameters were clear then, the boundaries drawn. The lights validated me. In the light *I* was to be observed. *They* were the observers. Then I could do it. But otherwise I was shy. This way of working was not good because no one really knew what I was going to do when it was time to shoot the scene. The crew couldn't focus the lights, the camera people weren't sure how I'd move. And the other actors didn't know what emotional pitch to expect . . . an example of how shyness and undeservability can be excruciatingly unprofessional. I remember the day I broke through it all. It was a picture directed by Daniel Mann called *Hot Spell,* with Shirley Booth and Anthony Quinn. It was a drama.

The set was quiet, the camera was too close for comfort (no lights were on). One or two of the crew lit cigarettes. Wardrobe sipped coffee and gossiped under their breath. Makeup and hair lurked behind the camera. The ceilings of the soundstage were so high, the walls so cavernously far away, that I felt insignificant and violated by the attention trained on me, but I knew the time had come to "act." I had to let myself go. I had to.

My character's boyfriend had just left me, and Shirley Booth (my mother) was trying to comfort me. Shirley walked into the bedroom, and I thought, This is it. I gathered my courage and went for broke. I launched into the scene, screaming and crying. Crashing around the bedroom set, I sobbed into my pillow, which I could barely see because the set was so lonely and dark. The more I got into the scene, the higher my voice rose. It stunned me that I seemed to revert to girlhood. Tears poured down my face. I could barely breathe. Shirley Booth was impressed and so was everyone else. The crew applauded, as did makeup, hair, and wardrobe. Danny walked over to me in the set. He sat down next to me on the bed. "How did you do that?" he whispered. "What did you think of?" he continued. "How does all that happen?"

I wiped my eyes and tried to explain that they were tears of liberation, breakthrough tears. I tried to explain to him how my shyness had made me feel selfish; because of it I had withheld the way I intended to play the scene, and I couldn't help it. When I broke out of my prison of shyness, I sobbed buckets of relief. I felt light-headed and mellow. I saw that acting was a way to feel emotions just for the sake of it. There didn't need to be a *reason* to cry. I had left part of my shy childhood behind.

Danny asked more questions about my feelings. I liked searching for them and I loved sharing what I found. He praised me and acknowledged my talent and said he would guard my private feelings. Days passed. I became acutely aware that I would do anything to please him; by searching deeper within myself, I wanted to gain his favor, make him proud of me, try risking more of my emotional truth. I soon realized I was falling in love with my first artistic, benevolent, openly vulnerable, patriarchal father figure. Because of my trust in him, I could summon my emotions anytime.

I was twenty-two, fragile, just learning about my feelings, instinctively knowing that I needed to explore them more deeply in order to become a good actress. But more than anything I suddenly found everything about my director an attraction.

I longed for contact with him at work. I reveled in his expertise with the other actors. I so appreciated his generosity in revealing his own life secrets as he probed with us to find our characters. Danny told me how, at the moment his father died, he could only focus on the spittle in the corners of his father's mouth. He told me of his first love. He shared his feelings regarding his wife and children. I hung on every scrap of information, subtly calculating in a lovestruck fashion how to motivate our relationship to become more intimate. He had, after all, been responsible for my screen test in New York. He hadn't required me to do a scene. He had allowed me simply to be myself as he asked questions and flirted with exposing my unformed personality on screen. He was there for me at the beginning, this man who had directed Brando and won Anna Magnani and Shirley Booth Academy Awards!

All my feelings of passion, both professional and personal, came crashing together. Suddenly I utterly understood why actresses fell in love with their directors. Directors were the fathers we longed to marry. They insisted that our emotions run free and then assisted in sculpting them. They adored our faces and bodies, but continually strove for improvement. They were our caretakers and caregivers. We were their wards. No one could hurt us, no one could criticize us. . . . Only they were commissioned with such trust and confidence.

And so the father-daughter combination got played out. Danny was twenty-five years older than me. That was a plus as far as I was concerned. What wasn't a plus was that neither he nor I could get past the fundamental understanding that this was only a movie. I would probably experience the same feelings again with another fine director and he with another actress who was just learning who she was.

The day of the wrap party I disintegrated. I said goodbye and drove back to Malibu. The family of shared feelings and artistic exploration had come to an end. I was sure those moments of magic would never come together quite like this again, and I was devastated.

Halfway home I turned on the windshield wipers. I thought it was pouring rain, but it wasn't. I was simply crying so hard I couldn't see.

The intimacies of people in show business are deep, searing, and can turn on a dime and be gone. I know that now. It was difficult then. Years later Danny and I met again and took a walk on the beach. We talked about how old he felt, and I remember he'd say, "God spelled backward is dog." It seemed so profound when I first heard him say it. Thirty-five years later, I realized, he was still relying upon past profundities.

As we walked he stopped with his feet in the waves

and said, "You remember our relationship on *Hot Spell?*" I nodded. "Well," he said, "you were like an open raw nerve. There was nothing you didn't feel. I remember thinking, This can be dangerous."

Danny died soon after that. His family showed me a picture I had dedicated to him after we worked together. I had written, *Darling Danny, you taught me how to fly.* I still feel the same way.

WHEN AN ACTRESS COMES TO THE DECISION TO "LET go," it is momentous. This is true for many reasons. You leave yourself wide open for hurt. You uncover buried characteristics you never realized were there, which can be alternately frightening and enlightening. You become, as Danny said, a raw open nerve susceptible not only to the whims of others, but also to yourself.

As you unearth your inner universe it can be shocking. I, for example, found that anger was one of the easiest emotions for me to play. I had not been aware of the anger I had locked within myself. Who knows where this anger was born. For me it wasn't bred only in my childhood. I have always felt I was born angry. I believe that I decided to come into this lifetime to resolve my issue of repressed anger. When I remember my temper tantrums as a child, I can also recall that I seemed to have a more than earthly reason for being mad. True, my mother was maddeningly phlegmatic, but there was more, and I believe that the "more" spoke to a rage that existed prior to my birth.

I believe that in lifetimes prior to this one I experienced such a profound lack of resolution with anger that I needed to come to terms with it and *literally* chose my mother because she would provoke me to resolve it. I don't know, intellectually, how this schoolroom for the soul works, but I *feel* that we humans are not only products of the emotional conditioning conducted in our childhoods, parental and otherwise, but also of the genetic memory still residing in the patterning of our souls' experience. The Hindus call it samsara.

I believe I was attracted to acting not only because of both my parents' unfulfilled dreams, but also because it enabled me to venture, once removed, into the area of full-blown, dramatically angry expression without threatening my personal existence. From the beginning of my life—this life—I've been drawn to the art and the act of emotional expression. And it isn't only because of the unexplained anger in myself as a young girl.

Many actors and actresses in Hollywood today are more conversant with the possibility that they came into this lifetime with unresolved issues that our business enables us to resolve and explore. We feel we are provided with not only an excuse, but a right and a duty to look into the vastness of ourselves and contribute what we find to our projects and characters.

This search for our interiors can be devastating for anyone else who doesn't understand. Sometimes we don't even know if we are doing it for the characters we play or for ourselves.

The line between professionally motivated emotion and the emotions of true personal feeling can be so blurred as to be blinding. That is why marriages are threatened with every picture, even marriages between partners in our business. Because my husband, Steve, had been an actor in New York, he understood what it took to investigate a character. In fact, he helped me. If an actor is married to a "civilian," it is usually an impossible situation. It takes a monumentally secure civilian to understand what we put ourselves and others through in the search for truthful acting. We can be self-centered and self-serving to the point of excluding all other humans. But then, we know somewhere way underneath that unless we are centered in ourselves, the character we're playing can spirit us away—literally. If we don't serve ourselves, how can we serve the character and the project? Our actions and feelings often don't seem grounded. We sometimes flail right off the wall. We become narcissistic beyond belief and still feel afraid to look at ourselves in the mirror.

To push our parameters and those of everyone around us we sometimes indulge in the grossest kind of exhibitionism. We can become so obsessed with personal perfection that we can actually believe the landing on the moon or the invasion of Bosnia is about us!

Yes, "becoming" a character and the search for it can make you a real mess. I was often reluctant to let a character consume my identity. It didn't feel good. I didn't like the abdication of the real me even though that was what I hoped to find. I was afraid I'd never come back, or more probably, I think I was afraid of what people would think of me.

I remember a little-theater play my mother was in when I was a child. It was called *Children of the Moon,* and my father thought she had turned into the character—a bitch who neglected her family, home and hearth. I remember hearing the arguments about the time she spent away from home to become another person at the theater. Dad was really upset. He thought our family had been neglected and the house was filthy. He wanted her *out* of that play and back home where she belonged. I saw Mother's frustration and finally her independent insistence as she decided to continue with the play. It opened, and Warren and I appeared as small children in it. It was successful, I think, but the memory of the price paid in our household was forever intense in my mind.

I elected to apply my disciplined technique to acting for many years. I developed into an astute observer and practiced the art of *emulating* what I saw rather than *feeling* it.

For example, when I played a victim I *acted* what I *thought* a victim felt like. I never really became a victim myself. I've often reflected upon whether the quality of my acting would have been higher had I let myself *become* a victim. I'm still not sure. Sometimes a feeling of controlled distance is more effective when playing the part of a sentimental person. A true victim who does not see herself as such is infinitely more moving than a victim who whines. Therefore, as the years passed, one of my deepest and slowest dawning revelations was the understanding that characters who held contradictions were certainly the juiciest.

In real life I was not so allowing. Contradictions in people I knew and worked with were anathema to me. I therefore missed so much in judging them on their inconsistencies.

To this day I have a hard time with inconsistencies in people's characters. I usually consider it a form of lying, which is much too harsh a condemnation.

But acting has shown me that contradiction is the spice that makes people and life worth being interested in. These are the characters that keep an audience interested. Now I can see that the same is true in real life. A person who is constantly predictable becomes boring. Unpredictable contradiction is fun.

In fact contradiction holds within it a kind of messy perfection, which is incumbent upon us humans to excavate.

The canvas and terrain of characters to play has offered me the lifelong pleasure of finding the harmony in messiness. This is what I loved most about Aurora

Greenway in *Terms of Endearment*. She was an impossibly difficult woman, but in the end she was usually right. She was essentially a heroine whose path to harmonious conclusion was strewn with the maimed and wounded who willingly would go through it again because she was fun.

Aurora affected my personal life because of the unpredictability of her contradictions. People like this are now an adventure and exploration for me. I have learned that a kind of harmony exists under chaos. The quest is to search it out. Then you have found a character on the screen and off.

If not for show business, I'm not sure I'd understand this. In fact show business has been instrumental in my deeper understanding of *real* life. Yet when I look back on the deeper lessons of my years in Hollywood, why do I first remember such strange, unrelated, isolated details, images that seem unimportant in themselves: the bright sunlight as I'd open the door of a dark soundstage, giving me an instant headache as I stepped into a blazingly white California day; emerald-green lawns, and sprinklers that go all year, wall-to-wall swimming pools, gorgeous fruit with no taste; 5:30 A.M. calls for making up and making love, 5:30 P.M. calls for giving awards for doing it . . . evening dress both times; thick makeup sinking into the pores of my face, separating me from the real world. Thoughts of dissatisfaction and restless boredom fluttering in me as I'd wait yet another hour for the lighting on the set to be completed. Even from the earliest days I considered that perhaps I basically did not enjoy making pictures. I never voiced this to anyone—I was afraid of sounding like an ingrate. I liked acting, but not making movies. There was too much waiting around for my temperament, which was basically impatient. I liked things to move fast, even at the risk of sloppiness.

Many times I can recall the feeling of just wanting to get it done and over with rather than done right.

This has been a serious defect in my approach to my work all my life. I don't know where the impatience comes from. I was born with it. It seems I've been intolerant of "dillydally" from the beginning. Perhaps this is another cosmic issue I came in with and I chose picture making as a course of investigation and resolution just because there *is* so much waiting around. To keep my character's emotional attitude afloat while camera people ditz around is sometimes intolerable to me. It causes anxiety and finally rage, to say nothing of bone-aching exhaustion. But it goes with the territory and therefore must be approached as a lesson in self-confidence and discipline. Time is different in Hollywood. It is a built-in part of the budget. It is paid for, so why not take it? I find this concept wasteful, dishonest, and indulgent and I usually say so, which doesn't help matters.

No, from early on I was not a happy candidate for moviemaking. There are probably many reasons as yet unmined in my psyche for my nagging sense of unfulfillment, my discomfort at being noticed and catered to. But I was not the only one with those feelings. Over the years I realized that many of us felt a raw dissatisfaction in the midst of what would be perceived by others as a perfect life. We felt we had a kind of emotional virus that afflicted us and was never really curable. It was treatable from time to time with massive doses of box-office success or, as the case may have been, a string of "deserved failures" to make us feel more ourselves.

But we were never really comfortable, cured of the affliction. We had each struggled with such intensity to achieve our goals, that "struggle" identified who we were. Without struggle we lost touch with ourselves. Success and achievement meant becoming someone else.

Because we were not prepared to be without the familiarity of conflict, we would often create it. I am only now beginning to understand that the stars in my little cosmos were so important to me in relation to my attitudes about struggle in a town as superficial and as deep as Hollywood; their talent, lives, behavior, and luminescence helped me see my own light.

Two of those stars had been there from my childhood—two who had a particularly strong influence during my first years in Hollywood. They behaved like no one I had ever met.

# 3

# CRACKING UP IN THE FUN FACTORY

## Dean and Jerry

*D*ean Martin and Jerry Lewis were my favorites when I was about twelve years old. How could I dream that eight years later I would be starring in a picture with them? Warren and I used to see every picture they made and at one point drove our parents crazy by cupping our hands and screeching around the house holding huge, invisible grapefruits the way we had seen Dean and Jerry do in *At War with the Army*.

I also remember registering the fact that Hal B. Wallis was the man who produced all of Martin and Lewis's films at Paramount.

I would never have gone to dinner with Hal B. Wallis when he came backstage to see me after I replaced Carol Haney in *Pajama Game* if it hadn't been for Martin and Lewis. Our destinies seemed intertwined. Or at least that's how it looks to me now.

Steve had arrived at the stage door to pick me up for dinner. We were not yet married, but when Wallis introduced himself and saw that there was an important man in my life, I saw a flicker of displeasure cross his face. Boyfriends and husbands usually meant trouble where female stars were concerned because the husbands saw their role as one of protector from the Hollywood predators. That was basically true of Steve too. He was thirteen years older than me, more sophisticated about life, and could spot a useful or an unuseful situation a mile away. It wasn't until much later that I realized the basis for that particular talent of his, a talent that had attracted him to me.

In any case Steve and Wallis and I had dinner. Wallis wanted me to do a screen test and, if he liked it, wanted to put me under contract.

I did the test (with Danny Mann), Wallis liked it, and Steve thought I should sign the contract. So I did.

I went back to the chorus. Then Hitchcock came to see *The Pajama Game* on the one *other* night that Haney was out—destiny again? He was doing a picture called *The Trouble with Harry* and was looking for an offbeat, "kooky" actress to play the lead. He asked me to be in *The Trouble with Harry* before I did anything for Wallis. That meant a location in Vermont and an immediate departure for Hollywood. I knew I had to make a decision about Steve, because he insisted that we marry or he wouldn't follow me to California. I didn't want to lose him, so I married him, and nearly fainted during the ceremony because deep down I knew I was doing something I wasn't ready for.

Nevertheless Steve was protective and supportive. He seemed to want to do anything that would ensure a successful career for me.

So having completed *The Trouble with Harry* (Hitchcock didn't like husbands either and banned Steve from the set), I was safely ensconced with Steve in a small apartment in Malibu, California, and I reported to work for my second picture: *Artists and Models* with Dean and Jerry. I could barely believe what was happening to me. I was twenty years old.

I was used to "well-kempt" Protestant behavior. This was my first experience with ethnic (Jewish and Italian) antics. I saw tourists and passersby swept up into Dean's golf cart, usually by Jerry, who had stolen it. I saw Jerry so unabashedly in need of attention that he'd do anything to get it. He was so free-flowing and openly demanding with his crazy antics, his spastic jokes, and his out-of-control inclusion of everyone in his path that I found him attractive. I was constitutionally incapable of acting that way and I sensed also that within that canny insanity brooded a really lonely man.

Dean was another matter. He was smooth, kind, subtly witty, good-looking, and seemed to be infinitely more complicated than Jerry. I didn't realize I had come along when their relationship was crumbling. I only knew they had been my childhood idols and they were still the hottest, funniest combination in every area of show business—number one in personal appearances, movies, TV, and radio. I was enthralled and fascinated by their combined talents. They were everything I adored.

To my surprise, Dean, not Jerry, was the funny one to me. His humor was subtle, spontaneous—a result of the moment. Jerry's was brilliant, but usually premeditated. I watched them carefully, scrutinizing every comedic antic, clocking why their zaniness sometimes worked, sometimes didn't. I sensed there was deep tension between the two, but I was used to behavior that *re*pressed rather than *ex*pressed.

The first day I worked with Jerry, I was supposed to

do a number on a stairway with him called "Inamorata."
It was a love song and I was dressed in a little yellow
sunsuit. My job was to leap up and down the stairs,
striking provocative, funny poses so that Jerry would fall
in love with me. Being a dancer, I was used to taking
orders from the choreographer, Charlie Curran (married
to Patti Page), and listening to the specifics from his
assistant. The assistant, however, was an aging juvenile,
an ex-dancer whom time had outrun. He was neither
attractive nor very funny.

Unless you've experienced someone demonstrating
your proposed material in an unfunny, forced manner,
you can't imagine how humiliating it is. You're turned
off the material, yet you know you haven't really given it
a chance. You know the assistant can't possibly do it
justice or he would be where you are. On the other
hand, the fear of ridicule is so strong that reason flies out
the window. More often than not, the fear makes you
cruel, which is what happened that first day with Jerry.

In those days, musical numbers were shot before principal photography on the script began. I didn't know
Jerry or how he operated. I wanted to tell him how my
brother and I had loved his scene with the grapefruit. I
wanted to tell him about the time when I heard people
laugh because of him—that was one summer in New
York when I was studying at the American School of
Ballet and he and Dean were playing down the street at
the Copacabana. Waves of laughter would float out onto
the street. But I never got the chance. Jerry rode onto
the set on a bike, threw his leg over the crossbar, and
swaggered toward Charlie Curran. I thought his swagger
was rather sexy, actually, connoting confidence and a
kind of unspoken intelligent arrogance. He nodded to
me, we shook hands, and then he gestured for Charlie
and his assistant to show him the number. I played my-

self, since I was a disciplined dancer from Broadway, eager to be prepared and to please whomever I needed to at any given time. I even wore my yellow sunsuit instead of rehearsal clothes and had body makeup caked on my legs so my freckles wouldn't betray my Scotch-Irish lily-white skin.

I did my part pretty well, I thought, but the assistant, as I said, was awful.

When we finished, Jerry said nothing and walked off the set. I looked at Charlie, wondering what I had done wrong. He shrugged and went to Jerry's dressing room, which was a little prefab box house on wheels, outfitted with a makeup table, a cot, a few chairs, and a telephone. I looked over at them, straining to hear the conversation. The door was open and I saw Jerry on the phone. I heard him say he didn't want to do the number.

I, of course, thought he either didn't like me or was being competitive with me. The assistant rolled his eyes and I sat down and waited. Within a few minutes, Hal B. Wallis appeared on the set. He was the producer. He went to Jerry's dressing room and closed the door. After a while they all emerged and it was clear that Wallis had prevailed.

As Wallis walked past me he said, "That young man is going to ruin himself. He's a great comic, but he tries to do too many other things. He thinks he's a producer, a director, and God knows what else. He should stick to being funny. We'd all be better off."

What Wallis misunderstood was Jerry's fear of not being funny. That's why he dabbled in everything else.

Jerry and I went back to rehearsal. He was not happy, but he was professional. I was having my first class-A lesson in how destructive the anticipation of being humiliated and outshone could be. The number was constructed to feature the girl (me). Jerry's character was the reactor to her comedy. But he was used to being the funny one. He was used to other people reacting to him. Actually he was very funny, but like all great comics he was afraid he wasn't.

The rehearsal for that number and others didn't last long. Jerry was nice enough to me, but what I didn't realize was that he felt his very survival was at stake. He and Dean were breaking up. He felt he needed to be funny every second and in control of every aspect of the movie, whether it was outside of his province or not. He was clearly a genius. That was obvious. But his genius inspired a kind of awestruck intimidation in everyone around him.

I felt something different. I felt I could be paralyzed by the tyranny of his insecurity. I understood his temperamental outbursts and cruel lashing out. I had done it myself. Unfortunately, his loyalists gave him more and more rope. They laughed at his jokes and fawned all over him. No one really told him the truth. No one said he needn't worry if Martin left the act, because no one even acknowledged that there was a problem between them. Wallis was right, but for all the wrong reasons. Jerry was wrong for all the right reasons.

So, Jerry began to lose himself in distractions—high-tech gadgets. His dressing room was outfitted with advanced stereo equipment and he had the first tape deck ever made. He invited me into the inner sanctum of his high-tech room and demonstrated his brilliance in technology as he experimented in plugging and unplugging wires and pushing buttons that gave his Al Jolson-like voice deeper resonance. Jerry would sing to me. I didn't know how to react. His voice had a piercing vibrato but it made me want to laugh. I knew he was serious, though. I repressed the laughter, wondering if I was doing him a great disservice. I liked Jerry.

After he got to know me better, he told me about his childhood. He said he had been plagued with fears of abandonment because his show-business parents were away so much. He told me how afraid he still was of being alone. That was why he needed people around all the time. He said he had developed into a control freak because that way he could refuse to allow anyone to leave. He spoke of himself in the third person. He never said, "I did this or that." He said, "Jerry did."

He told me he mugged so zanily and used his body in such a funny, bizarre way because he was afraid to let people hear him express himself in his high, squeaky voice. He was afraid to talk, to tell people how he felt. He said his comedy came out of these feelings, feelings about feeling like a freak. They were true feelings, he said. That was why people laughed. I couldn't believe that the great comic genius, Jerry Lewis, was sharing such intimate knowledge of himself with me. And yet in so many ways I was able to identify with him.

He showed me that expressing feelings about oneself was okay even if they sounded crazy. Whatever he had gone through in his psychological upbringing made mine seem like a day at the beach. In fact, I began to wonder whether deep deprivation was necessary to be good at your work!

Getting to know Dean was another story. The words that come to mind are those that describe a person cut *off* from feeling—purposefully cut off. Perhaps that was why he seemed so devil-may-care and so coolly casual. The Italians, I later learned, had a more apt word for it, *menefreghista,* which means "one who does not give a fuck." Dean Martin was basically a *menefreghista.*

He was so witty because of the way he saw the world. If he did a routine about the President announcing a nuclear attack, the focus of his humor would be the tie the President wore or how he, Dean, couldn't open his refrigerator door as he was listening to such a momentous speech. I remember once he called me about something, and the entire conversation was about the telephone wire he couldn't locate under his sofa. I was in tears of laughter. He would make observational jokes about things that no one else could see as fodder for comedy.

Dino Crocetti—Dean Martin—had been born into an environment where the Mob resided as neighborhood characters. In Steubenville, Ohio, he discovered the rackets early and he loved to bet on anything that moved. After school he'd make the rounds of pool rooms, cigar stores, and gambling dens. His offhand stories of the old days captivated me.

I asked him about Vegas and Bugsy Siegel, who dared to build the Flamingo Hotel and make it the first grand establishment for gambling, before anyone else was there.

Dean smiled. "Guess who was in the pit opening night, dealing blackjack?" he asked.

"Who?" I said.

*"Me!"*

He told me about some of the Mob characters, his stories making it clear they were "not gentlemen," but he was protective of my knowing too much about such people.

Over the years I saw that Dean was not impressed with the Mob. He grew up with them, and therefore, he shared many of their Old Country traits—privacy of thought and feeling that no one dared to violate, an emotional detachment from the world and everything in it, an unspoken belief in a Catholic God who would forgive even the most heinous crime through confession. But in his soul, Dean didn't want to run with the Mob. I always felt he didn't even like them. He didn't come when they called. Instead, he played gin, or drank, or did card tricks, or tried out new material for his act on whoever else happened to be around.

For them and everyone else, Dean was a *menefreghista,* one who simply did not give a fuck.

I did not know all this when I first met Dean. My initial impression was of a man who basically wanted to be left alone. He was nice to everyone; he just didn't want "nice" to go on too long. Often there would be parties at his home on Mountain Drive, where he and Jeanne lived with their seven children. Three of the kids were Jeanne's and four were Betty's—Dean's first wife. Dean didn't particularly want to be involved in the up-bringing of the children. He told me he felt inadequate, and his own emotional blocks prevented communication anyway. Whenever Jeanne asked him to have a stern talk with one of the children, Dean would take the child into his den and say, "I have nothing to say, but please tell your mother I bawled you out, okay?" The child would comply and sometime later would get a new car.

Dean insisted on being home every night for dinner with his children. It was a ritual that gave him the Old Country feeling that he was the head of the household and connected to his children's future.

Much of his humor on the set revolved around things that happened with his kids in what he called the "big hotel." He said he'd try to count them all, but he never learned to count that high. He said he had to eat standing up because he had "screwed himself out of a seat" at the table. His family humor gave the impression that his was an emotionally volatile, rough and tumble, interconnected Italian family. It might have been that, but Dean wasn't a part of it.

Even when Jeanne had dinner parties attended by the

most interesting people in town, Dean would usually just go to his room and watch television. More than once he retired to his den and called the cops, saying there was a party at his house and it was getting too noisy. Once I lost my pearls at one of their dinner parties. I wandered around looking for them and ended up in Dean's den. He was watching television while his guests were having dinner. He said I could sit down. I did and he told me he felt shy about not being educated and ashamed of his limited vocabulary and his lack of political and social knowledge. "I can't understand what the hell they're talking about down there," he said. "So I don't want them to know I feel dumb." He then launched into some new material for his club act, which was so funny I laughed until I felt like I had a hernia! Dean was terrified of the *intimacy* required to carry on a conversation, so he inevitably segued into comedy routines.

That was what I found the most intriguing aspect of Dean. When a man fears intimacy, I'm interested. I try to open him up. It didn't happen when we worked on *Artists and Models;* that came later.

On that first film with Dean I was awestruck at his and Jerry's antics. Even though there was always tension underneath, they seemed to share a compulsive need for the experience of creating and playing to an audience. Perhaps the tension fed that need, or maybe they were simply performers to the core and their world inevitably became a stage.

They careened around the Paramount lot on their motorized golf carts, clanging bells and tooting horns, stopping for a beautiful young starlet to cross the street as they drew a crowd by teasing her into red-faced embarrassment.

If they had an interview with a newspaper reporter, they might cut the tie of a man and perhaps set it on fire, or curl up like a baby in the lap of a woman reporter and suck *her* thumb. Nothing was out of bounds. They'd flop into cars driven by strangers and scream bloody murder that they were being kidnapped. Dean would light a cigarette with his solid gold lighter, blow out the flame, and toss the gold lighter from the window as though it was a used match. Someone, I noticed, always retrieved it for him.

There were custard pies thrown in the face, butter pats splattered on ceilings, golf clubs and balls slung around like children's toys. There was Jewish deli in Jerry's dressing room, and antipasto in Dean's; visiting musicians with sheet music of new song ideas, comedy writers who realized that the Martin and Lewis heyday was producing moments of genius that should be recorded, and the inevitable producers, directors, and agents who attended to the needs of the talented team Americans would never see the likes of again. The agents, Herman Citron and Mort Viner, were also my agents at MCA, so in many ways I felt part of a new family . . . a family that defied every value I had been brought up with. I had been schooled in a WASP middle-class environment, to say nothing of having been brought up to respect authority in the world of ballet. It was beyond my comprehension that Dean and Jerry could be so freewheeling as to play practical jokes on one of the studio heads and get away with it. Y. Frank Freeman was a southern gentleman with white hair and a hospitable manner. When Dean and Jerry spontaneously made him the brunt of their humor in the commissary during lunch hour, I watched with openmouthed astonishment.

Because he was the president of Paramount, he often entertained big, established stars at lunch meetings— Gloria Swanson, Audrey Hepburn, and Marlon Brando among them. I think he was proud to be seen escorting the likes of Marlene Dietrich or Anna Magnani through the tables to the executive dining room.

Whenever Dean and Jerry spotted such an event, the potential for deprecating humor was too much for them to pass up.

Their favorite rap was to stop Freeman and "visiting stars" in the midst of the big room and pose as inmates in a prison. "We don't need to eat this slop," they'd yell at Y. Frank while smearing butter all over his suit. (Butter was a big prop for their comedy.) They'd then pick up their food with their hands (lamb chops, tuna salad—it didn't matter), squeeze it through their fingers, and throw it around the table. Freeman would hover in gentlemanly shock, waiting for their next move. Marlene or Magnani would take a discreet step backward, careful not to provoke inclusion, leaving Y. Frank directly in the line of fire. That's when Dean and Jerry would really let him have it. One routine was their favorite.

"Okay," they'd say. "So you've called us all here. Tell the people why."

Freeman's mouth was painted open by now, causing speechlessness. The diners were just as nonplussed. They watched in shock.

*"Why?"* Dean and Jerry would yell.

"Because," said Dean and Jerry in unison, "because you are all fired!"

Everybody would laugh, including Y. Frank, because they were secretly acknowledging his power.

Jerry would then stuff french fries up his nose or throw spinach in Dean's face and tell him he should have washed that morning. Dean would shove cold cuts into his mouth and wag them like a huge flopping tongue. Marlene or Magnani would no doubt long for the Old Country as they smiled in abject terror, wondering when and how they'd be included in the insanity.

Then Dean would take Freeman by the arm and, like a Dutch uncle, lead him out of the commissary saying, "We simply don't like your attitude in here—*you* are fired." Jerry would bring up the rear and both would kick Freeman out the door. "Wash up, collect your pay—and *we'll* take care of the girls," they'd yell.

Marlene and Magnani had been around show business, but never like this.

By now the commissary would be in bedlam at the preposterousness of it all. There were two respected, dignified international icons stranded in the middle of the dining room while the boss of the studio had been kicked out by brash American upstarts. How would this routine end?

"One more thing," Dean would yell out at Freeman. "This studio is filthy. There're cigarette butts all over the place." (He'd light a cigarette with his gold lighter, take a puff, throw the cigarette down, crunch it out, and again throw the lighter away.) "Everywhere I look, cigarette butts!" Jerry came from behind like a spastic monkey. "And have our cars washed immediately," he'd screech. "In fact, have *all* our cars washed."

The commissary would applaud. Dean and Jerry knew this was their exit. They'd gallantly make their way back to the screen goddesses, open their arms, and lead the by now amused beauties to the executive dining room.

I would sit tongue-tied at the sheer audacity of it all. I'd never seen people behave like that. In my world there had been an inferred censor. A silent alarm that instantly sounded caution. I couldn't do what I had just seen Dean and Jerry do, not in a million years. The irreverence—the disrespect—the outrageous disregard for form and social appropriateness . . . Where had I been all my life? This stuff was great! It got laughs, it loosened people up, they didn't take their precarious jobs so seriously

—how could they? I'd not met that many Italians and Jews. The ethnic ethos of their comedy was what made Y. Frank squirm. He was from my part of the world. Him I understood. But *him* was no fun.

Later Freeman would offer Dean and Jerry money just to be quiet for one lunch hour. They'd turn him down, and Freeman would willingly offer himself up on the altar of their zaniness yet another time.

I guess that was it in a nutshell. When you went that far out on a limb, you were successful. If you pulled your punches, you sucked dirt.

Dean and Jerry were my primary education in spontaneous, Katzenjammer antics to let off steam, avoid ulcers, and touch the muse of comic insanity bubbling in each of us.

I observed the havoc Dean caused, however, by sometimes being funnier than his partner. Dean would come to work throwing away comedy lines that you could barely hear. When someone would say, "Huh?" he'd repeat it. A laugh would come, which he would top, then another laugh, then he'd top that until he was on a roll. Soon the entire set was engulfed in the more sophisticated, quirky, literal humor of Dean's words, which revealed the peculiar slant he had on any given situation. His humor was not as physical as Jerry's, although it could be—especially with his hands. Dean's hands were the size of ham hocks, with fingers that curled inward. He had broken several fingers boxing and they were strong from working in the steel mills. His hands encompassed so much space that it was easy for him to palm cards when he was a blackjack dealer. He could deal from the middle, the bottom, or wherever, and never be detected. He entertained me between setups with sleight-of-hand card tricks. In between the tricks he'd lob in his funny lines as though he was testing new material. People would crowd closer so as not to miss any of his subtleties.

When Jerry saw Dean capture an intimate audience, he would often double up in pain and run to his dressing room. The attention, of course, shifted to Jerry, and Dean's comedy roll was interrupted.

The doctor would arrive, pronounce Jerry fine but slightly exhausted, prescribe an early night, and recommend that shooting continue without him. It did. Dean would say nothing, but I could tell he was hurt. The next day, with new people around, Jerry would repeat what he had heard Dean say and use it himself to get laughs. Dean saw what was happening, but didn't say much. He'd just go on hitting golf balls and every now and then he'd look punchy at how obvious the manipulation had been. In fact Punchy had been his nickname in school. Since he drank J&B and made jokes about it, Punchy seemed as good a name as another. Whenever I saw that punchy look, I knew there was deep recognition of a pain he didn't want to touch. Dean and Jerry had a dance going between the two of them that was both obvious and hidden.

Since Dean was usually the quiet one, his punchy attitude allowed people to walk all over him. Because he was so laid-back and aloof and seemingly not desperate for attention, many people failed to recognize his real contribution to the Martin and Lewis combination. This began to grate on him seriously. Underneath, he acknowledged that Jerry did most of the work—the scripts, the production, the hiring, the planning. He knew that without all Jerry's work, and without Jerry's talent, there couldn't have been a Martin and Lewis phenomenon.

Yet slowly, Dean became more and more reluctant to continue with Jerry. He felt irrelevant and undervalued, but because he withheld so many of his feelings, he couldn't confront anyone about it. Not Jerry, not the director, not Hal Wallis, not Jeanne—not even himself. As I watched what was happening I could feel myself understand Dean more and more. He was a prisoner of his own growing rage and the control he had been taught to exert over it. "Never let anyone know what is within you," his mom had told him. Those could have been words out of my own mother's mouth, but for different reasons. To Mrs. Crocetti, holding your emotional cards was a survival technique in a neighborhood controlled by the Mob. My mother advocated such behavior simply because it was more polite.

In the meantime Jerry continued to control the set, plan the scenes, write the material, get raves for it, and seemed more and more obsessed with having everything his way. Though Dean was the singer, Jerry chose the musical directors. Then someone gave Jerry a camera, and suddenly he saw himself as the new Charlie Chaplin. He began to spend a great deal of his free time making home movies, insisting that Dean sing and perform in them. Dean and his wife didn't socialize with Patti and Jerry, so the personal family relationships were not there. Each wife thought it better that way, as did Dean and Jerry. In fact, Dean didn't socialize with anybody much, except maybe to play poker. But Dean felt forced to be in Jerry's personal motion picture scrapbooks.

Because Dean wouldn't confront Jerry the air couldn't be cleared and Jerry, in his own need for resolution, became even more controlling. One morning I heard them arguing.

"Anytime you want to call it quits, just let me know," said Dean.

"But, Dean," countered Jerry, "what would I ever do without you?" Half meaning it.

"Fuck yourself, for starters," said Dean.

"But we have a special bond together," Jerry said with a snicker. Psychological jokes were becoming the new communication, but it sounded like he really meant it. "We love each other, no?"

"Talk about love all *you* want," said Dean. "To me you're nothing but a fucking dollar sign."

Dean himself has quoted those words many times since, and is proud of them. I was stunned.

Jerry became more megalomaniacal than ever. Life as he had known it for ten years was in jeopardy. Like most funnymen, he had to believe he knew everything there was to know about what was funny, not only for himself, but for Dean as well. That need came out of his fear. I could feel *Jerry* feel that Dean was pulling away. He sensed that Dean might risk allowing their fame and fortune to slip through his fingers rather than face his problems full on.

The impending breakup of Martin and Lewis occurred at the same time that I was feeling the most vulnerable in my own life. During this time Steve decided to return to Japan, where he told me he had spent a great deal of time as a child with his diplomat father. Steve was interested in becoming a kind of impresario of Asian talent. He knew a lot about it and wanted to carve out his own identity. He didn't want to be Mr. MacLaine in Hollywood. He felt that I would be fine on my own with my work in Hollywood. But his departure left me lonely, so making movies became my entire focus and the people I worked with, my family.

My childhood idols, Dean and Jerry, were becoming like unenlightened children and in some way my own world felt jeopardized. Jerry's concern and fear sometimes disrupted the shooting of *Artists and Models*. Finally Frank Tashlin, our director, ordered him off the set one day. Jerry just shrugged, swaggered, and chuckled. "No," said Tashlin, "you're going home."

Jerry went home sobbing. I felt sorrier than ever over what was happening. Jerry hated Dean by now, but was afraid to go on without him. Dean simply couldn't cope with his buried feelings and wanted out. If this duo couldn't make a go of it, who could? I began to realize how much human emotion mattered to a professional relationship. I had been schooled to go on regardless. Nothing would block my living up to not only my ambition, but what was expected of me. It didn't matter if I had a broken neck, I mustn't break a contract. But with Dean and Jerry, I was seeing how much they were governed by their feelings and resentment. They seemed willing to let everything slip away because they couldn't get along. In some strange way I admired this.

I finished *Artists and Models,* coping as well as I could, realizing I was a part of a tragic demise. Working with Dean and Jerry during those end days was a lesson for me in not taking the spewed venom of others personally. There were times when I was caught in the cross fire of rage and was inadvertently wounded. My first reaction was to dislike them, especially Jerry, because he was more able to express his feelings. The cast did a portrait sitting in the still gallery . . . all of the cast together. Dean, Jerry, Dorothy Malone, Anita Ekberg, and Eva Gabor. I'll never forget it. Jerry was especially cruel in the way he ordered us around, desperately attempting to gain control of a frightening situation. I tried to be philosophical, but my feelings were hurt. The other girls just grinned and bore it, but I knew somehow that Dean and Jerry meant more to me than that. Perhaps my own self-investigation began while watching them flail away with no real understanding of what unconsciously motivated them. They were allowing and indeed *creating* a disaster for themselves because they were out of touch with what terrified them.

They each were trapped in the knowledge that their team was a prison as well as a bloodline for their survival. How they would decide to orchestrate their continuing partnership was the question. I had been involved with them a long time—long before I met them. I didn't want it to be over. I talked to them both, trying to play mediator, but I was just a kid hoping that my adult idols wouldn't part.

There were five more pictures to go under their contract with Wallis and Paramount and millions of dollars at stake, not only from their film careers, but from personal appearances and television as well. I couldn't understand how they could risk such hard-earned money. They were still the hottest act in show business. Even in their mutual animosity they went off to play a long-standing club date in Minneapolis. But that didn't work either. At one point Dean said "goddamn" on the stage.

Jerry stopped short, broke character, and said, "No one says goddamn in my act."

"Your act?" said Dean.

"That's right," answered Jerry.

"Then let's see you do it," Dean shot back. He walked off the stage, went to the airport, and returned to L.A.

Then something happened that would have motivated any other reasonable people to put an end to the feuding.

The Internal Revenue Service came down on them with a claim for $650,000 in back taxes. They didn't have it. Neither one of them had saved a dime. I couldn't understand that either. Incredibly, they each had spent everything they had earned. In every area of their lives they were out of control.

This was way beyond me. I still had the first dollar I ever earned and would always listen to advice (perhaps too often as a matter of fact) that affected my finances.

Agents, managers, Paramount and NBC executives, nightclub owners, and friends prevailed upon Dean and Jerry to come to their senses and resolve their differences so that they could pay their taxes and go on to make more money and have happy lives.

Dean swallowed his anger and loathing. They made a picture called *Pardners,* then, in 1956, their final picture, *Hollywood or Bust.* It turned out to be Hollywood *and* Bust. Again, the agents, managers, Paramount, NBC, nightclub owners, and friends intervened to smooth over ruptured feelings. A new script was written, engineered, and controlled by Jerry, of course. When it was ready to be presented, Jerry called Dean into the office. He outlined the idea to Dean. Dean listened and his blood boiled. The scene that followed has gone down in Hollywood history as the final nail in the coffin of their relationship. A number of people were present. Each tells it nearly the same way, including our mutual agent.

Dean stood up. "Are you saying," he asked, "that I play a cop in this thing?"

"Yep," answered Jerry.

"In a uniform?"

"Yep. In a uniform."

"No," said Dean. "All my life I ran from cops who wore those goddamn uniforms. I won't play a cop in a uniform. That's low-class to me."

"In my picture you have to wear a uniform," said Jerry. "A cop has to wear a uniform."

"Your picture?" asked Dean.

"That's right," said Jerry.

"Then you wear the uniform," said Dean.

With that, Dean walked. And that was it. It all came down to a cop's uniform and "You do it."

They never made a picture together again and, except for fulfilling one more club date, never worked together or talked to each other for nearly twenty years. I couldn't believe it. I tried to understand how this total rupture could have been prevented. But all the king's horses and all the king's men couldn't put Humpty-Dumpty back together again.

My childhood favorites were gone forever, and to me it felt like a parental breakup. Which one would I attach myself to? What would happen to all that zany spontaneity, that childish horseplay, which there wasn't enough of in the world? What about two people who had been a symbol of the science of comedy? The demise of this duo made me feel anxious. If a legendary partnership like this could break up, there seemed to be no guarantees.

The breakup of Martin and Lewis may have crumbled a certain sense of security for me and for many people, but witnessing what happened taught me that when people are completely dependent on one another, the relationship cannot last. Every individual alive needs to learn to stand on his or her own ground, claiming it for their own. A mutual respect for individual identity is necessary for any relationship to survive. And more than anything else, self-knowledge is essential. It was time for us all to grow up. I adjusted to their breakup and began in earnest a kind of search for my own self, because that was the only guarantee against loneliness in Hollywood.

The relationship between Steve and me became more independent. I relied on him for friendship and support, but both of us understood we would go through periods of separation with me in Hollywood and him in Japan as we each pursued what we wanted to do in life. I never thought to question the drive that Steve had to follow his dream in Japan. It was painful for me in many ways, but it seemed natural for him, and his support for me was always there—even if only by telephone.

On the homefront it was a foregone conclusion that Jerry Lewis would be fine without Dean. Everyone sort of knew that. He would continue to do pictures at Paramount that he would not only star in, but produce, write, direct, and stage the musical numbers for. His stage career was assured also. He was considered the talented one, the funny one, the one on whom the combination had depended. To illustrate how convinced everyone was of Jerry's survival as opposed to Dean's, most of the backstage writers, musicians, and even the conductor went with Jerry. Dean was in the cold, and he had walked out into it himself.

Jerry even expressed some concern for Dean's future and also for Dean's personal welfare. He went to Hal Wallis's assistant, extracting a promise that Wallis would do all he could for Dean because he knew Dean couldn't "do" for himself. It could well have been an ironic and empty request, but I've always felt that Jerry was more personally affected by the breakup than Dean. Dean simply wanted out—cold and cut. Jerry was arrogant and maniacal, but deeply concerned and unhappy that he was unable to put things right.

Nobody knew what to do with Dean—not Paramount, not Wallis, not even Dean. He and everyone else thought of him as a straight-man crooner who came along with the Martin and Lewis package. Few were aware of Dean's comedic talent, and Dean seemed too shy to flaunt it and risk the competitive ire of Jerry. Only those of us who could hear his subtle witticisms under his breath were privy to it. Dean floundered badly. He had no idea where to go.

I used to hang out at MCA, concerned about my own

career moves, and I'd hear the agents talking. Lew Wasserman, as head of MCA, was determined that Dean would succeed on his own. Maybe Lew's true genius has always been to turn an impossible situation into a triumph. In any case, he put Dean in a picture at Metro with Anna Maria Alberghetti called *Ten Thousand Bedrooms*. I guess he figured that the title would match Dean's smoldering sexuality. Or maybe he liked the idea of two Italians working together. At any rate, I was working at Metro when the film was being shot. Dean would saunter into the commissary, give me a peck on the cheek, then roll his eyes as he departed for the set again to make love to Anna Maria Alberghetti. Anna Maria Alberghetti? Even their singing voices were incompatible. And her screen image was too Goody Two-shoes. Dean needed danger around him, against which his laid-back nature could bounce.

With all his problems, Dean was still sweet and attentive, though he continued to treat me like a kid. He'd ask about my life and whether I was still driving my red convertible, a secondhand Plymouth. He swung a golf club everywhere he went and seemed generally unconcerned that his career was in the dumper.

And it was a deep dumper. *Ten Thousand Bedrooms* was a disaster. Reviewers said Dean was an uninspired, empty straight man, and certainly no actor.

It looked like the end of the beginning of Dean's movie career as a single leading man. He couldn't get a hit record either and no one wanted him in nightclubs. The agents at MCA scratched their heads.

Jerry, on the other hand, was doing his zany act in clubs all over America as well as singing on albums. He got his own TV show and signed a new contract at Paramount. He had a luxurious suite of offices at the studio, pretty secretaries, high-tech sound equipment, a new golf cart with his name in neon lights, a big desk, a swivel chair that turned as fast as his mind, a wardrobe to fill his "tuxedo" closet, pictures of himself mounted and framed by the still gallery, a projection room where he could screen anything at any time, researchers, legal advisers, gum, cigarettes, M&M's, the newest video equipment, fresh flowers, and about twenty flunkies who were there to laugh at his jokes.

He was surrounded by the loving support system he needed to become a genuine movie mogul. He would never be abandoned again. It didn't matter that Dean was gone. Now the studio would play straight for him. It said so in his contract.

Sometimes I'd visit the Paramount lot, which was basically my home base because of my contract with Wallis. Jerry's attitude had proved the validity of Hal Wallis's biggest fear. In his own head, it appeared, Jerry was a mogul, not a funnyman. He seemed to become an intellectual technocrat, far more interested in his gadgets and the powers they afforded him than he was in making people laugh. He'd usher me into his quarters, which had now expanded into a ministudio. He walked with more of a swagger now, his chin jutting out as he rolled his jaw with power. He flicked switches and ordered people around, speaking of himself in the third person. He would cackle the old Lewis outburst and feign some spastic jumps up and down, but it just wasn't the same. I thought of the grapefruits and the fun Warren and I had had imitating him. He had been the outrageous child we longed to be ourselves. Now he was like an emperor clown.

One day he shut the door, ordered everyone out, and offered me candy in a way that bothered me. There was nothing blatantly overt in his approach, but it was unmistakable. I had heard about Jerry's reputation with women, so I politely left his office and went to my car, the red convertible Plymouth.

The top was down as I blindly drove toward the studio gate. Was this the way it worked with the abuse of power? One of my childhood idols had, I thought, just come on to me. The other one couldn't get a job. I couldn't process the reversals of image. Jerry was, after all, a man just feeling his oats and Dean had been the one who walked out on the team. I was growing up by watching the fortunes and misfortunes of others. I wondered when it would be my turn.

What happened next taught me to live in the present, not the future.

Hal B. Wallis, my boss and discoverer, and the only producer whose name ever mattered to me, stepped out of his building and walked in front of my car. He stopped and smiled in a strange way. Then he strode over to me where I sat behind the wheel, leaned across my face, grabbed me by the shoulders, mashed his face into mine, and shoved his tongue down my throat.

He was strong and I couldn't wrestle away from him. It was a bad dream. I should have stayed in the room with Jerry and his candy and gadgets. I wanted to throw up in Wallis's face—I couldn't understand what he was doing this for.

This rape-kiss seemed to go on for days. No one else came by the car. The street was empty. I felt powerless.

I wouldn't classify this act as a "fuck me or you don't get the part" exercise. I already had the contract. It was a power move, using sex, and when I finally spat him out of my face and drove away, I vowed I would get him one day.

And I did . . . I sued him for extending my white slave contract beyond the California statute of limitations. Wallis was furious. I was the kid he had discovered and put under contract and I was acting like an ingrate.

In fact, in his opinion many of his children-contractors were ungrateful—Dean, Jerry, and me, Kirk Douglas, and Burt Lancaster.

Wallis would sell me out for $750,000 and give me what my contract stipulated, $12,000.

My Christmas bonus would be a cut-glass fruit bowl or a set of silver with the soup spoons missing because anything else would put him over budget. He was a penny-pinching tyrant and I hated working for him. I was glad when our contractual legalities were settled and I could walk away from him forever.

However, my experience as a contract player was valuable. It taught me that talent was up and down and bought and sold in Hollywood, but as long as you disallowed your soul in the bargain you'd be okay. One had to be soul-vigilant though. That is why Hollywood is good for the soul. You learn to appreciate and protect it more than anywhere else on earth.

In the aftermath of *Ten Thousand Bedrooms,* Dean was having so much difficulty finding work that people laid bets he'd be working at Larry Potter's, a small club in the San Fernando Valley, within a year. They weren't far wrong. He played small clubs around the country because no one of importance would book him. He was broke and he was not coming across. He couldn't find an attitude. He couldn't feel comfortable in his skin. He didn't know who he was. He had thought of himself as an irrelevant sidekick for too many years, and he was so prideful he wouldn't seek help. But a call came from Ed Simmons, a comedy writer who felt as low as Dean because of his breakup with his cowriter, Norman Lear. Ed offered his help. He had heard that Dean had gotten a job playing The Sands in Vegas, and Ed wanted him to succeed. Dean refused help. "I'm just gonna sing," he told Ed, not admitting that he needed to do more than that. Ed pressed him. "You've gotta find a character out there on that stage, you know that."

No truer words were ever spoken. To find your "stage legs" is the hardest quest of all. Who are you when you're standing there doing whatever you do? It's not enough just to sing, or dance, or tell jokes. You need a defined personality behind what you're doing in order for you and the audience to feel comfortable. Jack Benny, for example, was the skinflint; Gracie Allen, the ditz to George Burns's affectionate straight man; Perry Como, the ultimate in laid-back smoothness.

Dean realized that he had never been able to develop a character for himself when he was straight man for Jerry. Dean has always had an instinct for what is best for him. He realized everyone knew he was down-and-out. In a stroke of brilliance, Dean decided he might be willing to have Ed Simmons write comic material in which he'd be perceived as a drunk. He had loved Joe E. Lewis, who played the amiable drunk, and Lewis had recently died.

Simmons agreed, and the two of them came up with "Dean the Drunkie."

Dean's opening night at The Sands was something. It was well attended by celebrities because we wanted to be there for him. We were nervous because there but for the grace of God could go any of us. What would he do as a single? Many already thought he was a has-been.

Dean's longtime assistant and loyalist, Mack Gray, was with him that night. Mack was constantly with Dean. They had met through George Raft at the fights. Mack used to manage prizefighters. Since Dean used to box, they hit it off. Dean called him "killer," but the word was really derived from "killa," which means hernia in

Yiddish. Mack obviously had a hernia. Mack was as funny as Dean, and had had a long affair with Lucille Ball. I used to ply him with questions about his relationship with Lucy because I admired her so much. He would only say her red hair was real. I teased him that he blew it. He could have been half of "Mackilu."

Mack did not like Jerry Lewis because of the way he had treated Dean. He'd do anything to see his Dean outsucceed Jerry. Mack went into The Sands lobby and paid people out of his own pocket to come in to see Dean. He was broke by the time the show started.

Dean was in his dressing room, faced with another personal identity decision. Sy Devore, who made all of Dean and Jerry's tuxedos, had made Dean a special light gray tux to go with a pearl gray tie. At the last minute Dean ripped out of it and put on his old familiar Copacabana black tuxedo. Dean is a creature of habit. He doesn't really like to try new things. This black tux with the red satin lining felt familiar and comfortable to him, along with the black bow tie. It was then too that Dean decided he would never wear the same socks twice, no matter how clean and washed they might be.

So, armed with a glass of J&B scotch in one hand and a cigarette in the other, Dean walked out on the stage and became "Dean the Drunkie." At first the audience didn't know what to expect. They weren't used to seeing him alone. He peered out at them and waited for a reaction in that expert way he has. Then he stepped about a yard to the side of where he used to stand when Jerry monopolized the mike. "I'm just gonna stand here instead of there," he said, taking a long swig of J&B and making a face. He was laid back and in command.

The audience began to laugh. They felt they didn't have to feel sorry for Dean, which they appreciated.

He took another sip of J&B and said, "Drink up. The

drunker you get, the better I sound.'' (He kept that line in his act.)

He launched into a medley with a boozy sway and never finished a lyric. Instead of "It happened in Monterey . . ." he sang "It happened in Martha Raye a long time ago." Instead of "My darling if I hurt you, forgive me . . ." he sang "My darling if I marry you, forgive me . . ." He continued like that for his entire medley, and when he was finished he said, "I don't drink anymore." Pause. "I don't drink any less either." Then he headed into another bunch of songs that he introduced as coming from his new album, *Ballads for B-Girls*. And so it went. Dean had found his stage legs, his character without Jerry. He threw his whole approach "away." Acted as though he didn't care that much. He became a heightened version of himself, a *menefreghista*. "One who does not give a fuck."

The audience adored him, particularly those of us in show business. We understood what a breakthrough he had made. He had found who he was comfortable being. From that came the comedy.

Dean was on his way. I was proud to know him and it was only the beginning of his new identity. Twentieth-Century Fox put him in *The Young Lions* with Brando. He was back in the picture business.

A few years later Dean and I made *Some Came Running* together. The year was 1958, and I was twenty-four.

# 4

# MASCOT TO
# THE CLAN

The Clan and *Some Came Running* were the beginning of a relationship between Dean and Frank Sinatra and myself that endured for four decades. Dean and Frank had known each other over the years as fellow "dago" singers, but until *Some Came Running*, I don't think Frank was fully aware of Dean's brilliance.

People who act in films have an unstated appreciation for those who also perform on the stage. We know what innate force it takes to get up there and project past the bright lights. As Dean once said, "Those spotlights look like three goddamn trains coming straight at you."

Because of the acknowledged common experience of stage fright, just about every given moment in real life is used to create and rehearse "fun" and entertainment. Days are essentially devoted to the careful preparation of what will ensue in the evening. All of us who do stage work are night people. We come alive just after the moon comes up. As Dean once said, "I don't stop throwing up until noon."

During the filming of *Some Came Running,* I noticed that Dean and Frank's "friends" from Chicago seemed to think better at night too. We were on our movie location in Madison, Indiana, when The Boys from Chicago visited Frank. I didn't know who they were. I only knew that the nightlife of poker, jokes, pasta, and booze went on until five A.M. Our calls were at six A.M.

Dean and Frank had rented a house just adjacent to the hotel where I and everyone else lived. Frank's "friends"—Sam Giancana, who seemed to be the boss, and various princes and consorts—were "on the lam" (as they explained) from Chicago, visiting their good friend Francis Albert. Jimmy Van Heusen (real name: Chester Babcock and the man Frank secretly wanted to be) was there with Frank to oversee his creative needs by playing piano and serving as all-around court jester. Chester was a pilot and a daredevil, bald, rather rotund, and along with Sammy Cahn wrote some of America's best standards and Frank's best songs. Chester said he was in love with me and tried to persuade me to divorce my husband, and marry him. He, I'm privileged to say, wrote "The Second Time Around" to that end. I was sure I was not the only woman to have been on the receiving end of that dedication.

I was comfortable and friendly being around the guys in the group because I was perceived by most of them as a mascot. I was the only woman they allowed in the house, but that was because there had been a kind of communal decision made that I wasn't really a girl—I was a pal, maybe even one of the boys.

It would come as a shock (but a predictable one) to

me later when gently and separately both Dean and Frank visited my hotel room when no one else was looking. I wouldn't classify either of their approaches as a pass, nor was I offended in any way. As a matter of fact, their visits helped alter the sagging image I had of myself as a not very sensual woman. Except for the incident with Wallis, *no one* in Hollywood had ever made anything close to a casting-couch move on me. One producer had called me in *with* my agent to see if I was pretty enough to star with Glenn Ford in *The Sheepman*. I passed muster, but even Glenn came to look upon me as a pal.

Once I did have a director bellow and insult me for unprovoked reasons. I simply walked off the set (it was on location, and Sunday too—the golden hours of union pay), which concerned me not in the least. Shooting shut down. He came to my rented house and admitted that his behavior had been motivated by his desire to "fuck" me (as he explained gracefully), but he hadn't known how to tell me. I explained that I didn't want to do anything with him because I was involved with someone else. He understood and that was that. He didn't ask who it was.

I was married, but to most people it wasn't real. By now, Steve was living and working in Japan so much of the time that there was no perception of me as a married woman who was part of a couple. People knew I had a daughter, Sachi, who was two years old, and that her father was somewhere in the Orient. Many a Christmas and holiday Sachi and I would hang out with friends or whomever I was working with, and my intimate relationships with other men, though discreet, were common knowledge in Hollywood and accepted as a natural result of a long-distance marriage.

Before our marriage, sex between Steve and me had

been terrific. Afterward, not at all. Perhaps it was the geographical distance that resulted in sexual distance. Perhaps I was fearful of sustaining physical intimacy with someone I knew would be off again soon. Somewhere, somehow, and for some reason, I was afraid of committing totally to Steve. He was my friend and he had helped me a great deal, but the interplay of passion was absent between us. Yet he was definitely the person I cared most about, my primary relationship, and the man I would wait for until he had established his own identity in the world. Perhaps then, I thought, we would iron out our problems with trusting in intimacy. In the meantime I was free to operate in and around the hills and dales of Hollywood any way I wanted, and he was free to do the same in Japan or wherever.

Divorce was never an option, which was confusing to many of my friends and particularly to the men I had relationships with. In fact it was even confusing to me. Steve was only the second man I had ever been with, so I had not had much experience when I entered the Hollywood playground. I quickly learned that I needed to feel love in order to have sex with someone. So I created the illusion of love as an excuse to have sex. That was easy because the rich fantasy life inspired by scripts, love stories, and beautiful people guaranteed that I would fall in and out of love with people quite often. I thought it was real when it was happening and was frequently crushed to the earth with a splat when it was over. And it was usually over when the director yelled cut. . . .

In spite of that, the men in Frank and Dean's crowd acted more like adolescent boys around me than swinging seducers. They weren't interested in me that way. There were plenty of other women for them.

One evening during a night shoot, as we sat around Frank's house waiting for director Vincente Minnelli and his camera crew to call us to the set, there was the sound of screaming and a door being crashed open. One of the legion of women who surrounded the house twenty-four hours a day had broken through security and into the house. She barreled down the hallway and into the living room looking for Frank. "Frankie, I love you!" she wailed as she spotted him teaching me gin rummy. She pounced on him, began kissing him all over, and ripped off his shirt. He fell back and put his arms up in shock. I remember how helpless and ineffectual he seemed in the situation. He looked like a fallen stick figure, incapable of coping with someone who had taken control. He tried to wipe her kisses from his face. A security guard came and pulled the woman off him. Frank lurched to his feet. He looked around the room as though a bad smell permeated every corner. He brushed his trousers off, attempting to reinstate the crease. He threw the torn shirt under the coffee table and straightened his hair. "I feel dirty," he said. "I'm going to take a shower."

There was something chauvinistic about the way he said he felt dirty . . . as though women soiled a man's existence. I remember wondering why he didn't at least crack a smile or feel a little flattered that someone was that crazed for him.

Cleanliness was paramount to Dean and Frank. Whenever they took me with them for a little side trip to some gambling joints near Cincinnati, I'd sit in their hotel suite, fascinated at the spectacle of them primping for a night out. They didn't mind my watching them. They thought of me as a loyal pet. They splashed on their cologne, each dousing himself with his own favorite brand (Fabergé's Woodhue for Dean). Their white shirts were crisp and new, the ties well chosen, the suits expensive and impeccably tailored. But what got me were their hats. They wore wide-brimmed hats right out of the racetrack number from *Guys and Dolls*. They'd descend the stairs of our hotel and usher me grandly to the limo. They moved with self-assured pride, tossing away jokes and hundred dollar bills to bellboys. They adjusted their jackets and smoothed down their ties. Their shoes were uncommonly polished and I was certain their socks didn't smell. Underneath it all, I sensed their underwear was as white and fresh as soft, newly fallen snow. I also knew I would never see it. It was just better that way. Why was it that they who consorted with gangster types and worked hard at entertaining people insisted on being perceived as so impeccably clean? Maybe to them cleanliness was next to godliness and these guys saw themselves as gods. Or maybe they felt they needed to cleanse themselves of something. I was such an innocent then . . . an observer certainly, but unsure of what I was really seeing.

They took me with them everywhere, trailed by these friends who looked like gangsters. The "friends" adored basking in Frank and Dean's fame, fame that was earned legitimately. Giancana was recognized in some places; in others he went unnoticed. But when he was recognized it was with fear.

Sam Giancana was usually fairly nice to me, although once he gave me a glimpse of what he was capable of. It happened in Mexico City. I had a day off from the film I was making in Mexico, *Two Mules for Sister Sara* with Clint Eastwood, and had traveled to Mexico City to see Sammy Davis, Jr., perform in a club. I went backstage to congratulate Sammy, and Giancana was there. He was on the lam again, ensconced within a four-wall protected home. He greeted me (God knows Sam Giancana was not an overtly warm individual) and I shook hands with him. His grip was strong. He glared out at me from under hooded lids. His shoulders were more stooped than usual.

"Pasta?" he asked.

"No thanks, Sam," I answered. "I've had dinner."

"It's good," he continued. I sensed trouble immediately, maybe because he hadn't let go of my hand. "I want you to have some."

Much as I always do when anybody tries to force me to do anything, I balked.

"Oh yeah?" I challenged. "Well, I *don't want* to have some."

God, I was so green. I hadn't yet learned the art of feminine diplomatic compromise, in the face of possible trouble. No wonder the guys didn't think I was a girl. Well, Sam didn't either. He grabbed my arm and twisted it behind my back. It really hurt.

"Hey," I yelled, "quit that. I'm sure your pasta is numero uno, but I'm full."

He twisted harder.

Just then Sammy came out of his dressing room, jangling with gold chains and snappily dressed for the rest of the evening. He noticed my pained expression and my "disappeared" arm.

"What the hell are you doing?" Sammy asked Giancana.

I shrugged. "He wants me to eat his pasta," I explained, realizing as soon as I said it how foolish it sounded. Sammy suppressed a giggle and glanced at the pasta. He walked over to Sam.

"C'mon, Sam," he chided gently. "Let the kid go." (Everyone in our group still called me kid.) "She doesn't want any," he went on. "She's probably on a diet or something. You know how actresses can be."

Sam smiled that crooked, hooded smile of his and twisted my arm harder. I groaned.

Sammy touched his arm. "C'mon, Sam. Let go."

With that, Sam released my arm and slammed Sammy in the stomach with his fist.

"Okay"—he chuckled—"no pasta for either of you." Sammy doubled over. He had another show to do that night. I stepped back, horrified. Giancana went to the bar and made himself a drink. Sammy straightened up, took a deep breath, and said to me, "Why don't you come back later?"

I nodded and left. I wanted to deliver an exit line that would live in infamy, but I couldn't. I was confused. Sammy was in pain. My arm was wrenched. This man seemed to be a monster. Beyond those feelings I had not yet ventured.

Years later I saw Giancana with a woman he loved. I was startled to observe how she operated with such a man. "Dominatrix" would be a mild description. To his face she referred to him as a "cock-sucking sleazeball who's so chickenshit he loves to be whipped." He ate it up. For some reason that made inverted sense to me. Those who dominate must love to be dominated. I understood him a little better.

Perhaps Giancana was wary of me from the beginning because of something silly I did—in total innocence— when we were on location with *Some Came Running*. We were in Frank's house, sitting by the kitchen window, playing gin. I wore sunglasses to cut down the sun's glare and to disguise my reactions to my cards. Unbeknownst to me, Sam was reading my cards from my *sunglasses*. I kept losing—I couldn't understand why. Just then the doorbell rang. Since I was the official butleress, I went to answer it. It was a delivery of cannolis from Chicago. I brought them back to the kitchen, opened the refrigerator door, placed them inside, and noticed that one of the boys had put a toy water pistol on the first shelf. I pulled the pistol out and trained it on Sam.

"Don't I know you from somewhere?" I questioned, thinking of the wall of a post office.

Sam leaped to his feet and pulled a .38 pistol, a real one, out of a holster inside his jacket. Just then, Frank and Dean walked in looking for something to eat. They saw Sam and me with guns trained on one another and fell down laughing.

As I said, I hadn't processed who Giancana really was. His face was the texture of dough and his dark eyes were recessed under lids like protective ridges. I knew he was a hood of some kind, but at that point it was all so theatrically dangerous and amusing to me. I didn't have the background that Dean and Frank had, growing up on the streets. I played. They *knew*.

The incident passed, to be joked about for years. But as time went on and I grew to understand more, I was horrified to realize how glamorous our culture had made the Mafia. I actually felt it happening to me. I saw audiences' eyes gleam with glee at the secondhand thrill they received from watching performers who hung out with gangsters—their hands had shaken the hands of killers! What was it about us, that we glorified an individual so deranged he had no conscience? What did that say not only about us as a society, but about *me*? I too was hanging out with these guys, and found a lot of it fun. I was an innocent in the beginning, but when innocence departed and I slowly opened my eyes to their world, which I still didn't truly understand, I was faced with my own inner conflict.

As for Frank, he was nice to me but muscled others. He was attentive and sweet to me but often cruel and rude to others.

When he said to me one day, "Just let me know if

anybody bothers you and I'll take care of it," an electrical shudder went through me. It was a shudder of conflict. On the one hand, I basked in his protection; on the other—what would he do to someone who "bothered" me? What did he mean? And was the dangerous mystery of it all what made it attractive?

Years later, when I was doing my act in a hotel in Florida, there was a strike. My show was one of the shows targeted. I called Frank and told him how miserable they were making me: microphones shutting down in the midst of my performance, blackouts at inappropriate moments, static in the monitor system, etc.

"I'll take care of it, baby," he assured me. "Call me if you need anything else."

I didn't have to. I don't know what he did, but I had no more troubles.

Often when we'd speak on the phone after not having talked for some time, he wouldn't say, "Hello, baby, how are you?" He'd say instead, "Hello, baby, are you all right?" He somehow always implied that there was bound to be something wrong that he could fix.

It was because of Frank and his associations that I was beginning to understand the fundamental questions I needed to ask myself about human friendship, about power and morality. My eyes were being opened to other values and ways of operating. The ethics of my childhood and Judeo-Christian upbringing did not necessarily reflect how the country I lived in operated.

I was growing up in the twentieth century, and I happened to be doing it through the eyes and moral requirements of Hollywood.

I began to *think* more about what I felt and *feel* more about what I thought. Hopefully I could balance both against what I perceived.

Was honor among thieves at least honor?

Was loyalty of any kind better than no loyalty at all?

And where did fear come in? Couldn't people define themselves to a great extent by what they were afraid of?

I knew a violent revolutionary once who found through psychotherapy that he was suffering from a mental disorder defined as the fear of fear. When I read the biography of Sam Giancana, I realized what violent torture he had been put through by his own father—chained to a tree and beaten to a bloody pulp, within a heartbeat of losing his life for nearly a week. No wonder domination and violence were erotic to him. No wonder he couldn't allow himself to fear.

Dean and Frank also seemed unafraid of fear. They never appeared to weigh the consequences of their actions, and they never looked back. When Dean walked away from the cop's uniform with Jerry, he closed the book. When Frank walked away from a relationship, there was no way back. And one never knew when the ax would fall. When he broke off his engagement to Juliet Prowse she called me. "I just said I wanted him to meet my family in South Africa," she said. "And he regarded that as a slight. He won't talk to me now."

When Frank called me, he said, "She doesn't really want to marry me, babe. I don't need to pass muster with anybody."

We went to dinner to discuss it. He said he not only loved Juliet, but *liked* her too. Yet there was no way back. He had shut his own door on the relationship, and his Italian pride would never allow another opening. Yet I felt Frank respected you if you knew what you wanted and stood your ground, even if you were against him. He went in for the kill when he sensed weakness. I suspect he hated weakness in himself and therefore never allowed it in anyone else. Dean was the same way, but less direct about it. Frank made his opinions and temperament obvious. Dean was more subtle and held his feelings within.

There's a story about Dean that clarifies for me why the Mob never really pestered him. By pestering, I mean putting the strong arm on him to play Mob-owned joints.

Dean worked the Riobamba Club on Fifty-seventh Street in New York City. Riobamba was owned by Louis Lepke, a gangster who was awaiting execution on death row for murder. Louie Lepke was considered the hit man for the Mob.

Dean befriended Louie's wife when he knew Louie was in trouble; she ran the Riobamba in Louie's absence. It didn't matter to Dean what Lepke's morals were. Lepke had hired him and given him a chance; Dean would reciprocate the friendship with Lepke's wife. When no one else would associate with the remainder of Lepke's family, Dean did. He sat with them when Louie was executed—and was there for them afterward. The word got around that Dean was a good guy.

Dean didn't do this to impress the bosses. As a matter of fact, he ignored the bosses. They, in turn, left Dean alone. All during the time that Dean and Jerry played Mob joints, as well as when Dean played them alone, no one leaned on him. No one made calls in the middle of the night. No one expected his services at funerals or daughters' coming-out parties or weddings. If Dean went along with Frank (who did get calls), that was another story.

I watched Dean studiously distance himself from The Boys. He didn't run from them, he was just unavailable. Of course, he was unavailable to lots of people. He made Mob jokes and insinuated he had friendships with them, but there was a detachment that I admired. I wondered if it took courage. I wondered what would happen if they really leaned on him.

There was one man who did lean on Dean. That man was Ed Torres, who operated the Riviera in Vegas. I remember hearing Liza Minnelli call him Uncle Eddie because her mother had worked for him. He had sounded cozy and friendly. Jesus. I worked for Torres. He was rough. He used to purposely annoy Dean. He wanted to be Dean's *boss,* which was his first mistake.

Dean owned ten percent of the Riviera and as a result had a permanent suite there where he kept the wardrobe he needed when he played. One night Dean arrived a day earlier than planned with Mort Viner (his agent as well as mine). Mort discovered that Eddie had rented Dean's room out to someone else, clothes and all. He checked and found Eddie had been doing this all along.

Mort and Dean said nothing. Dean played his engagement, and on the last night Mort played rough. He paid off a bellboy to collect Eddie Torres's clothes and put them in the middle of the floor of Dean's suite. Just before Dean left the hotel, Mort set fire to Eddie's clothes and then rang the fire marshal and said he smelled smoke on that floor. Eddie gave up his need to control Dean.

Frank couldn't control Dean either. Through the years Dean often wouldn't take Frank's calls so Frank would call Mort to find out where Dean was. Frank wanted to socialize, tear up the town. Dean never liked going out at night. He liked to watch television and be alone. Many times I'd hear Dean say, "I can't go out tonight. I have a girl in my room." Of course, there was no one waiting for him but his faithful Western or a rerun of *Kojak.*

Dean's performance in *Some Came Running* was his best, I thought. He was a lot like Bama, a loner with his own code of ethics who would never compromise, so maybe it wasn't really a performance. Neither he nor Frank liked Vincente Minnelli. They thought he was too precious and pursed his lips too much. The two of them could dislike people because of small things that personally offended them. They couldn't overcome their judgment of a person's teeth or hair or smell. They'd make jokes under their breath. They would cast someone out of their lives because his jockstrap showed under his shorts. They were primitive children and their reactions adolescent. They put crackers in each other's beds and dumped spaghetti on new tuxedos. They would grab an ice cube from a drink and thrust it into the hand of a formally dressed fan and ask him to skate around on it.

One night, on an angry, moody whim, Frank just arbitrarily canceled the evening's shoot. No one could do anything. Another night Minnelli was taking a particularly long and artistic time of it. The shot involved a Ferris wheel in a scene at the end of the picture. Finally, after circling around the camera a few times with his lips pursed and much gesturing to himself, Minnelli put his head up in the air and closed his eyes. I tensed up. Dean and Frank and I stood waiting to do the scene. I could sense what was coming. The fans were screaming all around us. I looked over at Dean and Frank. The dawn was about to break. They were about to explode at Vincente's artistic indulgence. Vincente came out of his reverie and instead of saying, "Move the camera," he said, "Move the Ferris wheel." Frank bolted toward his limo, dove into it headfirst, and ordered the driver to the airport. He went back to Los Angeles, and Dean went with him. I stayed. Production shut down. Vincente was oblivious. After a few days the head of production at Metro, Sol Siegel, wrangled Frank into returning with a promise that next time the camera would move, not the set.

Frank could be just as ruthless with scripts. During an afternoon shoot, he invited me for a drink in his trailer. The assistant director came to the trailer to call us to the set.

"We're having a drink," said Frank, "because it's 'tini time."

"But, Mr. Sinatra," protested the assistant director, "we are behind schedule and we need to make up time."

"How far behind are we?" asked Frank.

"Two weeks," answered the assistant director.

"Say, buddy. You have a script handy?" asked Frank.

I knew what was coming.

The assistant director handed him his script. Frank counted off about twenty pages and then ripped them out of the script.

"There, pal," he said. "Now we're on schedule."

The assistant director fled, not wanting to put us ahead of schedule.

The pages never went back in. It was just like Frank. When he went on record that something was over, it was over. The writers had to piece the story together somehow. Frank realized later he had cut one of my big scenes, so he threw the end of the picture to me.

"Let the kid get in the way of the bullet," he said to Sol Siegel. "That'll make the audience feel sorry for her because she tried to save my life. Might get her a nomination out of it."

He was right. I got my first Academy Award nomination for *Some Came Running*. I wondered what would have happened had he wanted two or three martinis that day.

Where Frank was interested in martinis, I was interested in chewing gum. I always chewed it right up to "action." Frank laughed and was amused when I never had a place to put it. One day the director yelled "action" and I took my gum out of my mouth and stuck it behind Frank's ear. He mashed his ear up against it so it wouldn't fall. This became our game and no one could figure out why Frank usually touched his ear before a take.

For me, Vincente Minnelli was an excellent director, simply because he didn't direct much. He "let" us actors find our own characters and our own way. Dean thrived on the freedom he felt with Vincente—one reason his character of Bama was the finest of his career. But Frank was threatened by this way of working because the freedom of choice exposed him too much. Where acting is concerned, he likes the security of an autocratic, dictatorial personality, as long as he respects their talent. He did his best work for Fred Zinnemann (*From Here to Eternity*), a man who is renowned for getting the shot regardless of hardship, John Frankenheimer (*Manchurian Candidate*), who insists on infiltrating your psychological stability, and Otto Preminger (*Man with the Golden Arm*), an outright emotional Nazi.

Directors like that are okay with me too, because it is fun to please them, but I think I prefer a director who basically leaves me alone unless he or she can make a suggestion that is not really about ego.

Minnelli was agonizingly unperturbed, which guaranteed that he always got what he wanted. The camera crew, art department, costume people, makeup, hair, and special effects were well aware of his taste and control. They loved him and found no problem obeying his leadership. I felt the same way.

In fact, I guess you could say a really good director

doesn't need to do much but hire excellent people and act as a sounding board while they do their work.

The mythology of the Clan began with *Some Came Running* in 1958. We all enjoyed working together so much that with Frank's prodding we couldn't stop. I did *Can-Can* with Frank in 1960 and *All in a Night's Work* with Dean in 1961. When I worked with the two of them together, I usually played a cameo part in some stupid Mob-caper–Vegas movie and they'd give me a car or something as a salary. That was fine with me. It was fun and totally madcap.

When we got together and made pictures at the same time that the Clan was appearing in Vegas, there was an energy there that has never been duplicated since.

Two shows a night, seven days a week, for three months . . . while shooting a picture. No one got any sleep. Granted, these pictures were not award winners—*Robin and the Seven Hoods, Ocean's Eleven,* etc.—but the spontaneous humor on the stage and the set was unparalleled then and has never been matched since. The director never knew what was going to happen or how a scene would be played on a given day. But it didn't matter.

And at night the world came to Vegas to see Dean, Frank, Sammy, Joey Bishop, Peter Lawford, and, whenever they could inveigle me to the stage—*me.* Milton Berle used to love to come and interrupt, which was his stock-in-trade. Of course, Sammy knew that Milton was a filing cabinet of jokes and used to buttonhole him after every show for material that hadn't yet been heard. Milton was having a hard enough time himself, keeping up with the uncontrollable antics on the stage.

One night Dean wheeled out a table outfitted with a full complement of drinks. The audience howled, and he was off.

"Frank, do you know how to make a fruit cordial?" he asked.

"No, Dean," answered Frank. "How do you make a fruit cordial?"

Dean took a beat and shrugged. "Why," he said, "be nice to him!" He bared his muscles and said, "You know how I got these muscles?"

"No," said Frank. "How?"

"By carrying Jerry all those years," answered Dean.

Frank was playing the straight man for Dean. They both knew it. But sometimes Frank got sick of never getting any laughs.

"How come you always get the laughs and I don't?" he complained to Dean one night.

"You're not funny," said Dean.

"Well, let me try," said Frank.

"Okay, pallie," said Dean.

They went out on the stage and reversed everything. Dean played straight and Frank had the punch lines. Nobody laughed at Frank. In fact, they laughed at Dean's straight lines. Frank began to understand on a visceral level the depth of Dean's timing. No one could compare, and it was all because Dean had hit on the identity of Dean the Drunkie. He knew who he was with a drink in his hand, which, by the way, went with him everywhere. I have seen Dean carrying a "drink" on the golf course. His attitude is funny boozy, but the drink is apple juice.

Jerry, who sometimes played Vegas at the same time as Dean, couldn't fill the room. He still spoke of himself in the third person. Dean had decided not to be thrice removed from himself. He was blossoming without Jerry. He had found himself, and I began to find him really attractive—like a real girl! He made me laugh with his wit and sometimes his kindness and warmth were touching. We went on to do five more pictures together. After a while I was glad he and Jerry had split. That left room for me.

While we were filming *All in a Night's Work,* I developed a real crush on Dean. By now, I had finally become a ''girl'' to him too. I didn't know what to do about it. So, one night after work I stopped by his home to talk. I didn't know what I was going to say. Jeanne opened the door and ushered me into the living room, where seven children who had just finished dinner were playing. It was mayhem, the air thick with family interplay. I waited on the couch while Jeanne called Dean. The kids quieted.

He came downstairs, saw me, walked over, and embraced me.

''Hi, sweetheart,'' he said. ''Wow. You came to see me. Hey, kids, look who's here.'' They acknowledged me and returned to their play. We sat down together. I didn't know what to say.

''Well, sweetheart,'' he said. ''How can I help you?''

Jeanne yelled from the other room that there was a phone call for Dean. He looked into my eyes. Could he guess what I was feeling? I couldn't tell him. Young-lady crushes he was probably used to.

Finally I spoke. ''I just wanted you to know how much I've enjoyed working with you. I think you're brilliant.''

Dean held my hand and smiled.

''I feel the same way about you, sweetheart, you're the best.''

It was one of those moments when it is obvious that nothing more should be said. We looked at each other. I stood up and kissed him on the cheek. The kids had gone; the room was empty.

"I'll see you tomorrow, honey," said Dean. "Now, you take care of that sweet self of yours."

Oh boy. I excused myself as gracefully as I could and left. I felt like an idiot. I don't know to this day if he knew what was on my mind. Even if he had known, would it have mattered? I think not. He would much rather have watched television.

DURING THE YEARS OF WORKING WITH DEAN AND FRANK, I watched the two of them fall in and out of love with various women. I wondered how they actually conducted themselves in those relationships. Were they committed at all? Frank was in and out of engagements and Dean was married to Jeanne. Frank used to refer to Jeanne as the U-boat commander because he saw her as a Nazi who controlled Dean. Could they see women as real beings with needs and intelligence? Did they ever communicate on a fulfilling level? I was secretly grateful that I didn't really see them as potential lovers. Had anything like that developed, I would have been in real trouble. But it felt as if they were protecting me more than anything else.

Why had I drawn Jerry Lewis, Dean Martin, and Frank Sinatra into the formative years of my experience in Hollywood? Why them? *These* men were my friends and teachers. Why were Dean and Frank and I so comfortable together, given their backgrounds, which were diametrically opposed to mine? Sometimes I was flabbergasted not only at what I witnessed, but also at my reaction to it. When Dean and Frank took me places and our hotel rooms weren't satisfactory, Frank would punch a hole in the wall to make them satisfactory. I can't say I was appalled. It was like being in a violent cartoon. I'd watch the reactions of other people. Sometimes they were terrified. Sometimes they treated it as a joke he had included them in. That was always a mistake. Nobody was included with Frank unless you had earned it.

Once, when Frank and Dean and I were watching television at two in the morning, Frank suddenly got hungry and called the manager, demanding that somebody wake up and fix them something to eat. I could hear the manager mumble his irritation, but secretly he must have liked the idea of seeing Dean and Frank at two in the morning. Bleary-eyed, but with a smirk, the manager came bearing sandwiches and beer to our living room, where the TV was blasting out a rerun. The manager threw his chest out like a prizefighter's manager and gave Frank "attitude" about the late hour and loud noise. Frank offhandedly told the manager to go fuck himself, shut up, and get the hell out. The manager dropped the tray and called Frank a skinny *wop*. Frank took a swing at the guy and it connected. The guy swung back. Dean looked up. "If you're gonna fight," he said impatiently, "do it on the other side of the room."

Dean turned up the volume of the TV, opened a beer, and ate a sandwich. "Too much mayo," he said. The manager rubbed his jaw, mumbled something about how crazy they were, and left.

My stomach turned over. This really *was* crazy, wasn't it? I mean, I wasn't sure. I couldn't decide what I thought of their behavior. These guys were coming from a place that was so beyond my experience that I denied it was seriously sick. Of course my own proper upbringing in Virginia had nurtured in me an attraction to unruly, unseemly, rebellious behavior, because I always sensed that same repressed rebelliousness simmering under my own parents' surface. They never expressed what they were really feeling. These guys did. In a way it was a release. These were real and intense feelings. They lived their own code. Because I was so young, I think I saw their actions as simply an alternative code of behavior, not sociopathic, and I guess I thought they behaved this way only among themselves. It never occurred to me that either Frank or his "friends" would really hurt anybody.

I knew The Boys, of course, had been around when Frank grew up in Hoboken. They must have represented power and influence to him. But he was also a kid who told me he heard the music of the spheres in his head. The music sang to him, he said, calling him to his destiny.

As a loner with a strong-willed mother in control, he must have been attracted to the collective friendship The Boys provided. All for one—one for all.

I wished so often that I had had something like that in my life. In my world privacy was more valued than anything. "Hoe your own little row of potatoes" was the motto in our house. I longed to do outrageous things away from home. These people were always there for each other regardless of the morality involved. So I can understand why I wasn't appalled at some of what went on.

Still, I was intrigued with the unpredictability of Frank's behavior and what triggered it.

I don't think I ever met Frank's mother, Dolly. Whenever people try armchair psychology to analyze Frank's bizarre violence, they mention Dolly. His closest friends describe her as having been opinionated, emotionally intractable, unstable, foulmouthed, overbearing, and seriously unpredictable. Her son could do no wrong, she would say, and he would be "Big" no matter what. Frank told me he feared and emulated his mother simultaneously. He often spoke of her to me. "She was a pisser," he'd say, "but she scared the shit outta me. Never knew what she'd hate that I'd do."

As I watched his obsession with Ava Gardner's unpredictable behavior I could see the similarity. Was he addicted to being thrown off balance? Because Dolly had bullied him, did he need that from his mate? The fights and skirmishes between Frank and Ava were legendary. They couldn't live with or without one another. Ava hated Frank's gangster friends and wouldn't treat them with "respect," as glamorous terrorizers, the way the rest of Frank's group did—she lived with Frank. On the other hand, they thought she was a whacko and didn't act the way a real wife should act.

Since Frank clearly preferred the company of The Boys to a regular home life, there was no real competition between them and Ava. But Ava satisfied an insatiable need of Frank's to be bullied by a strong mother figure. Ava made him grovel. Ava humiliated him. Ava kicked him when he was down. Ava was unattainable, she was beautiful beyond words, and in her honeydripping voice she mouthed words that could make a longshoreman wince. Ava was the perfect combination. And if she was unattainable, how could she become boring?

Of course, Ava was as much a mystery to herself as she was to Frank. Therefore, he was strung out on her until she died, even after she had become a heavy drinker and a recluse.

Having dinner with Ava in her apartment in London explained so much. Her gorgeous body had become more ample, her exquisite face lined with sad bitterness around her tired eyes, but she was plucky. Her sentences were choppy as she spoke about her love for Spain and how much she *didn't* miss movies. Her two pet corgis had taken on Ava's personality. She was their beloved mistress, and they were angry, repressed little dogs, highly nervous and agitated, growling at her, demanding attention at every moment. They were so nuts that I said good night to Ava early.

But Frank loved all that commotion, the angry demands. Maybe with a mother of such force and a father of such passivity (Marty Sinatra was a fireman who let Dolly rule), it is understandable that Frank would admire and emulate his mother in order to gain her favor, and remain angry with his father for allowing such imbalance.

Frank could never say "I'm sorry" or admit he was wrong. It was as though he could not betray the expectation of perfection, and an apology would force him to face that imperfection in himself. And the fear he aroused in others was sometimes stultifying. People would literally shiver until they laughed when he erupted in a rage. For some reason, I never felt afraid of him. I don't know why. Perhaps I was afraid to feel fear. Perhaps I was too naive, and because I was never afraid of him, he trusted me.

He demanded total loyalty without deviation, yet he loved people who told him the truth. A point of view that contradicted his was okay if it was well thought out. But people never knew when they'd be met with revenge. He could change his own mind on a social or political issue with alarming speed.

For example he hated Richard Nixon with deep vitriol, then ended up campaigning for him. (Some say because Nixon personally complimented him on a stand he took.)

He told me that he thought Ronald Reagan was "a stupid bore who couldn't get a job in pictures, which was why he went into politics." He threatened to move out of California if Reagan ever got elected to public office. He thought Nancy was "a dumb broad with fat ankles who couldn't act." I heard him scream and curse at the television set when they appeared. It was a deep and personal hate that Frank felt for the Reagans.

But when Jesse Unruh, speaker of the California assembly and a Bobby Kennedy loyalist, decided to run against Reagan for governor, Frank decided to support Reagan. Why? Because Bobby had been responsible for his brother, Jack Kennedy, not staying at Sinatra's home in Palm Springs. Why? Because of Sinatra's association with the Mafia. Frank then supported Reagan to get back at Bobby.

His actions and values so often seemed to be motivated by what he perceived as betrayal or disloyalty. I wondered where such suspicion had been born. Or was it *because* the support and loyalty from his mother had been so unwavering that he required such unquestioning allegiance in everyone else? Frank never questioned his ability to succeed at anything he desired to attempt. His mother saw to that. Sometimes his methods were without conscience. His mother had seen to that too. No one ever questioned his right to succeed, regardless of what he wanted to do. He would have his way; that had been ordained from the beginning, with his mother, and it would ever be thus.

Even so, Frank was insecure when he was around people he deemed to be of a higher class than he. He felt inadequate and his response was to behave even more like a bum, unless they took the time to put him at ease, as Jackie Kennedy and Princess Grace did. He could relate to these women as a man with sex appeal; that was the common denominator.

Frank never said thank you for a present.

I gave him a cigarette lighter from Japan once. He adored it. It was thin and fit into his pocket easily. But he never thanked me. Instead he gave me a bigger and better gift.

That was the way it was with Frank. If you helped him more than he helped you, the friendship was doomed because the balance he wanted had been tipped. And if you worked for Frank and attempted to protect him from himself, you committed the most heinous of all crimes. *He* was the godfather, indisputably. He knew not only what was best for himself, but also what was best for you. And in that way he could be the most extraordinary friend. He was a happy man when he was able to come to my rescue. "Oh, I just wish someone would try to hurt you so I could kill them for you," he'd say when he was trying to express his feelings of friendship.

This point of view, this value system, this way of perceiving himself was not unlike the power he required on the stage.

In that spotlight, trodding the boards in his patent leather party shoes, swinging the microphone around as he made love to the sound of his own voice, controlling not only the rhythm but the volume of a forty-person orchestra, and sculpting the audience's feelings as they sat mesmerized, he was the godfather of the musical depths, of their sorrows, their lonely nights, their passionate silliness. In that compressed space and time— two hours in a club or theater—no one and nothing in the world was more important than that encapsulated experience. Nothing could disturb the genial perfection he created for his audience. He was a musical dictator because he knew best, not only for himself, but for them. He knew what would move them to feel. And he was a benevolent dictator, because in the final analysis he knew he was serving them. This, indeed, created the only fear he knew. Would he be able to give them what they expected? Would he be able to put aside his own ego to please the mother audience who came because they loved him and wanted to be proud of him, and would he thereby fulfill their expectations?

In this circumstance, Frank's inner world of conflict was eased.

He would see to it that the music was mathematically perfect, its harmonies made in heaven, duplicating the sounds he had heard in his head since he was old enough to be aware of them. His musicians were mere mortals who would unquestionably obey his unearthly commands because they recognized a gift from God in their musical father. His every gesture and move would be duly accounted for, appreciated, and respected because the light was trained solely on him. There was no need for him to command attention because the troops could see no one else. The emotional loyalty that was paramount to him was never in doubt. His audience was absolutely and without reservation his. He'd never allow their attention or focus to stray. Continual attention needed to be paid. And with all these components the audience became his obedient child as well as his mother. He knew what was best for it. And he was right. He had led it into the spheres of what he considered the divine. The spheres of heavenly music. This was the only realm of peace for him. Without it he would die. Yet, as a child of music, his survival was his mother audience. He desperately needed her to love him, appreciate him, acknowledge him, and never betray his trust. So he would cajole, manipulate, caress, admonish, scold, and love her unconditionally until there was no difference between him and her. He and she had become one. He became the mother basking in the image she had intended for him all along. And in that he found peace and a sense of completeness.

What was always so touching to me, knowing and experiencing so much of what Sinatra could be, was his exit line. He meant it when he'd say, "Thank you for letting me sing for you."

Without their permission he would have no reason to live. A tangled contradiction for a man who requested permission from no one.

In later years, when I had a club career of my own, Frank would sometimes wander onto my stage and kid around. He'd bring Dean with him. In the past I had been the mascot. Now the mascot required respect. I'd look over at them standing in my spotlight, and I would feel ill equipped to measure up to their stagecraft. As the spotlight shone in their eyes, I'd once again observe that magnificent strut of confidence and the mischief playing across their faces. I'd remember the old days when I wished I could be up there with them. How different it was from film. How carefree and raucous and un-planned. I wished I could be that way. Then, when they'd call me up from the audience and, in full view of people, teach me comedy tricks or show me how to hold a pose in order to milk a laugh longer, I was in heaven. They could make a joke out of anything. Once one of the showgirls left her sandal in the piano. Dean found it, held it up, and said, "Oh, I see Victor Mature was here." When I decided to go live, Frank took me aside. "Remember one thing, baby," he said. "You change the room by showing up." Sammy said, "Pull out all the stops." And Dean said, "What do you need it for?"

THOSE TIMES ARE GONE NOW. AND SHOW BUSINESS IS BE-reft because of it. When The Boys ran Vegas, they knew how to do it. Their hotels didn't care about a show room paying for itself. Gambling and a good time were the high priorities. The showroom and its entertainers were there to get you in the mood to drop your cash on the green velvet tables. If you were stupid enough to fall for it, that was their gain. Vegas was one of the only towns in the world that told the truth about itself. It wasn't in any way self-righteous. It existed to seduce you into throwing your money into its greedy pot. Everything was designed to make you have such a good time you'd even enjoy your losses, and furthermore you were warned.

Today, Vegas is a family resort town, with rides and circuses and cotton candy. It doesn't exist for the same reasons anymore. The glamour of its power hierarchy is gone now. There's no danger, therefore no vicarious pleasure. Vegas doesn't need "stars" anymore. It can't afford "stars." So it has no intimate, spontaneous interaction. Frank plays on his own. There's not much kidding around. The showrooms have to pay for themselves now because Vegas caters to children and their desires. It's got production shows and exploding volcanoes and pyramids and *Treasure Island* monsters and day care centers. It's no longer a place of underground mystery. Everything is aboveboard and boring.

So I look back with a certain sense of loss when I'm there without the old gang. Dean and Sammy are gone and everyone else is very old. The Boys have essentially moved from public view, exacting their brutal demands on governments and drug runners. Drugs were not part of our world in those days: even crime was cleaner.

The days of the celebrity train rides when twenty big stars traveled the rails in style while playing gin rummy for a hundred dollars a point are gone. The candlelight dinners at the Dunes, eaten to the sound of thirty violins around a waterfall of glittering turquoise peopled with every star in Hollywood are no more. The days of Don Rickles, Louis Prima and Keely Smith, Ernie Kovacs, or Vic Damone playing the lounge with hundreds of people lined up at four in the morning are over.

Liberace and Danny Kaye and Mitzi Gaynor and

Danny Thomas and Bob Hope and Bing Crosby and Marlene Dietrich and Nat King Cole and Elvis Presley and the Jackson Five used to trod the boards in Vegas. I would fly up and see three shows a night for three days.

It was a whirlwind of talent, gourmet food, specialty dress shops, absurd jewelry given as good luck thank-yous.

It was cars and furs bought with poker chips; Ramos gin fizzes at breakfast and anything you wanted all day long.

You don't find the stogie smoker with the ten-carat pinkie ring sitting ringside anymore. Today the high rollers are from Hong Kong and Japan and Europe. They win and lose in foreign languages.

Family mundanity reigns.

Mob mystery wanes.

The pictures have changed too, of course. Now no one can afford antics. Directors are auteurs now, or long-suffering traffic cops who just want to finish the day's work. It's all about the finished product's budget rather than the fun of the process.

The Clan tried to recapture the antics of yesteryear one last time by making *Cannonball Run II* not far from Vegas, in 1983. It was a disgrace, of course. Frank only worked half a day, and that was too long for him. He did one take and left. It looked as though he was never there at all.

Dean had deteriorated. I hadn't seen him in years and he seemed withered, drawn, with a grayish pallor. I noticed he put five spoons of sugar in each cup of coffee. With my new sense of health awareness I chided him for it and said he'd better quit. The next day he emptied a five-pound bag of sugar inside my trailer. Sammy tried to be funny, which wasn't necessary. Just dressed in his costume he was hilarious (he was a priest). I played a nun and Marilu Henner said if she had known I would win the Oscar soon after we finished, she would have treated me with more respect! As it worked out, *Cannonball II* was my all-important follow-up picture to *Terms of Endearment*. So much for calculating shrewd moves in my career. It did bring me together with my buddies of yesteryear.

In 1988, DEAN AND FRANK AND SAMMY WENT OUT ON THE road in the Together Again tour, a show Mort Viner put together for them. They believed they could recreate the old days. Booze, broads, bands, and badness. But things had changed. Dean was now seventy-one. And an old seventy-one at that. Frank had always been more active in every way, older in years but younger in spirit.

From the moment the tour began, it was clear that the differences in energy between Dean and Frank would be a problem. I was hearing the stories from Mort.

In Oakland, their first play date, Frank wanted to go out after the show and have some fun. Dean was tired and wanted nothing but to sit and watch television. Frank dumped his chair over. Dean did a pratfall and made Frank laugh, but Dean was upset.

They went on to play Vancouver and Seattle, and Frank became more insistent that the old days could be recreated. But Dean couldn't. He was slow and too late in his reactions. Frank couldn't accept Dean's advancing age. It probably reminded him of his own mortality. He began to make cruel jokes onstage and badger Dean unmercifully. Dean couldn't use his "I've got a broad waiting in my room" line anymore when Frank wanted him to go out at night. He just told Frank the truth.

"I don't want to go, dago," he said. "I just want to go to my room and watch TV and fall asleep."

Frank couldn't take that.

"What're you doin' this for, then?" he yelled. "C'mon, get your ass outta that chair."

Dean didn't move. He never liked being ordered around. He fell silent. That made Frank mad. He picked up Dean's plate of spaghetti and dumped it on his head.

Dean did a Buster Keaton and sat stone still. That made Frank laugh. Frank thought Dean was being funny, but he wasn't. Dean was making up his mind to walk . . . again.

When they reached Chicago, Frank was sure Dean would return to adolescence and tear up the town with him. It was, after all, Frank's town.

Frank, Dean, and Sammy were booked into the same hotel. But they were not all on the same floor. This was grounds for heavy disruption in Frank's mind. It didn't matter that they arrived by private plane at 2:30 A.M. It didn't matter that the hotel had not been designed to have three big suites on the same floor. It didn't matter that most of the hotel staff and indeed most of the town was asleep—Frank insisted they all be on the same floor, and that was that. He began making phone calls. He wanted Dean and Sammy to meet him in the lobby to facilitate the matter. Sammy very nearly complied, but Dean just changed rooms with Mort Viner so that Mort got the incessant calls for the next few hours.

When Frank had exhausted his inquiries to other hotels and could no longer reach Dean, he allowed himself to get tired and finally fell asleep.

There were three shows in a row in Chicago, which Dean was willing to complete. But on the last night, Mort arranged for a private plane to take Dean back to California, where he checked Dean into a hospital to make it look good. Dean needed some rest anyway.

Dean and Frank had come to the end of their road,

just as Dean and Jerry had. Frank called to inquire how Dean was doing, but Dean never took the calls.

Dean left our entertainment industry in much the same way as he came in: quiet, stoic, resolved to be left alone, essentially uninvolved with the passions of life and work. He was a true *menefreghista*. He was happy when he really didn't give a fuck. I miss him more than I can say, and every time I pass the Copacabana in New York, I remember the laughter I heard as a kid, which inspired me to wonder who was in there.

FRANK WAS UPSET ABOUT THE DECLINE OF DEAN. DEAN'S tired abdication of ambition and the joy of living worried and bothered and needled him. Frank's iron-willed drive ruled. Dean's passivity prevailed. Frank couldn't bear to observe Dean's deterioration. But the more he pursued Dean, the more Dean retreated. Dean knew what he wanted and didn't want in his life and none of it paralleled Frank's.

Frank went in the opposite direction. He knew in his heart that if he let go for a moment he'd die. He still needed to be appreciated, adored, and acknowledged.

# 5

# SINATRA
## Now—and Forever?

n 1992, when Frank was seventy-seven, he called and asked me to go out on the road with him. We'd play stadiums. I said, "Great, let's call it the 'The Team of the Ancients.'" Together we would be 135 years old. He laughed, thank God.

We never rehearsed. It was just like the old days. We met and reminisced and drank and joked, but we never rehearsed what we were going to do together. Our medley had been written and recorded so that we could learn it from a tape recorder. But it didn't matter. The tour wasn't about professional good work. It was about recapturing the old days. "We're gonna tear up the joint, baby," Frank said to me as he ushered me around his sunken curved bar at his home in Malibu. "So cool it. These big joints are just like Vegas, no different. It'll be a ring ding time." I blanched, not having heard this kind of dialogue in twenty years. Never mind, I thought. It will be an adventure just to observe and be a part of the way he keeps keeping on.

He sent me flowers on our opening night in Worcester, Massachusetts, and suddenly I was out there on a postage-stamp stage in a cavernous stadium. I had never performed in front of fifteen thousand people before. I was petrified. When I walked on I looked around and immediately felt myself wanting to fill the space all around me. The sound of the audience was thunderous. I could hardly hear the orchestra. There was a lag between the orchestra pit and me. I had been used to a self-contained band of eight musicians. Now I was working with forty. I finished my opening number and the people went crazy. Why are they acting like this? I wondered. I told a joke to find out if they could even hear my words distinctly. They could. They laughed. Jesus, I thought. This isn't so bad. I was only doing an hour (half the length of my solo show) so I timed my stuff a little differently. Then I tried something metaphysical. I felt myself expand my energy so that I filled the stadium. It seemed to be working. The people seemed to like it. And when it was over, they gave me a standing ovation. It was one of the great thrills of my life—up there with my opening night at the Palladium in London.

I took a few bows and ran to Frank's dressing room, somewhere near the shower stalls for the ballplayers.

"Great, baby!" he said. "Didja like it?"

"Oh yes," I said breathlessly.

"See, it's no different than a small room. You killed the people. I could hear it. We got a great combination here. We're gonna tear up New York when we get there."

So it went. The people loved me because I was with Frank. Just his presence gave them a kind of confidence that the past was not only not dead yet but could perhaps segue into the future. Somehow he made the young people, of whom there were thousands, understand their parents better. He was a bridge across decades.

We toured for a few months in Frank's private plane, one huge indoor stadium after the other. Frank could go right from the airplane to the stage. I needed some warm-up time. And when the show was over, if I wasn't in the limo he'd leave without me. Frank loved to end, then leave town like a modern day Roman warrior.

He insisted on a police escort (even at four in the morning in empty streets) with flashing lights and cops on motorcycles leading the way. We looked like a moving, real-live Nintendo game. Sirens wailed, horns honked, lights flashed, waking up the countryside, and if a lone driver who worked the graveyard shift happened to be traveling home on the freeway, the cops practically put him in custody until Frank left town. The tab for such extravagant waste boggled my Scotch-Irish brain, to say nothing of the expense of the extra limos that were on standby just in case we'd inherit some friends who might "wanna eat somethin' after da show."

The eating itself was out of an old Coppola film. Almost always Italian and usually a place outside of town, conveniently located for those running from the authorities. From the outside these restaurants looked identityless. Once inside, however, we were greeted by a set of bouncers with cauliflower ears and big heads. They would escort us to a long table laden with sumptuous antipasto and $1,500 bottles of wine. Usually there was a gangster or former boss waiting to eat with us. He would stand, Frank would introduce us, I would get the once-over, and then he would invite us to sit and partake of his spread.

These were the nights I wished I had the audacity to

bring a tape recorder. Not only because of the freedom with which Frank revealed his past, but also because of the subtle power plays that ebbed and flowed between him and the gangsters. Actually I needed a video camera with a real good close-up lens. The subtleties were awe-inspiring.

Giancana was long gone, of course, but the other regional bosses were still in place. I felt safe to regard them with an amused scrutiny. Why so many of them had hooded eyelids is a matter for the professors of "consciousness-creating physicality." They looked out at life from under those eyelids like paranoid survivors. Nothing escaped them. No move, no untoward laughter, no half empty plate, and no gesture of discomfort. They were psychological masters of summing up the environment.

At the outset of dinner, Frank was usually rather deferential to The Boys, the balance of power seemingly acknowledged and food given the higher priority. But as dinner progressed and Frank had finished his second martini and was about to break open one of the wine treasures, the mood changed. He'd hold the bottle, regard the year on the label, look around the table at The Boys, and say something like, "What the fuck is this?"

The Boys would blink and stiffen, and then they answered him. That was the moment when Frank knew he had control. They *answered* him. He had psyched out too many audiences to be perturbed by the potential disapproval of a couple of hoods. He needed to prove who was the real Boss.

The answer to his question wasn't what was important. The fact that they didn't call him on his rudeness *was*. And that hurdle having been jumped, Frank would proceed to drive The Boys into the ground for the rest of the night. In between eating their food and bad-mouthing their wine, Frank would systematically insult them: their work, their clothes, their big noses, their lack of education, and ultimately the fact that they were serving him "too much fucking food. Get it the hell off the table, for Christ's sake." He'd say, "Bring me a Sambucca with three coffee beans." The food would be whisked away and Frank would light up an old-time Camel cigarette. He used a cigarette lighter I recognized from years ago. It was thin and fit in his pocket without protruding. It was the lighter I had given him. He didn't remember.

Waiters, maître d's, and The Boys hovered in anticipatory anxiety as to what Frank might wish next. It was never the same. Sometimes he'd eat dessert, and sometimes he'd just drink. Once he threw a salmon soufflé on the floor. The point of tension, however, was most deeply felt by his manager, Eliot Weisman, who knew that there was the rest of the night to contend with. Wherever we went after dinner would have to include a piano player and a bar. Eliot's problem was figuring out where that might be. Where would the Old Man (that's what everyone affectionately called him) want to go? Would he want to go somewhere in this town or get on his plane and find a piano bar in the next town? Frank knew piano bars that no one else knew. Eliot understood the consequences of not being prepared. Piano players and good-time bartenders were lined up in every region, close to Frank's whereabouts, because one thing was for sure—the Old Man would not go to bed until five in the morning, regardless of the city he was in. That's why we usually traveled the night of the show: if we waited until the next day, he might not get up in time to be on his plane.

Frank's state of mind, what he ate, how long he slept, whom he talked to, how much he drank, and whether or not he was in a good mood were the subject of concern and conversation among everyone who worked around him.

They had reconciled with his demons, and his musical genius commanded their respect. To me, having witnessed so much of his self-abusive history, it was amazing he was still able to perform. He still preferred his old-time tuxedo for night shows (for matinees he wore his "Sunday school suit"). He pranced around in his black patent leather "party heels" with the grosgrain bows, and by the end of every performance he was wringing wet. Vine, the black woman who has been his maid for many years, would wipe him off and dress him either in the limo or on the airplane. Vine was the only person Frank would listen to. She was the first person he saw when he woke up and the last person before he went to bed. She told him when she thought he was out of line and otherwise melted into the woodwork. Vine was always included at the dinners and Frank was her life. She tended to his meals, his vanity, his clothes, and his sleep. She knew when he'd had a bad dream and whether he was lonely. She nursed him when his longtime friend Jilly Rizzo died and tended to him when he was suffering from a sore throat or the ravages of advancing age. She had been there all the years I knew him and will be there at the end.

The end, however, seemed aeons away. Energy-wise, Frank outdistanced everybody, including me. I could understand that his destiny was to be a legend that lasted long after his time. But the source of his energy was unfathomable. I don't think it comes simply from drive, or ambition, or the pulsating fear of being left behind. Nor is it only the need to be recognized and adored. All of the above are true but rather irrelevant. It has more to do with remaining a perpetual performing child who wants to please the mother audience.

It was my birthday when we were in New Orleans. Frank had been apprised of this and gave me a birthday dinner. My daughter, Sachi, her husband, Frank, Bobby Harling (who wrote *Steel Magnolias* and the screenplay for the sequel to *Terms of Endearment, Evening Star*), Mort, and several others were visiting.

We all met at the bar of the hotel. My conductor, Jack French, came along. Frank had worked with him years before. The two of them stood at the bar nursing drinks and chewing the fat about music, two artists who communicated in half sentences about a subject that needed no words at all.

When we went into dinner Frank handed me a present. It was an exquisite gold clock. He thanked me for all the years of our friendship and for always telling him the truth as I saw it.

We sat down to dinner and he drew me a clown on my napkin. He said it reminded him of me. Then he sang "Happy Birthday" to me. It was worth being a year older just to hear Sinatra sing "Happy Birthday." He directed that the wine bottles be opened. Someone leaned over and said each bottle cost $1,500. When the Mob spent that much money on wine to impress Frank it was so much easier for me to accept than when Frank did the same thing for me.

I knew he could afford it, certainly. That wasn't the issue. The issue was whether I deserved it. Frank's lavish spending habits and his generosity over the years had made me examine my feelings about his freedom of spending and my resistance to it. My instinct was to protect myself for the rainy day that I was sure would come. I had been raised this way. Neither of my parents would spend a thing on themselves. Whenever I gave them money for Christmas with express instructions to spend it on something wonderful, they'd put it in the bank. Once I asked Mother why she did that. She said she would need it in her old age. She was eighty-three.

Frank's relationship to money, on the other hand, seemed so outrageous to me that I felt I was observing a monetary value system from another planet. Once again I seemed to have drawn a person into my life who painted lessons for me with vivid primary colors. I painted with pastels, or maybe I just sketched with gray pencils. He showed me a kind of spending art.

He not only exemplified the freedom to give and spend freely. He exemplified the freedom to take and "lift" freely, like Peck's bad boy. One night after the show in New Orleans he pulled a caper that was the best of its kind I had seen.

Our entire party was transported by the usual contingent of flashing lights and motorcycle policemen to the front of the glass-walled restaurant, Emeril's (five stars and a New Orleans must). I could see people stopping in midchew. They must have thought the Pope had arrived. Not far wrong. Slowly we were ushered in, about twenty of us, and ceremoniously seated at a long table in view of everyone. It was a full-dress, New Orleans–style evening with cooking to match.

Frank sat down next to me, against the wall. A first course awaited him, and what was it? A beautifully decorated appetizer of French spaghetti. Oh God, I thought. How could this be so wrong? Frank waited for everyone to sit and as if on an action cue, looked down at the French-looking pasta, and gently moved his plate away. The waiter standing at attention behind him leaped to the rescue and cleared away the unwanted food. That meant that the Old Man was ready for the second course and no one else had even begun the first.

The clatter of forks and spoons audibly speeded up. One or two people declined to eat their spaghetti as well, and waited for what was next. I looked over at Frank. He had stuffed something in his coat pocket.

The waiter brought the second course. A fish dish with spicy sauce. Frank picked it up and smelled it. "Too rich for me!" he said, taking a bite as though to be polite. At least he was trying. The rhythm of "clear and serve" was now clearly out of whack. Should the waiters track themselves according to Frank, or to the rest of the party, who obviously were enjoying the food? They broke rank. Some attended Frank. Others took care of the rest of us.

Frank stuffed something else in his pocket. I looked over at Mort. He rolled his eyes. By now, conversation was in full swing. Frank's guests, as was usually the case, became interested in their own experience and started to ignore Frank's autocratically eccentric eating habits. In fact, no one was talking to him. Frank ordered a drink. A waiter snapped to attention. It was there before Frank could repeat the request. One course after another of the specially designed delicacies was placed in front of us. Frank ate bits and pieces. He would clearly have preferred eating pasta and antipasto in a Mob joint. But he remained civil. I noticed his pockets bulging. A waiter leaned over and said, "Mr. Sinatra, I just wanted you to know how much you have meant to me in my life." Frank smiled and waited for the expected request for an autograph. It didn't come. He turned to me and said, "Nice kid. It's the first time nobody's wanted anything from me."

Frank asked permission to smoke. It was readily granted since others wanted to smoke too. The main entrée came. Emeril had outdone himself, preparing food fit for royalty. Wine was flowing, and even Eliot and Mort were relaxed because Frank was deeply engrossed in telling me a story I had heard fifteen times. I had been through this with my parents not long ago. One simply enters the reality of the aging and the repetition can be fun. Slowly, Frank would lift a bite of food, examine it, turn it over and around, and finally make the decision to commit to eating it. With each involved commitment, Eliot and Mort knew they were off the hook for the length of time he took to chew and swallow.

People were now enjoying the famous Emeril's desserts, five auspicious creations of sugar shock apiece. Suddenly Frank pushed his chair back. Eliot dropped his spoon and pulled out his cellular telephone. He called the Windsor Court Hotel, where we were staying, and spoke to his assistant, who was waiting for instructions on Frank's next move.

"Is the guy at the piano bar?" asked Eliot. "The Old Man's getting ready to leave, I think. We've gotta have the guy on standby. And the girl bartender who looks like the librarian. Get her. He likes her." Eliot hung up.

The rest of the party froze. Were they supposed to leave too? Was that the protocol? Frank recognized the dilemma. He stood up and announced that he was tired, needed to hear some music, and we could join him in the bar at the hotel later. When he turned around I saw him unbutton his jacket so the pockets wouldn't bulge so much. His waiter leaned over and in a friendly, conspiratorial voice whispered in his ear, "If you want a whole set I can get it for you." Frank winked and handed him a hundred-dollar bill.

I wondered what was going on. Eliot left with Frank. The rest of us finished our meal and about an hour later returned to the hotel bar to thank Frank. He was holding court with two traveling-salesman types at the bar. When we arrived he made a new party. It was now about 2:30 A.M. Around three, there was a lull in the conversation, which Frank recognized as a perfect moment. He stood up, reached into his pockets, and turned them inside out. Half a dozen pieces of silver clattered to the floor. We all stared.

"I never go anywhere," he said, "that I don't steal something."

Frank held court until five in the morning. Finally most of us begged off and went to bed. He found some people at the bar. It didn't really matter to him who they were. He knew they would sit with him because of who he was. They knew he was lonely.

Perhaps lonely is the wrong word. In the way that old people have of making time stand still, he'd get comfortable with his Camels and Jack Daniels, kick back, and bend elbows with people until they wished they had no arms. People working with him would take turns doing their time. It was understood as part of the territory. Those who had the graveyard shift faced the next day with positives and negatives. The bad news was that they were walking on their knees with fatigue. The good news was they had been privy to stories Frank either hadn't remembered until then or had never before wished to recount.

The stories would die in the haze and blur of drinks and strangers. Only the memories of those present would keep them alive. But I could see indifference setting in even with them. The nostalgia for yesteryear was short-lived, seemingly without value where today's ambitions were concerned. The people of the night would turn away, get on with their own lives, and Frank, even though he was the King, would be left, as most older people are, with the feeling that he was grateful someone had stayed up all night and talked to him.

The next day Frank was up about noon to fly to the next city on our tour, Jacksonville, Florida. We landed twenty minutes before the show. He was fine with that. I was a basket case. He was particularly good that night, in an easy mood and having fun with the crowd, so I decided to confront him about the medley we were supposed to do together.

Frank, above all, does not want to embarrass other performers on the stage because of his mistakes. He doesn't mind being cruel and insensitive when he's in control. But when he feels he's not in top form, it's hard for him to accept that other performers don't mind.

I knew he couldn't remember his lyrics and the monitors were direly necessary to him. That was okay with me. The medley was made up of songs he knew and had been singing for years, but I still knew that I would probably have to jump in, just to keep it going. Frank was worried for me. He didn't know how I'd react to his memory loss. He doesn't like being anxious and afraid of anything different. Up until now he had refused to try our medley before we opened in New York. So, during the sound check, I said, "Do you like my new dress?"

"Sure, baby," he answered. "Do you want to make thirty-five cents?"

I let that one go.

"So, Frank," I said. "It takes a lot for me to get into this dress, corset-wise. So I'm going to put it on and after you sing 'My Way' I'm going to walk out onstage and we're going to do our medley."

He looked at me funny. "You are?" he asked.

"Yep," I answered. "So be ready."

He shrugged that Italian shrug that could mean okay, or could mean you're dead. The fact that we'd never had a rehearsal was something Frank didn't remember.

I finished my part of the show. He came on. I changed

into my sexy chanteuse dress with the corset, and when he finished "My Way" I wandered onto the stage. Frank had forgotten our conversation, of course, but he did hear the audience go wild when they saw us together. He couldn't remember my last name, so there was no point in introducing me. I pointed to the monitors and Frank, Jr., leading the orchestra, began the first number.

The monitors had spelled out who was to sing what, but Frank couldn't read them. He was going to have to fly by the seat of his pants. Well, he did. With every great performer, rising to the occasion is an occupational challenge usually met, and this was no exception. I had learned enough from him and Dean over the years to understand that I would have to find an attitude to play with him when we worked together. Dean was his side-kick drunk, Sammy had been his step-and-fetch-it talented friend, Steve Lawrence and Eydie Gorme had been his singing buddies who led him around while they kidded each other, Liza Minnelli had related to him as Uncle Frank, and now it was my turn.

Up until then he had not worked with his sexual energy relating to any of his partners. Perhaps I could work with that. People probably thought we had had an affair anyway. But I still needed to find an attitude. I found it with the first song. When he began to sing "You make me feel so young," I just stared at him. And when he sang "And even when I'm old and gray," I said, "You *are* old and gray." The audience loved that because I was stating what they were thinking. Frank laughed, thank goodness. I had found my attitude. When I saw him laugh at my making fun of him, I knew I was home free. Because of my own tenure in the business I had earned the right to give back at him, from a female point of view, what he had been dishing out all these years. And he was great about it. In fact he had a really good time. I put suggestive moves on him and he said he'd tell Barbara. I said she'd never minded before. He said, "Yeah, but now I'd probably do it and forget that I had." We hardly finished a song because the byplay became what our little time together was about. He saw that there was nothing to worry about, and from then on we did our medley together, never knowing what would happen.

I took to purposely standing in front of his monitors so he couldn't read his lyrics. He'd just laugh and berate me. I'd tell jokes while he was singing so he'd get mixed up. Once Frank, Jr., began a number and Frank, Sr., decided he wasn't ready. He refused to begin. Frank, Jr., kept going. Frank, Sr., said, "Wait a minute, who the fuck told you to start?" (It's considered tasteless form to use that word on the stage, but with Frank, there was no form.) Frank, Jr., played right ahead. I looked at the monitors. The operator didn't know whether to follow the orchestra or follow the Old Man. Frank wouldn't sing. He turned to me and said, "Why does he keep playing?" I said, "I don't know. He's your son."

Frank, Jr., kept right on with the orchestra. "So what do you want to do, Frank?" I asked, the song half over. "I don't know," said Frank. "What do you think?" It had now become a sketch instead of a medley.

"Well," I said. "I guess I could do it, but you know I can't sing that good. You could do it, but you'll have to talk to this monitor guy because without him you'll just get lost again. Or you could go speak to your son and we could start all over."

Frank just looked at me. Then he said, "The hell with it. I'm going to the races." And he walked off the stage. It was like that.

Once, at Radio City, he was suffering from a bad throat and we had to cancel the show. The next night he said he was fine, and I reassured the audience that he would follow me after intermission, not to worry. I finished my set, walked off the stage, bathed in sweat, and Eliot was standing in the wings, ashen.

"He's on a plane, Shirley," he said. "He left for California. Can you go out and do another hour?"

"Are you kidding?" I said. "I don't have my orchestrations with me. C'mon, Eliot, you must be kidding."

"Oh," he said. "Well, will you go back out there and tell them that Frank isn't here?"

"Are you kidding twice?" I asked. "You do it. You're his manager. What's wrong with him anyway?"

"I don't know," said Eliot. "He said he had a bad throat."

"Sure, right," I said sarcastically. "Well, now what? If he's in California, how do we continue?"

"We'll postpone for two weeks," he said. "Can you come back?"

"I don't know," I said. "I thought the Music Hall was unavailable because of the Christmas show."

Eliot grimaced. "Lots of things suddenly become available when you face losing money."

He picked up the intercom. The audience was leaving for intermission. "That concludes the program, ladies and gentlemen," he said. "Mr. Sinatra will not be performing."

That was all he said. I couldn't believe it. I felt like such a jerk for having reassured the people that Frank was there, when he wasn't even in the city anymore.

But that's the way it was. Energy to be really bad and energy to be soaringly good.

Traveling back to California in his plane, across country, after our last stadium show, Frank didn't want to sleep. It was late at night. He thought everyone else was asleep. I watched him. He went to the back of the plane and quietly retrieved the snack food from the galley. He got down on his hands and knees and surreptitiously stuffed everyone's shoes with popcorn, peanuts, jelly beans, gumdrops, crackers, and nuts.

Frank Sinatra, my friend, legend, and glorious survivor, would do anything to have some fun.

THE IMAGE OF SINATRA ON HIS HANDS AND KNEES STUFFING gumdrops into people's shoes seems to be the true Sinatra to me. This was the man-child that moved me. This was the coworker who reveled in the mischief of stashing my gum behind his ear.

Since Frank was an artist of music, I saw him as an artist of life. Because he heard and trusted the sounds in his head, I believed he was acquainted with the reality of other dimensions. I always saw something in his eyes that recognized that truth was more than it seemed.

I wondered if his Karma would catch up with him while he was alive today. Or would it wait until some other time around?

I believe the reason for so much of Frank's emotional violence was his need to be understood on command. He couldn't wait. He, like many true artists, lived in the moment. That moment was so expansive, so full of uncontrollable feeling, that those who didn't "get it" were visited by his cruelty. His music was mathematical perfection with no room for imprecision. He saw the truth in the same way. Absolute—no deviation. He had to live in a world he created in order to control it, and his talent and street-smart shrewdness enabled him to get away with it.

I have never had the driving audacity to chisel such chunky drama in my life. I preferred to be an observer and in that respect I have been afforded uncommonly extravagant entertainment.

In much the same way as the American culture is attracted to the *Godfather* films of Coppola, I was attracted to observing the real thing with Frank and company. I admit to an interest in gangsters—almost like a child watching a car wreck with my hands over one eye. I couldn't stop gaping. How could these people behave the way they did? How did their minds work? Did they derive malicious pleasure, or was it just part of the job, motivated by a sour deal or an unpaid debt?

I have always been curious about people who push the perimeters of human decency beyond the pale.

Frank Sinatra never restrained his need for drama, or his feelings, or his behavior. It was constitutionally impossible for him. He cut a swath through his friends and his life.

I knew several of the wives and girlfriends of The Boys Frank hung out with. They fundamentally denied that their men were gangsters. In fact, a few were very involved with New Age thinking, holistic healing, and Buddhist principles of never hurting or killing.

One girlfriend invited me to her house many times. She grew her own organic vegetables, had an ecologically perfect landscape and garden, and meditated several times a day. She said God was her best friend and talked openly about the laws of Karma and how everything she put out would come back. She loved her man and thought that his reputation had been badly damaged by negative gossipmongers. Because of the bad vibes people directed his way, she had to live in a house surrounded by lead walls and bodyguards around the clock. I found her blindness paralyzing. How could she be so closed-minded? Was she a mirror for me? Here I was, galli-

I was aware of the camera angles even then.

Warren loved our
grandmother's perfume

My daddy was a Southern
gentleman: conservative, yet a
bawdy teller of tales.

Warren and me then and -- sort of -- now.

Archive Photos

It's all in the family.

My first dancing partner.
His name was Moe.

At eighteen I dreamed of
being a prima ballerina.

Did this herald my
interest in angels?

THE WASHINGT

Me in the chorus of *Me and Juliet* on Broadway. I had one line: "It seems like only yesterday that Suzie left the show."

*The Pajama Game* on Broadway: I enjoyed holding up Eddie Foy, Jr.

Hitchcock was my first director. I had memorized the whole script.

I could only stand still for Edith Head.

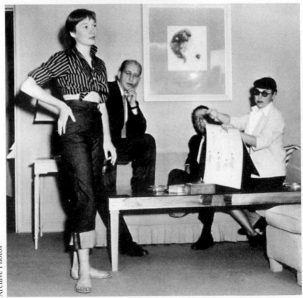

*Artists and Models*:
This was the scene
Jerry hated doing.

*Artists and Models*: To me, Dean and Jerry were both sexy.

*Some Came Running* with Dean and Frank: The beginning of the Clan relationship.

Archive Photos

Archive Photos

The set of *Can-Can*: Frank made even Kruschev fun.

*All in a Night's Work*: While I had a crush on Dean, neither Elvis nor Hal Wallis fazed me.

Dean and I tore this silver ranch mink during a love scene.

Archive Photos

I was just back from India, and Dean and Frank didn't understand anything I was talking about.

Being on the stage with Frank: a dream that became real for me.

We were all still out there— live. Left to right: Steve Lawrence, Frank, Eydie Gorme, Liza Minnelli, and Dean.

Long Photography, Inc

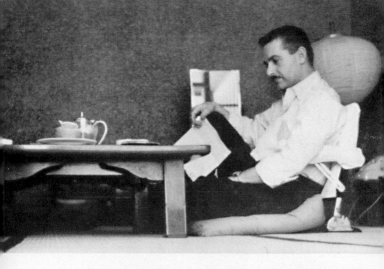

Steve, Sachi, and me at our Shibuya home. Steve was handsome, intelligent, reflective, and cultured. All necessary qualities to fall in love with —and to learn.

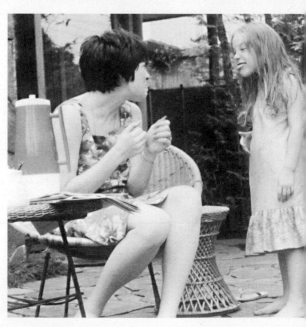

My greatest teachers.

*My Geisha* with Edward G. Robinson, Yves Montand and Robert Cummings. No one knew what was going on between Montand and me. Courtesy of Paramount Pictures. *My Geisha* ©1995 by Paramount Pictures. All Rights Reserved

With Yves Montand: I had just declared Steve the love of my life.

*Two for the Seesaw* with Robert Mitchum: I should have pulled harder.
But he made me laugh too much.

What can I say?

vanting around the world, working, playing, and openly consorting with the same people. What was happening to my sense of right and wrong, my morality, my boundaries? I actually enjoyed what I was privy to. I found it harmless and I didn't know why.

THEN SOMETHING HAPPENED THAT WAS A MAJOR REVELATION.

A close friend of Steve's and mine who worked in Vegas came to see me in L.A. He wanted to talk alone and away from my house.

We walked on the beach. I couldn't understand his need for such privacy. Then he reluctantly opened up.

"I hear rumors in Vegas," he said.

"What rumors?" I asked.

"From The Boys," he answered and looked over his shoulder.

"You mean the Mob?" I asked.

"Yes," he said. "There's some talk that they will kidnap your daughter."

My mouth fell open.

"What do you mean?" I said. "Why?"

"In order to appropriate your talent," he said. "They want to own you and this is how they'd threaten to do it."

I'll never forget my reaction. I feel it viscerally even today.

I felt the molecules of my blood boil in every inch of my body. I was prepared to kill, and I would have.

"You tell those people to go fuck themselves," I said. "If they so much as cross to my side of a wide street or come within the same city as my daughter, I will call the President of the United States and every fucking reporter I know. I'll blow the whistle publicly on not only them but their wives and girlfriends too. You tell them I think they are scumbags and I am not amused.''

My friend stopped dead in his tracks.

''And one more thing. Tell them to shove their horses' heads up their asses.''

He looked too shocked to react. Finally he spoke. ''Look,'' he said, ''I'm not even sure it's true. I just thought I'd tell you.''

''You're right,'' I said. ''It's not true. Those cock-suckers are never coming near me or my daughter. On that you can depend.'' I walked away from him. ''Thanks for telling me,'' I said. ''Now you make sure they know my reaction.''

I called Steve in Japan and told him what had happened. He was horrified. ''Sachi should come to Japan,'' he said. ''She should go to school here, where she'll be safe.'' After much soul-searching I agreed.

Soon after that, we enrolled Sachi in an international school in Tokyo, where she would live with her father during the school year. She would come home to me during the long holidays (one month at Christmas and Easter) and during the three-month summer vacation. In addition to the Mob threat, I wanted to get her away from what I perceived to be a growing drug culture in the Los Angeles schools and the fate of being a movie star's daughter.

I was too frightened to ask Frank whether what I had been told was true, but I never hung out with the guys again. I had abruptly grown out of my morbid fascination with danger.

Of one thing I am certain, though. If the threat was real, Frank had nothing to do with it. He adored Sachi and invited us to Palm Springs and to his home in L.A. many times. In fact, it was not long after that Frank's own son was kidnapped. No one ever got a straight answer as to who did it. I had my notions, of course. I just couldn't figure out why.

There was one thing I did figure out, though. I had a reservoir of rage in me that would serve me well against injustice for the rest of my life.

# 6
# POWER

*I* suppose you could say that my survival quotient speaks to my acquaintance with the knowledge of how to get power and how to use it.

Once I was through the act of being born, and out of my mother's protective body, I engaged in the manipulation of my environment so that I could survive. I cried, I flailed, I smiled, I grabbed for food; I did whatever I had to do so I wouldn't die. That's what we all do because the squeaky wheel gets the grease and the grown-ups have to know what we need. Therefore, exerting control was one of the first of my human endeavors.

That hasn't changed much. Even though I listen to advice, I'll still do things my way. I personally am not so much interested in power as I am in doing something the way I want to do it.

Intrinsically, this point of view carries power with it. I didn't know that when I first came to Hollywood. I just knew I didn't want "them" to curl my hair, paint my face, force me into PR relationships or even into going to premieres of pictures I didn't want to see.

I made a compromise sometimes. I'd drive up in my red Plymouth, have the valet take my car to the back of the theater, parade down the red-carpet aisle, all smiles, then duck out of the theater without having to sit through the film.

I had heard what everyone else in the world had heard about Hollywood . . . that it was all about money, that people's very souls could be bought and sold for the sake of fame and the chance to be a star.

I have never understood why the concept of being famous—a star—never motivated me much. Perhaps it should have but it didn't. I wanted to be good at my work. Frankly, now I consider my thinking to have been astonishingly limited and narrow. Why shouldn't I have stardom as a goal? But I didn't. I wanted people to like what I did. I wanted to be prepared, be professional, be imaginative, be a performer and an actress that people got a kick out of. As I said, my goals in Hollywood were limited. Yet, what I didn't particularly care about was probably the secret of my success.

I never knew or cared about the deals being made—including my own. I cared about the script and whether I liked the people I was working with.

I read the trade papers but didn't understand much other than Army Archerd's column and whoever was writing trade gossip for the *Hollywood Reporter*. The manipulation of money and power went right over my head. And I was extremely impolitic when it came to playing the Hollywood game.

If studio heads or producers solicited my opinion, I

told them the truth, unpleasant though it often was. And I had no diplomatic finesse in expressing my displeasure. On top of that, I almost always turned what should have been a creative or commercial discussion into a psychological interview about them.

Stumbling and offending at every turn, I couldn't refrain from rushing in where angels feared to tread. I was a fool.

The Hollywood studio bosses seemed to have one kind of power and the artists had another. I didn't understand either.

The artists knew how to speak to the subconscious, how to move people, how to make people identify with them. The bosses recognized that they didn't know how to do that, so they exerted their control with money. They liked to make artists feel subservient, yet at the same time knew there was no industry without them.

Our business was called the "motion-picture industry," not "motion-picture artistry." But I saw that the real power lay in the artistry. Artists were the ones the people came to see. We lived the life the public identified with.

When Bette Davis did Regina in *The Little Foxes,* she elected to play the part the way it was written, with the darkness of a manipulating woman in complete control. Willy Wyler, the director, wanted her to play against the writing, which is to say, with more sweetness and a deceptive, likable quality. Davis said this wasn't what the audience expected from her and refused.

There were arguments and emotional scenes on the set. Jack Warner called in Wyler and told him to leave Davis alone. She was the box-office queen on the lot, and he said Wyler shouldn't "screw around with whatever the audience liked." Wyler capitulated because of the power of Davis's "queen bitch" quality.

I remember how Y. Frank Freeman, at Paramount, or Sol Siegel at Metro, or Zanuck at Fox would look into the faces of us actors and wonder what secrets of theirs we could perceive, things that they themselves were not aware of.

In fact, as the years passed I often thought about developing a relationship with a studio head just to see how they lived and functioned, but I never got that far because most of them weren't around long enough. Studio power became a revolving door, particularly after Jack Warner, Harry Cohn (Columbia), Benny Thau (Metro), and Skouras at Fox retired. The old moguls who lived and breathed the "industry" were a breed apart. After the agents took over, I couldn't remember anybody's name because they were in and out so fast.

So what was power, then? Those people weren't going to enable me to march to my own drummer, I was.

I was also developing a political point of view, so I became vigilant as to how my position in Hollywood could focus public attention on a cry in the dark, how I could help change those things that had been ignored for far too long in our society. I was learning that within the independent artist there resides the power to effect change in areas where the powers-that-be are too entrenched, too budget-conscious, or finally too embarrassed to do it themselves.

I was learning something else. Real power could reside in the seemingly most insignificant of crew members.

I remember a scene in *Around the World in Eighty Days* that we were shooting with thousands of extras. Filming ground to a halt because the propman had forgotten to put the champagne in the balloon with David Niven and Cantinflas. That's power.

A supporting player I worked with was so good he

made my male costar insecure to the point that he refused to work. The supporting player was fired. That's power.

Another man I worked with had been having an affair with the cameraman's wife. He had had such a bad night with Mrs. Camera that Mr. Camera couldn't shoot his face in any light. We lost a whole day. That's power.

A director who insisted upon waiting a week for the right cloud formation ran up nearly a half million dollar tab because of his "artistic integrity." That's power.

A small child I worked with in *The Children's Hour* hated to take direction, brought the set to a standstill, and ended up being more powerful than any adult on the lot that week. That's power.

Power, then, was a question of the moment. Those who had it one year would scarcely be remembered the next. So what did having power really mean? Why did people seek it, and why was it so important for me to respect it?

I think I was simpleminded about its relevance, but try as I did, I couldn't see the true and deep advantage of having power because it was an illusion anyway.

I could understand being independently wealthy; that guaranteed a kind of freedom. I could understand being popular with the public; future jobs would be assured. But even that came at a price. Many of my fellow stars were popular playing one type of character and wished to expand and grow into another. The problem was that the public sometimes didn't want to grow with them. So how much power did the star really have?

People who have the vision to express a film create dilemmas for studio heads. The executives know they can't visualize what the filmmaker has in mind. The filmmaker knows that too. But the filmmaker needs the money. So the better part of valor for both is just to jump in and hope for the best. That's the essence of our industry anyway: hold your nose and dive in. You know that for the duration of the filming your buttons will be pushed and your dreams will be buffeted about. Still, where else is there such collaboration of art and industry? Where else can you indulge your childhood fantasies until you feel you've become an adult? Where else can you leave a legacy of human expression that might affect billions of lives?

Therefore, to me, power is finally the courage and audacity to believe in yourself, to believe you have something important to say, and to see to it that you have the stamina to follow it through.

Nowhere is stamina more evident than on a film set. No one who hasn't been through a three- or four-month shoot can conceive of what it takes.

The days begin at five o'clock in the morning, with the actors in makeup and the crew setting up the lights and camera for the shot. The producers and editors are usually there as watchdogs, spies, and friends of the court.

If you're lucky you get your first shot by nine. That's rare, however. Rare because when the above-the-line people come together with the crew, somebody always feels uncomfortable. Perhaps the structure of the scene itself is faulty. Perhaps an actor doesn't want to say a certain line because it's bad for his image. Perhaps an actress feels her character is demeaning to women. Perhaps the director has a shot that is so oblique the actors feel they aren't being seen. Perhaps an actress has eaten too much salt over the weekend and her face is retaining so much water the camera picks it up and she won't even match herself elsewhere in the film!

Perhaps two costars truly can't bear each other, as was the case with Laurence Harvey and me on an innocuous picture called *Two Loves*. I found him insensitive and pompous. Once, right before the director called "action," Harvey leaned toward me and scrutinized my left cheek. "What on earth is that?" He acted as though I had a hickey the size of Mount Fuji. Just as I was about to ask for a mirror, he said, "Never mind, they'll never notice, it's not your face you should be concerned about." I did a slow burn but went right on with the scene. The next day was the love scene. I ate a clove of raw garlic before beginning it. That settled his hash.

I worked with a woman who wouldn't allow her left side to be photographed. The entire set had to be redressed, the camera moved, and the scene restaged.

Sometimes a dramatic scene stimulates such deep emotion in an actor that he breaks down and sobs. Many actors dread crying scenes, because they are not able to cry with a hundred people in the crew looking on. Others are terrified that if they start crying, they won't be able to stop, which would mean a new two-hour makeup and hair redress. I used to dread shooting dancing sequences because of the inevitable perspiration and humidity that ruined my hair and the base coat of my makeup. If the hair and makeup don't match an earlier part of the scene, it will interfere with the emotional response of the audience.

Many times during a rehearsal, either I or some other actor has a brainstorm that means that everything is thrown out and we begin again.

Many is the time the crew sits around while actors and the director go over and over a nuance, or experience a disagreement, a staging conflict, or a temper tantrum.

I did a picture just recently where the three stars, me included, sensed a weakness in the director and decided to go for the jugular. The unexpressed insecurities we had about the way the scene was written drove us to quarrel about a simple staging move that had to do with looking out a window.

While the crew sat around we argued for two and a half hours about nothing. The director became more and more entrenched, and so did we. The producer was a weakling and couldn't control the situation. Our own exhaustion finally wore us down and now I can't even remember if we looked out the window or not.

These problems are never about what they seem to be about. They are usually about unexpressed anger, vulnerabilities, a feeling of endangerment, undeservability, vanity, or an all-around fear that nobody will love us.

Making pictures is like being in therapy. Every unresolved issue we've ever been plagued with will surface, depending, of course, on the material and the personnel involved. But if it doesn't get you sooner, it will get you later, and so the jangle of discord continues throughout each working day. At lunchtime there is no letup. More discussion, arguing, creative differences. There is a slight slowdown after lunch, but soon it all heats up again.

The day continues until at least seven, but more likely nine. In the old days, we women used to have a "no close-ups after six o'clock" clause in our contracts. Today, because of spiraling costs and other economic factors, we usually shoot until the day's allocated work is finished. That is often two in the morning (close-ups included). Screen Actors Guild requires a ten- or twelve-hour turnaround rest period, but many times the director, whom you are endeavoring to please, prevails upon you to waive your turnaround—if you don't, you are responsible for the film's running a day behind.

After the day's work is finished, you don't go home, or to your hotel if you're on location. You go to the dailies. Dailies, or rushes, are many takes of the previous day's work. To me, viewing them is necessary so I know how I'm doing. Some actors don't like to see themselves on screen while they're shooting; it makes them self-conscious. Some directors don't like their actors to see the dailies for a variety of reasons. Sometimes they feel an actor will become unnecessarily self-critical, depressed, antagonistic to the camera angle, etc., etc. I had one very fine director who allowed the actors to view the dailies, but not to comment.

Even in a more open emotional environment, the moment after the lights come up can be painfully self-conscious. The silence is thunderous. Should you speak up if you didn't like what you saw? What if everyone else liked it? You're flummoxed at what the camera caught compared with what you thought you were doing. The back of your hair looks funny. Yet you know the director thinks you shouldn't even be looking at your hair. You've blinked your eyes too much. Your voice is too high or indistinct. You ponder whether you're too close to judge or whether the audience and critics will render the same verdict.

I remember not being able to see many of the dailies when I was in Mexico shooting *Two Mules for Sister Sara*—the delay in processing back and forth from California made it difficult. I was playing a hooker posing as a nun and wore fake eyelashes. They were too overstated, but by the time I saw how awful they looked, it was too late. If I took them off, my face wouldn't match the scenes already shot.

So you sit in the projection room, withholding your feelings until someone else speaks. Unfortunately, regardless of what you just saw, the first words are usually, "Great dailies. Just great." The die is cast. Who among you is willing to cast the first stone? On a film there is nothing worse than creative sabotage. Belief in what you are doing is everything. Without an inordinate degree of creative self-belief, it is impossible to go forward every day, making astronomical economic decisions and accurate assessments of whether you've got what you want or need to change something. The dailies are usually the pudding of proof, and when the projection-room lights go up, the moment of truth is upon you. If you object to something, it must be done in the most oblique and subtle manner because all filmmaking is so personal, and that is how criticism is almost always taken—personally.

If a comment is particularly abrasive, an eruption can occur, which leads to hurtful arguing and raw, vented feelings. This doesn't often happen because nobody will really tell you the truth anyway. First of all, they might be wrong. Second, it might cost them their jobs. And third, it's always easier to refrain from rocking the boat.

So people who are considered difficult are usually those who come closer to expressing what they honestly feel. That is not wholeheartedly desired either. Some people in Hollywood are so megalomaniacal, and nurture personal agendas of such perversity, that it would be far better if they never expressed their truth at all.

On the other hand, some of the most obnoxiously crazy people are the most talented. If you can get past their insanity, there is sometimes creative gold underneath.

So moviemaking is like a continual group therapy session without a therapist each and every day. Usually it ends at midnight, and you have five hours to recuperate and prepare yourself for the next day's "fun."

Front-office people don't know what to do with the emotional intensity of filmmakers. They don't know how to react when they have prepared themselves for an explosion, but, out of genial manipulation, we artists instead withhold what we're feeling, which drives them crazy. But they are rendered helpless at the sight of a truly talented person self-destructing. And when a creative person gets into that self-sabotage mode, nothing and nobody can help.

What does a studio head do when an actor freaks out because the scene reminds him of the time he was beaten by his father or an actress is positive she's ugly because her mother instilled such insecurity? Neither can face the camera, and the "regular" people (crew and front office) try to cope as they watch time and money flow down the drain. The producer, particularly a creative one, usually acts as the go-between. He understands at least some of the emotionality involved, yet his indulgence is tempered with pragmatism, because wasting time and money won't be tolerated for long.

I've always seen the producer's role as that of a two-way diplomatic ambassador—an economic ambassador from the front office to the set, and an artistic ambassador from the set to the front office. The producer is on the scene of the production, but represents the home office. A director needs a powerful and good producer to be on his or her side because the director is also a diplomatic ambassador to the cast and crew.

The tempers that flare and the creative differences that escalate to open warfare often require peacemakers. In our business, however, the peacemakers are not blessed. They are usually vilified and judged to have no fighting backbone, no courage of their convictions, and that's because "peace" is not the goal in moviemaking. Having your vision served is the goal. Yet an artistic endeavor must have the backing of the front office—hence a standoff.

There is no solution or formula that works for every picture because each filmmaker is different. Some are more paranoid than others. Some don't care as much as others. Some are in it for the games, the hidden agendas. Because human emotions are the tools of our expression, financial people are in for a rocky ride if they want to save money while they make movies. It takes a special kind of mind to negotiate the rapids of free-flowing temperament because at the bottom of it all is the understanding that money flows from an enterprise only when the artistic impulse is protected from drying up. What a tightrope walk! What a poker game! A producer must evaluate his cards, weighing the positions of both front office and director. A director does the same with the cast and crew. The game is played with both poker faces and melodramatic antics. The ante is raised when you want someone to fold. The jokes, the camaraderie, the suspicions are cards played close to the vest. Pretty soon you realize it's never about who wins the pot or even how the picture does. It's all about what you're learning about yourself while playing the game.

Hollywood is a place that puts you in touch with your desires. Only when you desire something deeply can you be corrupted. I was alone in this land of temptation, alone by choice. I had given up the pleasures and support system of my husband and child in order to pursue my desire to be successful, to be respected, to be hired, and to be loved. There were times when I felt both selfish and guilty about turning over my child to Steve's supervision for so many months of the year, but his promise to care for her allowed me to feel comfortable; certainly the Hollywood alternative was not perfect either. Yet my desires in Hollywood did not include the kind of power the bosses had or even the power of fulfilling a perfectionistic artistic vision. More than anything I wanted the power of communicating to people.

I wanted to be artistic, but I also wanted to be commercial. It mattered to me whether my pictures made money, and not only because I'd get paid more. It was because those with the financial means would respect whatever secret quality I might possess that made me appeal to the public. Everyone in Hollywood wants to be appealing to large masses of people, particularly the bosses.

So as I questioned myself about my potential corruptibility, I realized it had to do with how much I wanted from Hollywood.

Possessions have never meant that much to me. I don't have ·paintings and valuable works of art or the knowledge to collect them astutely. I've never erected a lifestyle for myself that would put possessions in a position of controlling me. I think I don't have the strength of character to let myself be tempted. For that reason, I've also never really been involved with a super-wealthy man. It would jeopardize the control I would otherwise have in the relationship.

Yet Hollywood has carrots to dangle in front of every human being alive. It is a test site for determining your price. Did I have the confidence in myself to live and work around temptation? Was I purposefully ignorant of some of the most despicable power plays in town because I was afraid I might be drawn into playing the game the same way? I've often wondered whether I was afraid of real power because I might abuse it. Power is a Tar Baby. Once you touch it, it never lets you go. No amount of it would be enough. No amount of money generated by it would be enough.

Perhaps choosing not to perceive corruptibility was my way of tolerating the ugliness that went on; otherwise I'd have to leave.

A few times over the years I played around with the idea of giving away everything but I never had the guts. I became interested in Buddhism and particularly in the personal values of the lamas. Those who completely divested themselves of wants and desires were incorruptible.

That was impossible for me to do in Hollywood. The tyranny of success, money, fame, the tyranny of desire, seemed to accompany me because I needed to communicate. At the same time, though, I was learning that real power came from the inside out—not from the outside in.

When I became interested in metaphysics, I conducted seminars in relation to what I had learned about internal values and spirituality. I didn't see myself as a teacher but more as a student who was imparting her experience.

For a while I deeply enjoyed the people who came for the weekend communal get-togethers. But then they began to mushroom into what I felt was a metaphysical steamroller with New Age groupies hanging from the sides, heralding that I had changed their lives.

I found this intolerable. I didn't want the responsibility of that kind of power. I didn't know what to do with it. I stopped the seminars.

But the question still remains in my heart and mind. When does the God-given right to control my own destiny become an insatiable need for power over those around me?

Am I so afraid of the question that I deny the materials to sculpt my own answer?

Just because I seem to have survived the minefields of Hollywood's power play doesn't mean I understand why.

Hollywood helps me to continue the search.

# 7
# COMING TO TERMS WITH *TERMS*

here are those who say that "difficulty" is what makes a picture good. I'm not sure I disagree with that. Certainly *Terms of Endearment* was a singularly difficult experience, and maybe the shooting circumstances contributed to its artistic success. Maybe not. In any case, *Terms* taught me a lot about the Game.

Jim Brooks, who wrote and directed *Terms* from the Larry McMurtry novel, is brilliant. He is shrewd, caring, and possessed of a certain take on human nature that celebrates the defects in us all. The experience of making *Terms* was analogous to his slant on life.

When Jim first came to me with his script, I loved it. He says I took him aside and whispered in his ear, "This could be important." I don't remember that, but if so, my psychic abilities far exceeded my awareness. In the two years that it took for every studio in town to turn the script down twice, he vigilantly kept abreast of anything else I might consider doing. So . . . I didn't work anywhere else. I even walked away from a Steven Spielberg production (the part of the mother in the original *Poltergeist*) because I wanted to be available for him. Jim makes a street-smart evaluation of other people that puts your own self-awareness to shame. That's why the picture became important to me.

Paramount finally acquiesced to financing Jim's dream, and we were on our way. He asked for $8 million, knowing it would cost more, but "once they see the dailies, they'll be so committed they'll give me more," he said. Street-smart, I guess, but the studio also could have pulled the plug—which they came close to doing.

There was some talk of Sissy Spacek playing the crucial role of my daughter because she looked so much like me. But Sissy turned it down. Mary Steenburgen was another possibility, but she and Jim didn't connect.

Debra Winger had just had a big success in *An Officer and a Gentleman* and Paramount was high on her. Even though she was a dark-haired beauty, unlikely as my daughter, Jim felt that her spunk and intelligence would make her a perfect Emma. So did I. I loved her smoldering intelligent eyes on the screen. Up to that point I had never met her. Her reputation for being difficult preceded her on every film, but that was true of just about anybody who was any good and who cared about the work.

I met her at a NATO (National Association of Theater Owners) convention. She was pleasant, witty, and said she couldn't wait to begin working on the film.

We rehearsed in New York during the winter of late '82. I took the opportunity to wear, as Aurora, all my old fur coats. I did not wear them anymore myself, but for the character they were perfect.

I'd walk across town from my apartment on Fifty-second Street to Jim's midtown place, bundled up in a fur coat, trying not to feel conspicuous, but knowing that it was exactly what Aurora would do.

Debra usually wore miniskirts, combat boots, and knee-high socks, and had her long black hair swinging around her shoulders. She looked mod and offbeat in a studied kind of way, rather obstreperous and defiant. I liked the look, almost wished I could dress that way, but by now I was forty-nine and into my more conventional and straight period. Slacks, blouses, sweaters, leather, and high heels.

It all began with Debra being ticked off at the way I dressed.

"What is that piece of shit you are wearing?" she asked, referring to a white leather dress I had dragged out of my trunk and found very comfortable.

A little taken aback I said, "Well, I like it."

She turned to Jim. "My hair . . . what do you think?"

He shrugged, not terribly informed about anything women put on their bodies or did to their hair. She opened her tote bag, extracted a pair of shears from it, and disappeared into his bedroom. We chatted and waited.

She came out of the bathroom and said, "Isn't this Emma?"

She had chopped her hair off to chin-length. I was impressed. This was real commitment to a part and an abdication of her own vanity.

We then launched into a scene in which Aurora tells Emma that she should be more aware of her limitations. We stuck to the script and then Jim asked us to improvise. Debra, as Emma, sprang back with admonishments about my (Aurora's) way of being and dressing. I, as Aurora, chose to play my reaction as one of detachment. Whatever Debra-Emma said, I-Aurora ignored her and went on with other dialogue and action. I thought that would be Aurora's weapon. Debra became more and more upset. She walked out of the living room and called Jim into the next room. I couldn't really hear what was being said. A while later Debra and Jim emerged saying that was the end of rehearsal.

Debra left. I looked at Jim. "Don't worry," he said. "She's just emotional. She's finding the character. It's about the work."

I took that at face value.

We all returned to California and preproduction.

Jim had written the part of the aging astronaut who becomes Aurora's lover for Burt Reynolds. Jim had worked with Burt in television and liked him. Burt, however, didn't want to work without his toupee and he insisted on his daily regimen of working out and watching his diet. So a middle-aged spread was not something he was willing to allow for the sake of a part. Vanity got in his way, I was sorry to see, and Jim moved on to someone else: Jack Nicholson.

Jack is an actor who doesn't count close-ups or how many scenes he's in. His only exercise of that ilk would be "How much do I get? Which days do I have off so I can go to a Lakers game?"

Talks proceeded between Jack's agent and Jim's people. In the meantime, Jim wanted Kim Basinger to play the role of Emma's best friend, Patsy. The part called for someone extremely beautiful who could also provide competition for Aurora.

From my living room in Malibu, Jim and Debra and I

called Kim. She was upset that we approached her directly.

"Why are you guys doing this to me?" she asked. "This is a supporting character with you guys and Burt Reynolds has asked me to star with him in *The Man Who Loved Women*." I could feel the anguish in her voice as she turned us down, feeling deeply put-upon.

I understood Kim. From her point of view, a picture with Burt was more of a sure thing. Unfortunately, though, she took a calculated risk and lost. *The Man Who Loved Women* didn't work. An unknown actress was cast in the part of Emma's friend.

Our rehearsals proceeded with what I would call chaotic exploration. Debra was hyperkinetic and insistent upon having everyone's full attention.

With cozy friendliness, she sat down next to me one day. "You know, you're the most important person in the room to me," she said. "Never forget that."

"Thanks," I said, pleased that we had finally connected.

"Do you have a cigarette?" she asked.

I brought out a package with two smokes remaining. I handed Debra one.

"Oh no," she said. "You only have two left."

I said, "That's fine. No problem. We can always get more."

"No," she said.

"Oh, go on, take it," I said.

"No," she said.

"Why not? You wanted a cigarette. Have one."

"No," she said. "You'd never forgive me for taking your next to the last one."

I didn't know what to say. I replaced the cigarette. I didn't know if we were doing an Emma-Aurora improvisation or if she was angling for a fight.

A few days later Jim and I and two actors, playing my suitors, were immersed in concentration over a comedy sequence so that it wouldn't go OTT (over the top).

Debra arrived at rehearsal with a ghetto blaster turned up to eardrum-bursting level, set it down not far from where we were rehearsing, and began to dance. Jim looked up. His focus was broken. He walked over to her and said something I couldn't hear and an argument erupted. Debra had achieved her goal: full attention.

Perhaps tension between actors created tension between characters on the screen because it was authentic? Was this about *non*-acting?

I called John Travolta, who had done *Urban Cowboy* with Debra.

"Tell me about Debra, Johnny," I said. "How does she work?"

"She's difficult on herself," he answered, "and can cause, how shall I put it, consternation among her co-workers."

He went on to say he wouldn't like to repeat the experience, but he was reasonably friendly with her and liked her. All of that made sense. I could live with someone being difficult on herself. God knows I had walked that road myself, but being a well brought up, middle class "lady" from Virginia, I never liked rocking other people's boats. It was socially inappropriate—not polite. In other words, I never had the guts to be outright difficult where others could observe it. In some ways Debra was refreshingly unrestrained.

With Jack Nicholson finally cast as Garrett, the company moved on to Houston where we would continue rehearsals, along with the wardrobe and hair fittings. The day I was to leave for Houston the storm of '83 hit Malibu. I was stuck on Malibu Road and couldn't get out. I was alone in my house because no one was allowed to leave or enter. The old houses built on wood pilings in Malibu were not safe. As I looked from my window I saw several collapse and be swept away with the undertow. Then the pilings from Paradise Cove began to flow south. Two of them hit the pilings under my house broadside. I thought my place would collapse. But it held. Then I looked out over the churning ocean and saw a Dodge car tossing its way directly toward me on top of the waves. This is it, I thought. I held my face, as though that would help, and put my hands over my eyes. I waited. I didn't feel the thundering, crunching thumps that I had come to identify from years of living above water. I waited another few seconds . . . nothing . . . I braved the balcony outside to see what had happened. The Dodge had crashed into the house next door. A man on the *other* side of me was taking pictures from his balcony about thirty feet high. A wave was gathering force. I could see that the man busy photographing the Dodge was directly in its path. I screamed for him to get off his balcony. He couldn't hear me. The wave washed over him and dashed him to the rocks below. I panicked and ran inside to call 911.

The phone rang. It was Jim calling from Houston.

"Why aren't you here?" he asked. "We're starting a picture in a week and you are not here."

"No," I said. "I'm here in the middle of a hurricane."

"Oh, good," he replied. "So you have a chance to study your script."

"Well, yes," I said, "but not right now."

I looked out the window to check on the man next door. There were people and sirens and lights. I could see help had come.

"What kind of accent are you going to use?" Jim

continued. "Have you decided on it yet? We have to know so Debra can take hers from yours."

I heard the frightening rumble again. I knew it was a mountain of water coming straight at me. I couldn't speak, I was so terrified.

"Are you there?" said Jim.

"Yes," I whispered.

"Speak up," he said. "I know you'll be all right with whatever's going on out there. I just have one worry."

"So do I," I said.

Almost on cue, the mountainous wave hit. It crashed through my living room. The sound was something I had never heard before. I was sitting high on a kitchen bar stool. The water inundated everything. Then, as quickly as it had come, it was gone. My furniture, walls, clothes, and carpet were soaked or dripping with salt water.

Miraculously, the phone still worked. Jim continued as though the world only existed from his end of the line.

"Listen," he said, "whatever happens, I don't want you to get out of character."

He hung up. I sat surrounded by the mess in my living room.

So he didn't want me to get out of character.

I never was one to get "in" character until the moment the director yelled "action," and even then half the time I'd be thinking about what I was going to have for lunch. I wondered what he'd think of that.

Directors who have written their own screenplay are more territorial about their material and their characters than they are about their own children. They live and breathe their creations, and nothing, absolutely nothing, will deter them from realizing their vision. This intensity of focus is what studio heads find so intimidating. To a creative filmmaker it is *not* just another movie. To a studio chief it is what will fill the autumn time slot.

Jim's focus was so complete that he was determined that nothing would disturb mine. Death was the only excuse for getting out of character. And he would use any means necessary to accomplish what he needed, regardless of the side effects.

Early on, when he was still uncertain whether I should play Aurora, he took me to a restaurant that he knew had questionable service, but was pretentious and expensive. He watched me with the intensity of a hungry hawk as I dealt with the waiter's ineptitude. I tried to be civil and patient with him for a while. Then I erupted and let the waiter have it. Jim fairly drooled with delight that I could call on my imperious aspects so readily. Aurora was mine.

It was the tactic he used throughout the shoot, but while it was happening I was either too naive or too stupid to see it. It was my agent, Mort, who suggested Jim's attitude was a method, but by that time I was already beginning to see how our human defects could be a grist for any mill. It was an idea that had never before occurred to me, not at this extreme. I was a novice when it came to such exquisite manipulation. How could I have been in the business thirty years and not seen this? But, of course, until I worked with Jim Brooks, I hadn't worked with such a master. I had been used to a method of work where the director simply told me what he wanted and I'd try to accomplish it. William Wyler was famous for not telling you what he wanted but getting you to do it another way . . . namely his. During a scene in *The Children's Hour* he made me run up and down the stairs for nearly thirty takes. When he finally yelled "print" and I asked him why, he answered that he wanted me to be tired! Why he didn't just say so in the beginning he never told me.

One of Jim's unexplained directions came the night before we were to begin *Terms*. During the rehearsal period in Houston, I had worked with a River Oaks–Houston accent at Jim's instruction. That was where Aurora lived and it wasn't too much of a stretch for me because I was from the South anyway. So, I conceived the character as a Texas belle who lived on the lower end of the right side of the tracks. She spoke with a Texas drawl, had bouffant hair, many chiffon dresses in her wardrobe, and cared desperately about her kitchen and the impression she made at every turn. I always work on a character from the outside in, not the other way around. If I know how she walks and laughs and places her feet when she sits in a chair, I know her. In other words, I work like a dancer. When I know how a character moves, I know how she feels.

We had completed rehearsals in Jim's hotel suite and were ready to shoot the next day. Jim lay down on the couch and put his head in my lap. Everyone else had gone. He talked of his demons and a dark-spiritedness that frightened him. I was touched, but perplexed as to how to react. I decided to emphasize the positive, which is usually my MO. He sprang to an upright position and said, ''Why don't you let yourself come down here in the muck and the mire with the rest of us? What makes you so fucking stable and on top of things?''

I was stunned. Oh my God, I thought. Was he serious? Yes, it seemed so, but what was he serious about? Did he want me to change my values and personality for the film, or was he just trying to provoke Aurora?

A Russian play was not as Byzantine as this. I pleaded a headache and said I needed to get to bed and left.

My call was at six in the morning. Jim telephoned me

around ten o'clock that night. "I've decided that Aurora shouldn't be from Texas. She shouldn't speak with an accent. She should originate from New England and we find her here in Texas. Okay?"

"But, Jim," I said, paralyzed, "what about all the wardrobe, the hair? I mean, I don't know what to say. We start in the morning and you're changing it all to-night?"

"Yep," he said. "It'll be more spontaneous. You'll adjust."

He hung up.

Jim Brooks knew I was basically a gypsy, which means a dancer, which meant I would take direction without question because I had been taught to fear and respect, without reservation, the choreographer-director. I grew up that way. Whatever the person with the stick said was law. Otherwise I'd be cracked over the back. Many a choreographer—man and woman—had hit me with a stick or thrown me across the room by my earlobe (freshly pierced, as luck would have it) or twisted my leg up behind my ear until I thought I would pass out with pain.

Jim knew this about me. So he understood I would make the adjustment because I respected him. He took the gamble that it wouldn't destroy my confidence. But more than anything, by putting me in an uncomfortable emotional position, he succeeded in getting another layer of reaction out of Aurora because she was a woman who hated to be thrown off balance. That's where the comedy came from. If he could throw *me* off balance, he figured he'd force me more deeply into character. Maybe he was right. Maybe his method worked. Maybe I would have done it anyway. Or maybe he really just changed his mind at the last minute and left the burden with me. You could go crazy trying to figure out the motives for his methods. At least I knew one thing. Jim Brooks was not a man to try to outwit, outsmart, or even outprepare, and for sure, there was a purpose in his madness every step of the way. My problem was functioning with it.

The first day Debra and I worked together in front of the camera, the assistant called us to our marks. She got to hers first.

"Hey, Mom," she ordered, "hey, get over here. These are yours."

"Okay," I said.

The first day in front of the camera is one of jockeying, of establishing boundaries, of assessing your fellow actors as well as letting the crew know that regardless of how brilliant you might be, you realize it means nothing if you're not in your light and you don't know where the camera is. You know that they know that you know this, *and* you are also scared.

I moved toward my marks, trying to adjust to the tailored slacks I wore now instead of a bouffant dress. I was not yet used to my toned-down wig and I had no idea what kind of accent would come out of my mouth. I tried to sustain my dancer's discipline. As I walked I wondered what the hell would be the damn pecking order this time.

"You're over here," Debra said.

The crew stopped talking. They could sense a stakeout.

"I heard you," I said. "I know marks when I see them."

"Good," she said. "How's this for a mark?"

She turned around, walked away from me, lifted her skirt slightly, looked over her shoulder, bent over, and farted in my face.

"Do you always talk with your mouth full?" I asked. She laughed.

God, I thought, maybe this was the new, modern, hip way of finding a character. I felt about two hundred years old.

So was this Debra Winger's conception of Emma, who was, after all, disdainful of her mother and rebellious? Where did her character end and Debra begin? Aurora existed to be thrown off stride. Did Jim and Debra really feel I needed auxiliary assistance in my acting?

During the shoot I was living at the Houstonian Hotel, where I slept on the floor next to a permanently closed window they had chiseled open specially for me. Outside my window was a tree that blossomed into springtime and rustled in the wind with sweet murmurings. That tree saved my life. I will never forget it. It was real . . . no complicated antics bred out of God knows what. It simply *was*. It was a constant for me in a surrealistic illusion that was unfortunately becoming more and more my real world.

I would often pass by Debra's room at night and hear her crying into the telephone. I didn't want to stop and listen. I was afraid the conversation might be about me. I was as lost as she was, but for different reasons. She told me she slept very little, but she was still beautiful every morning. Once, after a rough night, she bent over the table while we were rehearsing the dinner scene and whispered that she had a sliver of glass in her eye and needed to go to the hospital. We stopped rehearsing and I gestured for Jim. She looked up at him with such anguish, saying she couldn't sleep and her eye was bleeding. Jim complied immediately. He was sweet and compassionate and properly sensitive to her turmoil. We went on to shoot without her.

The next morning Jack and I were shooting our "morning after" scene in Aurora's bedroom.

We had had a rehearsal and after touch-ups (the heat in the low-ceilinged set was unbearable) we were ready to shoot. I got into my side of the bed, and Jack got into his. Jim climbed up behind the camera for a good vantage point and called "action."

I began the scene—I was on the telephone with Emma while Jack slept.

Suddenly, under the covers, I felt a tongue on my ankle. It went up my leg and then it stopped. The setup had been so difficult for the camera crew that I didn't want to stop the scene.

I realized it was Debra under the covers doing what she considered sexy mischief. Apparently she was doing the same thing to Jack when she left off with me. He didn't have any dialogue, though, and besides, he's never been one to turn down a sexual adventure.

The scene seemed to go on interminably. I looked up at Jim. He knew Debra was under the covers, but he kept the cameras rolling. He didn't seem to know how to handle it.

Finally, he called, "Cut."

I kicked Debra away from me. She threw back the covers and announced, "You shouldn't knock it if you haven't tried it."

She grabbed my legs and held them apart under my nightgown. Jack then mischievously pinned my arms over my head. The crew instantly became a solid unit of voyeurs led by the cameraman, who had endured the cruelty of the communist regime in Poland and must have welcomed a set with a little sexual horseplay.

I was, by now, pinned down by Debra from below and Jack from above.

She started with her tongue again, sliding up my leg. I looked over at Jack. He had that maniacal, devilish expression we've all come to know and love. Obviously he was going to play this out to the fullest extent. What the hell, he was only in for two weeks. What did he care?

I wrestled my arm from his grip and grabbed his balls and squeezed as hard as I could.

"Tell her to get off me," I said sweetly, tightening my grip.

"You heard the lady," Jack said in a high voice. Debra let go. I kicked her away. She sat up. I slithered away from the set feeling like a schoolteacher from Pasadena.

All night I thought about how else I could have handled what had happened. I had no way to relate to their antics, and more than anything I was embarrassed at *myself*. Why couldn't I just laugh it off and allow them their good-time behavior?

The *Terms* experience was rapidly becoming exactly what Jim had suggested at the outset: "coming down into the muck and mire."

The war stories were filtering back to the Home Office. We were falling behind the schedule. On a film, if the antics affect the schedule, budget, or potential profit, the top brass gets involved. Actors and creative people can indulge in any behavior under the sun as long as the money isn't affected. Schedule and budget mean money. I wondered when the Paramount people would send wranglers for us crazy actors.

I had a few days off, and was relishing some time away from the madness, when the assistant director called. "Debra's crying," he said. "She wants you or she can't work. A driver will be over to get you and bring you out here."

When I arrived at the swimming-pool location, Debra was pacing up and down beside the pool with zinc oxide smeared on her nose. The crew and Jim stood watching. I walked up to her.

"What's wrong?" I asked.

"He's evil," she sobbed, pointing at Jim. "He's dancing at the end of the street and I know he's evil for me."

She put her arms around me. I held her while she sobbed for over an hour. Jim didn't come near us. I just held her and rocked her. Finally her anguish subsided. She was exhausted. A while later they finally got the scene. I went home thoroughly cross-eyed.

That night she called me. Her monologue was all about how Jim couldn't be trusted because of his own personal flaws. She said she was able to discern things about him that nobody else could. As she talked she wove a tapestry of convoluted, highly rococo observations and opinions of Jim, none of which seemed rooted in reality. They sounded so well thought out, though. I felt thickheaded and incapable of hanging on to my own sense of reality. I began to count the days until the film would be over, and we were only halfway through.

WHEN JACK NICHOLSON ARRIVED BACK TO SHOOT HIS scene, he sensed there was trouble. Jack is a master of the intuitive. His nose started to twitch. He was like an animal perceiving a negative vibration—a monstrous dynamic in our midst.

When you've been around our business as long as Jack had, you grasp the dynamic on the set immediately.

I could see he didn't like it. The crew was operating in a disjointed, fragmented way . . . taking too long . . . arguing over inane things. Jim was slightly wild-eyed, but looking for a way to use the chaos. The dynamic was insinuating itself, working its destruction.

We were doing the kitchen scene, where Jack had pages of dialogue describing what it was like, as an astronaut, to walk on the moon. Then he noticed the camera crew was not together. The prop guy was late with the food we were supposed to eat in the scene and no one was in charge. The dynamic permeated the set as though it had a personality and an intention. It became an invisible being who was about to jeopardize Jack. Jack was up for practical jokes regardless of how bizarre, but not for the dynamic of unprofessionalism. I sat across from him, watching the buildup of an explosion. Suddenly his eyes narrowed as he did a quick sweep-of-a-look around the set. He was ready to work and they weren't.

"Hey," he yelled. "Motherfucker—hey!"

Suddenly he slammed his fists onto the top of the kitchen table with a violence that literally shook the set. The crew froze; *no* one moved. Everyone had been put on notice and they knew it. Then Jack collected himself. He smiled that devil smile. I could feel the dynamic slink away.

Jack's is not a petty temperament. When he is threatened or angry, he can be *truly* impressive. His repressed violence is nothing to trifle with, certainly not to be manipulated. And he's not in the same class with those who tinker with danger, as Jim does. Jack is *real* danger—class-A danger—smiling danger. The kind that renders a crew paralytic. The kind that makes your blood run cold because he's willing to pay the price. Which is what happened that morning. And from that flashing moment on, the set was reborn into a professional unit inspired to make a movie the way it should be made.

It was a miraculous transition. God, it was wonderful. Even Debra straightened out, expending most of her hyperkinetic energy within Jack's trailer. He called her "Buck." I later found out Buck was short for buck and wing (Winger). He definitely knew something we didn't know.

Jack was without cosmetic vanity and every take was different. He was a chameleon of talent, changing his colors and his skin according to whatever occurred to him, and this evoked a spontaneity in me that I was thrilled to feel again. Jim cackled with pleasure as he saw his characters come to life.

Jack-Garrett teased Aurora unmercifully while she provoked every minute of it.

There was one scene, my favorite, that ended up on the cutting-room floor. Aurora is watching Garrett topple over one of his garbage cans after a particular dizzy night with a blond bimbo. She glares at him from behind her tree. Then, as he's lying drunk on the pavement of their adjoining driveway, she walks over to him, stands just above his head, looks down, and says, "It's all I can do not to step on your face."

The scene in the water where Garrett puts his hand into Aurora's bra had me laughing so hard I could hardly play it. I was beginning to see that the Garrett-Aurora relationship was what was going to make the picture work. *And* we were having fun. Was this the way it *should* be? I wondered how long the fun would last.

The dailies on the picture were looking very good too. Of course, the characters Jim had written were so well drawn, I felt any good actors could have made them sing. But, maybe not. Maybe *we* were the only ones meant to do them. Perhaps it *was* worth it after all. In between setups we talked about acting. Jack told me that the way to play a drunk scene when you're walking is to believe that the floor and every piece of furniture around you will break if you touch them. He said that withholding emotion is what moves an audience because they identify with their own inability to express their feelings. It was an acting lesson and a few weeks in the emotional sunshine. Everyone took their cues from Jack. He simply wouldn't tolerate the dynamic of negativity that forever lurked around our perimeters.

When Jack left, the dynamic moved in again. Debra

became so hyper one night during dailies that she began running up and down the aisles, singing between reels, carrying a can of Coca-Cola with brandy in it. She plopped down next to me. The next reel began and she whispered in my ear, "Wait till you see this!" Becoming more and more agitated and gleeful over what she saw, she threw her arm over my chest and pulled hard on my right breast. I shrieked in pain, rammed her with my elbow in the stomach, and said, "Get the hell away from me." She retreated like a wounded, manic child who has provoked discipline but is terribly hurt after receiving it. She bolted from me with aggressive tears. I felt terrible. I wished I hadn't done it. But at least I was finally fighting down in "the muck and the mire." Jim could no longer accuse me of being above it all.

It was soon after I hit Debra that Jim banned me from the dailies. For me, to make a film without watching my dailies is like painting a picture with my eyes closed. When I protested, Jim said it wasn't in my contract.

So I took to sitting outside the projection room on a little bench, looking wistful and hoping to make Jim feel guilty. It worked, but I had to watch the dailies by myself. The crew was humiliated for me too but they knew that above-the-line talent was crazy anyway.

What was more disturbing about the "daily" situation was what happened when it was my turn to watch. Jim would come in and sit himself on my lap and talk to me so I couldn't see the screen, while Debra careened around the room with her brandy can. It was total madness. Then one day the Paramount brass arrived. They came to the dailies. Jim allowed me back in to watch with them. How could he have explained my sitting outside with my head hanging low and a scarf pulled around the sides of my face, purposely engendering pity?

The Paramount people brought a dose of normality.

They knew what was going on. They sat and talked to me before the lights went down, asking me how it had been to work with Billy Wilder, William Wyler, Bob Fosse, Alfred Hitchcock, and so on. The implication was clear. . . . Have you ever been through madness like this before? I knew Jim was listening to my answers and I could feel his rising insecurity. I tried to keep my replies circumspect.

The dailies began. And the scene was great—Jack and me in the car, driving on the beach and ending up in the water.

We saw many takes, and when it was over the lights came up. The Paramount guys were grinning. "Well, what did you think?" one of them asked. I couldn't contain my excitement. I said, "I really liked what I saw."

As is usually the case, the brass looked to the director. Even they won't say what they think without some assurance that it's okay. Jim said nothing. They said nothing. Silence. Then Jim said, "So you thought they were great?"

"Yes," I said, sensing an ambush in the making.

"Well," Jim went on, "that's why I don't want you in the projection room."

The Paramount people blinked. Jim waited for my reply. I picked up my purse and walked out. I went back to the hotel, called Mort, and said they could shove the Oscar I was probably forfeiting up their asses. I was walking off the picture.

He said, "You're kidding."

I said, "Nope. I mean it. I want out. Let them get Bette Davis or Joan Crawford or somebody who can handle this. I can't."

"What will you do?" he asked.

"I'm coming home tomorrow," I said. "First thing smokin' I'm out of here."

"Do you have a call tomorrow?" he asked.

"Yes," I answered. "So what?"

He hesitated. "Okay, that's good enough for me. See you tomorrow."

I packed, called the airport, made a reservation, and went to bed.

Never had I walked off a picture. It wasn't in my nature. I was thrilled I had the guts.

I woke early, registered that I should have been on the set, and went back to sleep.

Around nine the phone rang. It was the assistant director.

"Where are you?" he asked. "Did you oversleep? We're waiting for you."

"I know," I answered. "I'm not coming in. Now or ever. I'm out of here."

I hung up.

I puttered around, muttering words of confidence to myself.

Half an hour later the phone rang. It was Mort.

"Well," he said, "the shit hit the fan. Jim is crazed. He says he understands why you feel this way. He wants you to know he has a warped sense of humor."

I didn't say anything.

"Are you there?" asked Mort.

"I'm here," I answered. "Fuck his sense of humor. I'm done."

"Wait a minute," said Mort. "I told him how you felt about everything. By the way, Paramount knows how nuts this shoot is—why do you think they keep showing up? Half the crazy stuff you don't even know about."

He hesitated. I hesitated.

"By the way," said Mort. "I told him I agreed with you. Debra doo-doo is one thing, but not letting you see the dailies is just not professional."

"Nothing is professional around here," I said. "It's amateur night in Dixie. It's nuts. I hate it. And please don't tell me that Jim is doing all this on purpose, to get Aurora-like reactions from me. I know that too and I don't give a shit. I can't stand it anymore. I have to get out of here."

"You've got to let him call you," said Mort. "He's begging to speak to you. He keeps saying over and over that it's his sense of humor."

"Oh," I said, "and where are the laughs supposed to come?"

"Can he call you?" asked Mort.

"I can't really walk out, can I?" I asked.

"No," said Mort. "Not unless you've got ten million dollars to spend on it."

"Yeah," I said, "I know. But I can't stand it. And you know how I get when I can't stand something."

"I know," he said. "But just take his call."

I sighed down to my toes, knowing that whatever Jim might say, the dynamics on the picture were set in motion and they wouldn't run their course until the film was completed—if then.

I knew how talented Jim was and basically how profoundly wise and sensitive. Yet, would I allow myself to be destroyed if I continued? It was only a movie after all. But not to Jim. It was his life.

As I measured my feelings I tried to determine why I was willing to walk away from a potentially huge success and a possible Oscar nomination. No matter what had happened, I knew the script was extraordinary. But the truth was, I *was* willing to walk away from something that was making me miserable. I was then, and I am now.

However, I couldn't argue with Mort's assessment. The reality was I couldn't afford to be sued.

"Okay." I sighed. "Tell him to call me."

"Listen," said Jim, "I have a really weird and warped sense of humor. I think you're really doing extraordinary work on this film. Your choices are brilliant and I don't want anything to interrupt what we're getting here. Okay?"

"Okay?" I asked. "You don't want anything to interrupt what we're doing? How about a man in a white coat?"

"Okay," he answered. "So I'll be seeing you soon? Okay?"

Jesus.

"Yeah," I answered, vowing that I would make ten million dollars one day. *That* would be power. I was learning.

The shoot continued. But not only did circumstances not improve, they got worse. In Hollywood the shadow is always darkest just before it gets darker.

We finished our work in Houston. Then the company moved on to a New York location that didn't include me. At least, that's what I thought.

It started as soon as the company arrived in Manhattan. The calls would come at six in the morning, California time. It was usually an assistant director on a cellular phone calling from the hallway outside of Debra's room. He'd say she was terrified of the comedy to be done that day and wouldn't go to work unless I talked through with her how to play the scene. This went on for a week.

Sleepily I'd call her. She'd go over, word for word, her intention, her motivation, her fear that it wouldn't work. I didn't think I was much help, but usually our conversation somehow satisfied her. She'd hang up and tell the AD she'd be ready in a while. Soon she'd report for work—still, I'm told, uncertain of how the scenes should go. Actually I thought she had a point. I never understood the necessity of the New York portion of the story. She, in her intelligence, had picked up what I thought was the one flaw in the script and was saddled with making it work.

The company left New York and flew to Lincoln, Nebraska, where the remainder of the film would be shot.

Debra was doing a fair amount of research on cancer deaths because of her character's fatal illness. I remembered that Travolta had told me she insisted on sleeping in a graveyard on *Urban Cowboy,* causing worry among the crew and others, but that was how she worked.

Perhaps the identification with her character caused what happened next, I don't know.

We were shooting in a hospital in Lincoln, which is where the action actually took place. I walked out of the elevator on the floor allotted to us. I couldn't hear anything. The normal crew noises weren't evident. No one was milling around. I spotted the AD. He pointed to a room and rolled his eyes. The crew had shrunk up against the wall. I heard Debra's voice.

I walked over to the room. Jim was sitting on a chair, bent over at the waist, his head hanging low. Debra stood over him, berating him. She used language I'd never heard before as she admonished Jim for his insensitivity and all-around comportment.

As I watched I realized there was a dance between two masters going on. The lower Jim's head hung, the more vitriolic Debra became. Both of them understood that the crew was observing everything. A director knows that he is the captain of the ship; democracy does not exist on a movie set. The person who sits in the chair is a dictator. His vision, his word, his conclusion, whatever it may be, is law.

Yet what I was witnessing was a purposeful abdication of his position of authority.

This was doubly interesting to me because I would never dream of chewing out a director. I'd just leave. But here she was, a fragile-looking, dark-haired, vulnerable young beauty spewing venom the likes of which I had never heard before. And Jim was not only taking it, he was bending to it, as though inviting her to hit him harder, preferably below the belt if she was so inclined.

I looked over at Jeff Daniels, who played Emma's husband.

"What's going on?" I whispered.

He shrugged. "She thinks he wasn't being sensitive to our scene. She dies today, you know."

Yes, I knew. As a matter of fact, I wondered how I'd react to seeing her take her last breath. I figured it was going to be difficult for me to be devastated.

"Was Jim being insensitive?" I asked. A rhetorical question, I realized.

"Who knows around here?" said Jeff.

"Did he say anything mean?" I asked.

Jeff shrugged. "Who knows?"

Debra continued to berate Jim. She was on a roll. A roll of such precise and definitive annihilation that the rest of us stood mesmerized.

Crew members slowly tiptoed to the craft service table and I drifted away, waiting for the diatribe to end. By observing any longer, I felt I would be contributing to Jim's emotional keelhauling.

Soon Debra left the small room. She went to the hospital room where her scene was to take place. She climbed into bed.

Then Jim emerged. He straightened up somewhat and stroked his beard. He walked toward the set with a hurried shuffle.

"Okay," he said. "Now, is everybody ready?"

The crew scurried to their assigned positions.

I went into wardrobe and dressed. The wardrobe girls busied themselves with panty hose and bras. No one spoke of what had occurred.

I had my face touched up.

People sipped coffee and ate doughnuts.

A few seconds later we were all on the set. The camera was ready. The lights came on. I sat in my chair by Debra's bed. Jeff took his place next to me.

Jim took his place by the camera. He called "action." Debra began the process of dying. She raised her hand in a meek little wave as though signaling good-bye to me. I watched anxiously. Jeff was properly alarmed. Then Debra took her last breath.

She had played the scene beautifully.

The nurse came in, reacting to the machine attached to Debra's arm. She took her pulse. The nurse shook her head and said, "She's gone."

I wanted to leap into the air and shout for joy, but I quickly recovered what was left of my professional's sanity and made the acting choice to hyperventilate. Up to that moment I did not know how I was going to play the scene. Why I chose to hyperventilate—breathe in short shallow breaths—I can't say. There were many reactions Aurora could have had. Breathing quickly in order to control her emotions seemed as good a move as any.

Debra lay still. Jeff rose from his chair. I rose from mine. He held me and I decided Aurora should finally break down.

"It's so hard," I cried, quoting the script. "I never realized it would be this hard." I let myself go completely. I sobbed and sobbed into my son-in-law's shoulder. I felt my shoulders heave up and down. I wanted to cry for days. Only I wasn't thinking about the death of

Emma. I was thinking of how hard it had been for me to be in this picture.

A YEAR AFTER *TERMS* WAS COMPLETED I CALLED JIM ON New Year's Day to wish him happiness for the next year and ask for a recap of the year we had just been through. I told him I was still confused and unresolved about what had gone on during shooting and I asked for clarification. He was wonderful. Short and sweet.

"Listen," he said. "Winger and I need a certain amount of chaos and Sturm and Drang in order to work. That is the way we commit to our task. You and Nicholson are different. That's all, forget it."

Does one need conflict and struggle in order for artistic creativity to flourish? The oyster needs the irritant of sand to make a pearl, but do human beings? I had been working toward peaceful, straight-shooting situations, where communication was direct but noncombative. I felt that chaotic stimulation was not only unnecessary, but destructive. Maybe I was wrong, *or* maybe some pictures make it in spite of conflict, or maybe they make it because of conflict.

Debra inhabits her parts to the point of misery. She's willing to lose herself—in fact, is compelled to do that. It might seem crazy, but it is her way of working. From her I learned that the creative impulse is pockmarked with soul scars. Each of us brings a different life experience to our work, making demands on our very different memories. Therefore, each of us has something to say and a contribution to make.

Debra's style of working is risky and, above all, honest. Though it's not my style, it held a lesson for me—that I was just as entitled to express my needs in order to create a working environment that was nurturing for me.

That was what Jim meant when he said, "Why don't

you come down to the muck and mire." I was trying to be cooperative—a nice guy. "Christian-like and disciplined," as Jim put it.

So, when I won the Oscar and walked down the aisle to collect it, I leaned over to Debra—even then I couldn't be totally honest—and said, "Half of this belongs to you." She *was* honest and replied, "I'll take it." Perhaps her honesty inspired me to raise the Oscar above my head and say, "I deserve this."

# 8

# FOSSE

## Once Again, Please
## . . . Forgive Me

 can't tell my Hollywood story without celebrating one of the great talents in the cosmos of creativity. Bob Fosse was an extremely complicated person who thrived on knowing the worst about himself. When he died at sixty, none of us was surprised. He had been attracted to his own death for many years. In fact, his greatest film was a depiction of just that. The erotica of his demise, *All That Jazz*.

Bob Fosse and I started as dancers, he in Hollywood Metro musicals, me on the Broadway stage. When we worked together on the film of *Sweet Charity* we remembered that each of us had helped the other get to Hollywood. He had taken me out of the chorus of *Pajama Game,* insisting I could do more. I had brought him to Hollywood, insisting that he could direct a movie. We shared a destiny that each of us recognized—from a respectful distance.

I was eighteen years old, dancing in a Broadway show called *Me and Juliet*. Bill Hayes, Isabel Bigley, and Joan McCracken were the stars. Fosse was married to Joan. They had been dancing partners, doing clubs, etc., and had survived the wars of the Metro musicals.

McCracken was a small, yet powerful woman with a foghorn voice and a sense of "in your face" comedy years before it was fashionable. She had a long history on Broadway, beginning with *Oklahoma!*, where she played the original "fall down girl" as choreographed by Agnes de Mille. I had done the subway circuit of *Oklahoma!* years later when I was sixteen years old. McCracken was part of Broadway myth. Now I was working with her in *Me and Juliet* for Rodgers and Hammerstein.

Joan was a tried and true gypsy, as well as a consummate character actress in comedies on the stage, and she possessed a generosity about other people's talent. On matinee days during the run of *Me and Juliet*, Joan formed an actors' class for chorus kids she thought had talent. I happened to be one of them. She gave us little scenes to memorize and enact. Then she'd give us her observations, critical and praiseworthy. She was smart, fair, and encouraging.

Joan's husband, Fosse, was back and forth between New York and Hollywood, depending on where the work was. The word went around the company that he was an imaginative dancer who had worked some with Gene Kelly and an offbeat dancer named Carol Haney. I hadn't seen that many Metro musicals because I was concentrating on Broadway. But I remembered that Fosse had danced in a vignette with Carol Haney in *Kiss Me Kate*. I could see he had not been trained in ballet, but he was a superb jazz dancer.

Every now and then Fosse would wander into our acting classes, which took place on the stage with a simple work light in between shows, and watch us. He didn't say much. Just watched, a cigarette dangling from his lips as he hunched and paced up and down the aisles of the theater. I couldn't take my eyes off him. He exuded a kind of creativity just by the way he moved in and around the seats of the dark theater, watching and pondering. I wondered how the marriage between him and Joan worked, with a continent separating them because of their profession.

I loved McCracken. She was direct, honest, and very sensitive. She seemed to take me under her wing, sensing how serious I was about becoming an "acting" dancer, and helped me a great deal with my speaking voice.

I loved being in the show too, but I didn't want to find myself, a few years down the line, still in the chorus. I had no idea what I would do instead. As I've said, I never thought about being a "star." But I did want to play good parts, even though I knew little about acting and I wasn't sure what a good part for me might be.

I wanted to be funny and dramatic and musical and glamorous. I wanted to make an audience feel something. I wanted to be individualized and not lost in the background. I wanted to be noticed and loved. But I never really saw myself in motion pictures, although I couldn't focus on exactly what I wanted to do on the stage.

The nature of ambition is very different for different people. It never occurred to me that I wouldn't become successful in show business. I felt somehow that I should *expect* to make it, that I would only be fulfilling my destiny.

I could feel the tendency in myself, however, to want to be comfortable and quiet and safe and not dare to put myself through the humiliation of the firing line—auditions and lessons and painful training and the necessary competition that was expected if I wanted to "make it." Yet whenever I felt that anxiety, I remembered how much effort and money and pride my parents had invested in my future. Not that they ever demanded in any overt way that I "become" anyone special. But "good genes, pioneer stock, excellent bloodlines," and the like were phrases that echoed in our house so often that my destiny seemed to be to live up to what my family and the good Lord expected of me. I guess I didn't want to let them down. Their dream became my dream. I hated taking even the smallest amount of money from them. I was in my teens and I felt old enough to support myself. It wasn't easy.

The memories of my early days in New York are still visceral. I can smell the greasepaint and steam heat of our chorus dressing room on the fifth floor off of stage right. One of the dancers sharing the dressing room was married and had a child. She bought the evening and morning papers every night and headed home to her husband and what she called a "settled life." She was thirty-one at the time and seemed ancient to me.

I lived in an apartment over the catacombs on West 116th Street. More than once I returned to find everything gone . . . the furniture, clothes, dishes, etc. I was so naive, I didn't realize I was living in one of the most notorious dope sections of Manhattan. I'd simply take my paycheck and furnish the place again with wooden furniture I bought wholesale and unpainted. My surroundings didn't matter much to me anyway. I didn't intend to be home much. I was always out mapping my dreams.

During the run of the show I was in, *Me and Juliet,* a new show was being planned. George Abbott, the grand old man of the Broadway theater, who was directing *Me and Juliet,* was contracted to codirect, with Jerome Robbins, a new musical about unions and management written by Richard Bissell. It was called *$7^1/2$ Cents.*

Investors were wary because the show sounded so political, but in addition to George Abbott and Jerry Robbins's involvement, there were three very creative people producing it: Robert Griffith, Freddie Brisson, and a bright young man named Hal Prince. The choreographer was young and bright too—Bob Fosse.

Some of the backstage personnel in *Me and Juliet* were going to move on to the new show. They and the producers came to the cast of *Me and Juliet* looking for investments in the production of *$7^1/2$ Cents.* I remember so well that I couldn't afford the thirty-five-dollar investment increments they were requesting from us.

I decided instead to audition for *$7^1/2$ Cents,* despite trepidation about my singing voice. I was a strong dancer, but because there were only to be six girls in the chorus, each would have to do everything—sing, dance, and act.

At the audition I sang "Blue Skies," and I began before the pianist was ready. But because my voice hit the balcony and my legs were long and I laughed a lot and seemed relatively believable when I read the lines, they gave me the job.

George Abbott and Jerry Robbins conducted the auditions along with Richard Adler and Jerry Ross, who wrote the score. Pacing up and down the aisles, shoulders hunched from nervousness, darting furtive glances at the stage, was Bob Fosse. He was as I remembered, intense and magnetic. With Fosse as choreographer and Robbins codirecting and staging some of the musical numbers, I would be working with the resident geniuses of the Broadway world, but I was too young to realize that. Things were happening so easily for me—there hadn't been that much struggle. As I said, it felt as though I should *expect* this. I wasn't particularly grateful. I was comfortable with things happening as they should!

Rehearsals began. The show's title had been changed from $7^1/2$ *Cents*, which the producers thought too political, to *The Pajama Game* (the industry the union was involved with). My first exposure to Fosse began.

Bob loved rhythm. He derived much of his inspiration from it. I had read that he came out of a burlesque background, and I wondered if that was why he loved the bump-and-grind beat so much.

Hour after hour he'd pace around the rehearsal hall with his rhythm metronome on and his cigarette hanging from his lips, the smoke curling into his squinting eyes. He could adjust the machine to any combination or rhythms he wanted. He'd feel a rhythm and start to move. The movement created a style. The style became the character of the dance that then seemed to choreograph itself.

Bob appeared fragile, not just because his body was thin and wiry, but because he seemed to make an apology every time he spoke. He didn't have the hard-driving, fascistic cruelty that most choreographers possess. The world of dance, especially ballet, is the world of pain. When you grow up accustomed to and conditioned by pain, it becomes a way of life, a requirement for creativity, a familiar companion. Therefore, that which is inflicted upon you, you will inflict on others. It's inevitable. It's familiar territory. You're comfortable with it. In fact, you feel a job well done should not be rewarded unless there has been pain involved.

Fosse came not from the world of ballet, but rather

from the world of jazz. That's different. Ballet is the repetitive training of the body for the purpose of executing steps in traditional fashion. It is tied to and bound by the past. It is a disciplined beauty consciously preserved in the image of the old days in societies that were class-conscious and appreciative of elitist physical expertise.

Ballet had been my world since I was three years old. When one is a ballet dancer, there is precious little time or room for anything else; family, fun, love, children, and relaxation all go by the wayside. It is all-consuming, because to force the body into such unnatural positions requires all the perverted sense of discipline one can muster. The strength required to live up to the traditional technique is superhuman, to say nothing of the mental persistence and stamina required. Ballet is one of the most beautiful of all art forms, but it is unnatural. In order to devote yourself to it you have to be willing to be an artistic soldier, a follower of commands, and a creature of repetition. You have to eat food that will keep your energy and strength up to par, but will not put on weight . . . almost impossible. Smoking and drinking are forbidden, yet nearly every great ballet dancer I've known has indulged in both. Sex happens in between tours, and having children is a flight of ridiculous fancy if you intend to be a real parent or a real artist.

Because ballet dancers are always touring, they rarely know what's going on in the world beyond the barre, the rehearsal hall, the stage, the dressing rooms, the airports, the trains and taxies and hotels. Sleep is snatched whenever possible and love is rarely permanent if it interferes with rehearsals and performances.

Fosse was definitely not a man from the world of ballet. His expressive talent and creativity came from movement that was specific and turned inward. In ballet, all movement is turned out. The five positions, from which everything else springs, require that feet, legs, hips, and arms are forced outward.

In jazz, the movement is generated from a feeling of inward coolness, a kind of inner rebellion that sneaks up on the body, expressing itself through unpredictable twists and turns that surprise rather than please with beauty.

Fosse's movements were expressions of the man himself. He liked to have mischievous fun, and although he was obsessive about his work, he rarely turned down a good time, good drugs, good jokes, or good women. His choreography depicted those aspects of his experience that had formed him and he was fearless in expressing himself. Yet he thought of himself as a character out of *Peanuts*. He'd come to work with a Mickey Mouse lunch box and a baseball cap with Donald Duck on it. He sometimes lisped like a small child (usually when he wanted something) and when he really wanted something, he'd apologize.

"Forgive me," he'd say. "But I'd really like you to try it this way."

In fact, he conducted rehearsals as though he was apologizing for being there—yet when I began to tally up what was actually happening, I could see that with his apologetic approach he was putting us through more grueling physical repetition than most choreographers would.

In fact Fosse was the king of "Forgive me, but once more from the top."

We'd do it again and he'd pace back and forth, dressed in his black slacks and button-down black shirt, his cigarette dangling, writhing in indecision as to what he should change.

He was choreographing a number that closed the first

act. It was called "The Picnic." In it he was able to indulge all his childhood movements of mischief.

Carol Haney had been hired as the lead dancer, brought from MGM at Fosse's recommendation. She had worked with choreographer Jack Cole for many years and Cole's style was obvious in her movements, which were hard-driving lunges close to the ground, supported by thunder thighs of strength. There was a lot of oppositionary arm work associated with Jack Cole's style. The torso went in opposition to the arms. Difficult to do. Fosse had been a Jack Cole dancer too. Therefore, they both understood that it was necessary to develop a new style. Jack Cole needed to be out. Bob and Carol needed to be "in."

The "Picnic" number was rambunctious and freewheeling with cartwheels, long running glides, and pixielike wiggles. It was exhausting, which was part of the point, because not only were people supposed to be having a wonderful time at a picnic, but we also closed the first act. That meant Fosse didn't have to worry whether the dancers had any wind left or not. . . . Intermission would take care of that.

At one point he choreographed a section that entangled the arms and legs of all the dancers in complicated, fun-loving, and intricate ways. A little like the way he saw relationships!

A few days into the rehearsal my not-yet-husband, Steve, took me to a party, and, thinking I was drinking fruit punch, I chug-a-lugged several glasses of what was mostly fruit-flavored vodka. It was the first time in my life I had ever been drunk. Steve took care of me and carried me to a cab. I was nineteen years old and I guess it was about time to experience a hangover. It lasted three days. Three days of nausea, vomiting, and searing headaches. Steve nursed me.

So there I was in the middle of a pile of intertwined dancers' bodies, trying to hold down waves of nausea while attempting to execute Bob's strangling, fun-loving movements. I felt like I was trapped in a drunken picnickers' orgy, not unlike Bob's actual fantasies. The memory makes me ill even today.

Carol Haney led the enthusiasm in the number and was fabulous. But that was nothing compared with her stamina and body strength in "Steam Heat."

"Steam Heat" was a classic number, devised by Fosse to open the union meeting at the top of the second act. It was with this number that Fosse made his mark. Haney, Buzz Miller, and Peter Gennaro were the trio of dancers. Fosse used to direct their movements by explaining that each movement should come from the pit of their stomachs, where warm brandy bubbled.

The number was done in black tuxedos and ties, black jazz shoes, and derbies. Fosse loved hats. He used them as props all the time. Hats inspired movement that was eye-catching and magical, a studied sleight of hand.

He worked with moves that required incredible strength in the thighs . . . Deep, dragging lunge-falls coming up to pixie, gaminelike poses.

Buzz and Peter were the finest jazz dancers of the day, but it was Carol who carried the comic intention of the number.

Fosse forced the trio to execute the hat tricks in the basement of the theater until, sometimes, two or three in the morning, explaining that technique had to be second nature. The tricks must be effortless so that the attitude of their execution could bleed through.

Fosse and Robbins worked together on staging other musical numbers. They never got in one another's way. Whenever a line needed to be sung by a chorus dancer, Fosse would suggest they give it to me. If a bit of comedy business needed executing, he asked me to do it. I think it was mostly because he had seen me in Joan Mc-Cracken's acting class and she had told him she thought I was talented. Such is the nature of show business. If someone you love and respect puts a bug in your ear, you pay attention. Robbins paid attention to Fosse. Fosse paid attention to McCracken. I was the beneficiary.

Robbins and George Abbott also watched the genius of Fosse develop. They left him alone. It was just as well because when we had our first preview in front of an invited audience, several things became evident. The audience laughed at Carol Haney, and she was just doing the dancer's role of Gladys. Charlotte Rae, the comedy lead, was playing the part too broadly. Too many faces, too much slapstick. The audience didn't laugh at her. Abbott tried to hold her down, but she found it difficult. So he fired her and combined her part with the dancer's part that Haney was playing. The result was one of the most sought-after Broadway roles for comedy acting dancers in the business.

Usually, after that, whoever played Gladys in the national or road company's production of *Pajama Game* went on to do bigger things—Neile Adams, Juliet Prowse, and Debbie Allen, to name several.

We, in the meantime, were treated to seeing a star born because Fosse had choreographed Haney into a comedy dancer and subsequently Abbott directed her into a comedy actress. Her foghorn voice and understanding of comedic movement were unique.

The question then arose, who would understudy her? That's when I came in. I had no notion that I was capable of doing it. It was Hal Prince, one of the producers, who suggested that I take home the script, go over the words, see if I liked acting, and then audition for the understudy's role. Hal helped cue me so I could get the hang of how to memorize dialogue. When the audition day came, I was ready.

Three people sat on high stools watching as two of us from the chorus auditioned. The three men were Abbott, Robbins, and Fosse. Hal Prince didn't rate a chair. He was just the young producer. Carmen Alvarez was the other dancer who auditioned with me that day. Carmen was tall (5′8″) and big boned, a striking Puerto Rican beauty with a long, dark pony tail and swaggering body movements. She was not the obvious type to play Gladys, but she was funny and she could act.

We went through the scenes with the stage manager reading the other characters.

I had had a long red ponytail in *Me and Juliet,* but the stage manager told me it was distracting on the stage. One day he dunked my head in the sink of the basement chorus dressing rooms, turned the water on, and when I came up for air he chopped my hair off into a strange bowl cut. I didn't object really, and I've had the same haircut ever since.

So hair-wise I looked more the Gladys type. Haney had a bowl-shaped pixie cut too. Such a hairstyle is necessary if you're a dancer who sweats a lot and works with hats as part of the choreography.

In my audition I tried to give the part a little extra something instead of doing exactly what Haney was doing, which wasn't easy because she was so wonderful. Then Carmen did her audition. She was funny and spontaneous and good, but my resemblance to Carol's physical type was a big advantage. I got the part.

I got the part, but I couldn't seem to get a rehearsal. There was no time. We were playing in Boston and ready to come in to New York. Fosse was busy with last-minute changes and he needed his assistant with him all the time. The only way I could learn the part was to watch from the wings. That is what I did, which is where the story started that I psyched Carol out.

As a matter of fact, I never expected her to miss a show. She was a gypsy of the first order. She'd go on with a broken neck. Fosse thought so too. What was the point of having a rehearsal for the understudy?

Even so, I wanted to be as prepared as possible. So I got a derby and found that I became more obsessed with the "Steam Heat" hat tricks than any other part of the role. Fosse had said such tricks had to become second nature. It was necessary to be able to do them while carrying on a conversation or reciting poetry.

No amount of work can prepare you for the moment when they tell you, "You're on."

The show had opened in New York. It was a huge hit, earned great reviews, and a new star was born in the person of Carol Haney, a new choreographer discovered in Bob Fosse, both newcomers to Broadway by way of Hollywood.

Two or three nights after the opening, during a Saturday matinee, Carol fell and badly sprained her ankle.

I, in the meantime, had applied to the company of *Can-Can* to understudy Gwen Verdon. Gwen was out of the show from time to time. Perhaps I would get a chance to go on for her. I was *positive* Haney would never be out.

I had the application in my pocket when I left the subway—fifteen minutes late for my half hour call before curtain—and turned the corner to the stage door of the St. James Theater.

The stage manager, Abbott, Robbins, and Fosse were lined up waiting for me!

"Where have you been?" said Fosse.

I lamely explained that the subway door had gotten stuck in Times Square.

He said, "Haney's out. You're on."

My heart plummeted. And my first thought was that I would drop the derby in "Steam Heat." Then I called Steve at our apartment.

I rushed to my dressing room in the basement, and was summarily told to go to Carol's dressing room, where the costumes, props, and shoes were.

I remembered a pair of sneakers I had in my tote bag. Quickly the wardrobe mistress dyed them black so I could wear them in "Steam Heat." I luckily had a pair of heels with me, so I could wear them the rest of the show.

The orchestra conductor asked me what key I sang in. I hadn't the faintest idea. John Raitt, the male lead, tried to help. We decided *he* should sing some of the songs I had never rehearsed. I felt fairly secure about the dialogue, knowing I could make it up if I got into real trouble. For some reason, neither the dialogue, my acting talent (none at that point), nor even the songs made me nervous. I was nervous about what I knew how to do best—dance. I didn't know enough about the other aspects of performing to be anxious and the dancing was what I naturally concentrated on. It was the most difficult dimension of the character anyway. As for the comedy, either I was funny or I wasn't. No amount of preparation would help much anyway.

Haney's costumes fit me. My hairstyle was enough like hers that the hats were fine. The shoes were my own, as well as the tights and the bras.

I did some pliés and stretches and ran through the hat tricks, then went down to the stage.

I was ready to go on. It was as though my entire life had led to this moment; all the dancing lessons, singing lessons, and fledgling acting lessons; all the years of understanding movement and working with teachers and choreographers since I was three years old. All the days and nights of traveling on buses and streetcars to and from rehearsals and classes and performances . . . the depressions when I'd fall off a pirouette during a critical variation; the frustration that I didn't possess a natural turnout or beautiful insteps on pointe; the anxiety over losing my balance in an adagio without understanding the fundamental reason.

I breathed deeply and said a prayer. The stage manager turned on the microphone and announced that Carol Haney wouldn't be performing. The crowd groaned and whistled in displeasure. Then he announced my name. The noise was even worse. Some people threw things onto the stage. Carol was *the* new star on Broadway and she wasn't there. I swallowed hard. Humiliation was not my idea of a good time.

The stage manager hung up the microphone and went out to clean up the stage.

The conductor took his place and the overture started. The strains of "Hey there, you with the stars in your eyes . . ." rang in my ears. Even today, when I hear that song, my stomach turns over and I feel slightly nauseated.

The curtain opened and I was on.

The audience didn't scare me. The cast did. They were lined up in the wings, some standing on each other's shoulders, watching with mixed shock and awe to see how I would do. Someone had torn a long strip of paper roll and quickly passed it around the company for everyone to sign good luck wishes.

I found that paper roll a few months ago, after my mother passed away. I had sent it to her and she kept it. As I sat in her attic poring over past treasures I could feel it all happening again.

I suppose the audience identified with the underdog

me. They were wonderful. The more they responded, the more relaxed and attuned to them I felt.

The first act barreled along. John Raitt was supportive, Janis Paige sympathetic and really sweet, Eddie Foy, Jr., funny and thankfully lighthearted. Then came the "Picnic" number. I led it, and by the time the midway point came, I thought I was going to die of exhaustion. When you're leading a stage full of seasoned, trained, strong dancers, the impetus to stay out of their way is a question of survival, which meant I had to be stronger and possessed of even more stamina. Carol Haney had those attributes. I didn't. I was a good dancer, but I wasn't stage smart. I didn't yet know how to pace myself. I hadn't learned the trick of never breathing in—only breathing out, which will save you from collapse. I was also dancing full out, as though this were the only number I had to do. When the end of the number came and, as choreographed, we all fell down, I really meant it. I could hardly get up.

The stage manager rushed to me, picked me up, and the cast applauded.

I staggered to my dressing room to rest and prepare for "Steam Heat," which opened the second act.

I put on the dyed black sneakers. They were still wet. The dye ran all over my feet. Never mind.

I dressed in the black tuxedo and did a few hat tricks. How, I wondered, would I be able to see the hat with the spotlight in my eyes?

The spotlight is the biggest adjustment a performer must make on the stage. You are used to a rehearsal-hall mirror and daylight. The performing conditions are entirely different. Because of the spotlight, your front vision is nothing but black. You lose your balance because there is no identifying landmark in the midst of the black mass except for the exit signs and a few red emergency lights. The spotlights are so blinding that you almost feel protected in your exposure. You know that every inch of you is being observed, but you also know that the lighting makes you beautiful. You can see no one. Your reactions are as though you are playing to yourself because you can't see the audience's reactions. That is why performers develop a sense of feeling relating to sound and movement. You learn to sense with other faculties. You learn to feel the people somewhere in your heart, but more specifically, in your guts. You know when it's working and when it's not, and when it's not you change your approach, your attack, your rhythm. If that doesn't work, you experience what's called flop sweat. It's an awful feeling. It is sheer, unadulterated humiliation, reminiscent of all the times in your childhood when you felt completely helpless to do the right thing in order to be loved.

So, I stood behind the curtain waiting for the second act overture to finish. Fosse never left my mind. It was his number, his creation, his obsessive craziness that motivated such a classic as "Steam Heat." I couldn't brush his cigarette, his eagle eye, his authoritarian apologies, his hunched-over pacing and prancing from my mind! He hadn't given me any direction except one—"make the part, the dancing, and the comedy your own."

A dancer rarely dances for himself or herself, though. We dance to please the choreographer. That face is forever in the front of the dancer's mind. A face of delight or anger, depending on how you've done. Every dancer I know, including me, apologizes to the choreographer if we make a mistake. It's a bond of such symbiotically powerful threads that the synergy is palpable.

The director of a film elicits somewhat the same acquiescence, but there's not the same degree of submissiveness because acting is not as hard or as physically painful as dancing. A director deals with more individualized human passions, and that requires diplomatic cajoling and loving manipulation. A director knows he or she won't get the scene if the performer feels hurt or violated. With a dancer, a choreographer concludes that the art itself is based on human suffering, because it is indeed painful; just because a dancer is an artist does not mean that he or she isn't also a combat soldier in training. And so the relationship between the two is more that of drill sergeant and private, regardless of how talented the dancer might be.

The curtain went up. The clang of ''Steam Heat'' sounded. I went into the number with Buzz Miller and Peter Gennaro.

I had never rehearsed with the spotlight. In fact I had never even rehearsed the number. I had just watched it. Slowly I adjusted to the bright light in my eyes. Then came the first hat trick. When the hat crossed the spotlight beam I lost sight of it for a moment. I panicked, but it found its way back into my hand. I could feel Fosse smile.

I relaxed a smidgen, but not enough to lose control of my muscles.

Then came the tour de force hat trick. I stepped up to the light, threw the hat into the air and the spotlight seemed to swallow it up. I couldn't find it. Hours seemed to go by. Then I saw the hat descend. I reached up for it, rather than trusting it would find its way back to the precise spot Fosse intended. My fingertips caught it for a moment and then I lost it again. *I had dropped the hat!* My worst nightmare in life. Fosse would kill me, I was certain. Feeling as though I had betrayed the entire world of dance, to say nothing of how I had let Fosse down, I said out loud, ''Shit.''

The first few rows audibly gasped. I had added insult

to his injury. I wanted to die. I quickly retrieved the hat and continued on with the number. Fosse's face never left the front of my mind. Here was a chance for him to see that his number didn't rise or fall on Carol Haney's performance alone. I wanted him to see that it would work regardless of who performed it. But I had let him down.

It didn't matter to me that the audience applauded wildly when it was over. This was a repetition of the same emotional moment I experienced as a child running a relay. My father had come to see the race, and as our team was rounding the finish line and it was my turn to take the stick and run for the end, I dropped it! I dropped the stick in front of my expectant and cheering father. I let him and his expectations of me down, to say nothing of my teammates.

The humiliation of dropping the stick was with me for years. I couldn't resolve it. I couldn't let it go. So it followed me until the next time I had a feat to perform under pressure with a father figure whom I longed to please watching expectantly . . . Bob Fosse.

The audience seemed to love what I was doing, though, as did my fellow performers who were still piled on top of one another, watching from the wings.

When the show came to an end and curtain calls were the final act of our reward, I skipped out onto the stage with Buzz and Peter. The three of us took a bow and then Peter and Buzz stepped away from me, leaving me in the center of the stage to be acknowledged. I did not relish the moment. I wanted to meld back into the company of players. It was only their recognition—my peers'—that I wanted. I had never hungered for fame, or dreamed of my name in lights. And now at this moment, facing a standing ovation, when most people would have reacted with "Gee, I made it," I felt only the inclination that had motivated me all my life: *make something of myself and do it well*. Recognition, reward, fame, and fortune were not requirements of mine.

I've thought often of that moment in relation to my drive to carve out a place for myself in show business. Was it because I was young and not quite ready to accept stardom as my right that I didn't feel more elated?

Or was it something deeper? I was aware that so much of what had motivated me lay with my family and their expectations, unfulfilled for themselves. Why then wasn't I appreciative and hungry for more?

After the show, Fosse came to the dressing room that for the next week or so would be mine. He thrust his hands into his pockets and paced back and forth, his image reflected in the mirror.

"Good," he said. "You made the part yours. Are you all right?"

I nodded.

"Good. Take it. My assistant will help you tomorrow. You were good. Good energy."

Steve took me home and we went to work on the acting. Because he had been an actor, he understood some of my problems as a newcomer. We worked into the night on the lines and the attitude. "Remember what Fosse told you," said Steve. "Everything is energy."

It was from Fosse that I realized *energy* was the primary requirement for a good performance on the stage, on the screen, and in life.

It was many years before I'd work with him again. He and Hal Prince had given me the ball to run with. I would go for the touchdown.

Soon after my weeks of replacing Haney were over, came the offer from Hal Wallis to go to Hollywood.

Hal Prince tells the story on himself. "Don't go," he said. "You'll get lost in the shuffle. Stay in New York.

Do some more Broadway shows, and then when you're ready, another opportunity will present itself."

I thought about what Hal Prince had said. I went back to the chorus, and about two months later Haney was out again for one night. I went on again. That was the night Hitchcock was in the audience.

My future was assured.

Fosse went on to do *Damn Yankees, Bells Are Ringing, New Girl in Town, Redhead, How to Succeed in Business Without Really Trying, Little Me,* and *Sweet Charity,* each a hit in its own way.

In the meantime I established a career in Hollywood, acting. Fosse stayed in New York.

About fifteen years later Lew Wasserman, by then head of Universal Pictures, was interested in doing a musical. I had seen *Sweet Charity* in New York starring Gwen Verdon, who was now married to Fosse. She told me she had patterned the character of Charity after a picture she saw of me. I looked gamine, slightly lost, and my feet were turned in. She suggested I do the part on the screen. I told her of the time I nearly missed my break in *Pajama Game* because I longed to understudy her instead of Haney.

Sometimes it seems there are only twelve people in the world, all of whom play an important part for one another. Gwen and Fosse were two of these people for me.

I went to Wasserman with the idea of doing *Charity* on the screen. He liked it but wondered who could direct. I suggested Fosse. Lew said, "He's a choreographer and a Broadway director. What does he know about the camera?"

I said, "What did Jerry Robbins and Herb Ross and Stanley Donen know about the camera? But Fosse would be better than any of them because he's studied every-thing Fellini ever made, frame to frame.''

Lew saw how convinced I was. It was my career too, after all. He thought for a moment. He had no board of directors to answer to. *He* was the only boss.

''Okay, kid,'' he said. ''Let's get him.''

Bobby loved the idea. He came to California and *his* future was assured.

Since Bob was such a devotee of Fellini, and since Fellini had done the original *Nights of Cabiria,* on which *Charity* was based, Fosse was way ahead of the game. He knew exactly how he wanted to shoot it. There was a small glitch, however. Lew had assigned Ross Hunter to produce the picture. Ross was an aficionado of glitzy, glamorous big spending. Fosse didn't see *Charity* shot with so much Hollywood-ness. He wanted the picture to look like a tacky dance hall on Forty-second Street. There were long, rancorous meetings over the conflict of styles. Fosse's vision won, Ross Hunter politely left, and Robert Alan Aurthur took over, a man whom Bob felt comfortable with for many years in Hollywood.

Sweet Charity—Charity Hope Valentine—was origi-nally a hooker. But Fosse had an aversion to American hookers. He had no problem with French or English or German ones (as evidenced in *Cabaret*), but American prostitutes were not characters he was comfortable with. So Charity became a dance hall hostess. I had a problem with that because the toughness of her hard-earned atti-tude toward money would be compromised. And the milieu of a Forty-second Street prostitute was different from a Forty-second Street dance hall hostess's. Never-theless a dance hall girl she was. To watch Fosse conceive a musical number for the camera was like witnessing a master painter using celluloid instead of oil colors. He choreographed the film itself, coloring it, clipping it, slowing it, speeding it up, double exposing it, cutting it. He literally made you feel the film was moving, rather than the people.

From the first day, Gwen was there for me, helping me with a role she must have privately coveted for herself. She coached me in wily ways to execute Bob's steps without throwing myself off balance. Fosse was a genius at going against the flow of the body in any given dance movement. His body conceptions did not flow easily. That is what made them so startling to watch. They were mind-bogglingly unpredictable. That is also why many dancers hurt themselves doing Fosse's work. It was unpredictably countergravitational! One's own body was never really prepared for what it had been instructed to do. But Gwen showed me ways to prepare my legs, my back, and my feet. She had been performing his work for nearly fifteen years. Aside from being married to him, she was the finest interpreter of his movement. She could show me how to wrap my body around a move that belonged to the language of another planet—the Fosse Planet.

Chita Rivera and Paula Kelly worked on either side of me. When we danced together, they were so powerful it was like being between two disciplined and well-oiled steam rollers. They carried me along with their energy.

The three of us became very close. I was beginning a love affair with a TV journalist. This relationship entailed a great deal of traveling. Fosse liked to work late on Fridays because there was no union turnaround on Saturday. He also liked to work late because he knew I wanted to get away early in order to have a longer weekend. He never said that specifically, but it was understood. So, I would stand around behind the camera, in costume, warmed up and ready to dance as he moved bodies about in geometric designs, trying unusual visual compositions. Chita and Paula would feign exhaustion and cover for me so I could get out early. I was determined to have a personal life while living up to the demands of being a "star."

The most difficult part of *Sweet Charity* for me, which Fosse never knew, was that for the entire shoot I suffered from an infected root canal. Every step I took, every movement I made was agony. I didn't want to take the time off to have it fixed because I would have held up production. I would rather die than not be disciplined and dependable. During one number my fever was so high I don't even remember shooting it.

Then Martin Luther King was killed, and Paula was so upset she couldn't work. Fosse didn't understand. She said, "We've lost a great leader and this is only a movie." Fosse blanched. It wasn't only a movie to him. It was his life. But he let us all go early. I had my tooth fixed and was a new person.

Two months later, Bobby Kennedy was assassinated. I knew Bobby and his family, and I was destroyed. Seeing how upset I was, Fosse switched around the shooting schedule to include a new scene in which I had to cry. Everything in human experience is grist for a director's mill, particularly a director who feels he gives birth to films as a woman gives birth to a child.

It was this obsessive dedication that made Fosse great. He was a person addicted to detail. The detail of stitching on a dress hem, the detail of a swift movement of the eyes. He missed nothing. As a result, he saw too much. Being the repository of all he saw rendered him indecisive. That was the reason for the constant repetition. He was trying to process all that he saw. It wasn't so much that he was cruel with his demands of "once again from the top" it was that he saw something new and different each time. If he let it go by, perhaps he was missing a value in a movement or a scene that could be the focal point of creating.

Many times I watched him stew in the juice of his own awareness, remembering how he had been nearly fifteen years before in *Pajama Game*. He was unchanged, visiting upon everything and everybody the same alert, anxiety-riddled consideration.

One day early on in the shooting of *Charity*, he was stuck trying to decide how to move the camera on a tracking shot. I could see he was getting himself into a morass of possibilities. (If you were Fosse those possibilities were endless.) The cameraman was becoming so confused he couldn't help him. I made the mistake of offering a suggestion.

"You brought me out here to direct this picture, so let me do it my way," he said. He was absolutely right. And his way was to leave no stone unturned in the process of creative decision making. Again I thought back to the time he picked me out of the chorus, saw my "detail," and believed in me. Now the roles were reversed. I was in the position of defending his work style to the producers and the studio, because I so deeply believed in him.

Fosse once told me that he was reluctant to work with actors who were not performers. He didn't like or understand the indulgent "movie star" style of finding a character and coming to grips with the expression of it. "Performers," he said, "have the right energy. They know there's an audience out there who must understand them and hear them. Movie actors don't get that. Performers have a level of intentful energy that people in Hollywood don't have."

I understand what he meant. When you've done a lot of stage work, you understand.

In the fifteen years since I had left Broadway and been

in films, my level of "intentful energy" had dropped. I knew something was missing, but I couldn't figure out what it was. I was unconsciously forcing the camera to come to me, which in many ways makes for natural intimacy on the screen, but in other ways is simply not fulfilling and appears too underdone. Subtlety in acting is another issue. Subtlety on screen is accomplished, I think, by commanding the moment and, when you have the camera's undivided attention, making a clean, precise, *small* gesture. When you connect, it's because you filled the space you commanded with enough security to make broadness unnecessary.

I had gotten into the lazy habit of allowing the camera to *find* everything I was doing. It was an excuse for not exerting my creative intention. It was a lack of preparation. I wasn't doing much homework. I rarely studied a scene the night before. I had become a part of the "let spontaneity carry the day" school. The school that purports that too much thinking and rehearsal make it stale and contrived. The school of lazy intent.

What Fosse taught me, by rekindling my *performer's* intention, was that when I, as an actor, was acquainted with each nuance of thought, movement, and heart in my character, I could then throw that knowledge to the winds and start afresh. But not until I'd earned the right. Not until I'd considered each creative possibility through thought, rehearsal, and much respect for the terrain that was new to me. It was no different than his approach to the hat tricks in "Steam Heat": "Know the terrain thoroughly. Then you can throw it away."

I have to admit that even with Fosse's genial advice, I remained essentially lazy. I did learn to pay more attention to the memorization of dialogue, so that I wasn't fighting for my lines on the set. But because I, being basically a dancer, connected all memory to movement, I always found it difficult to memorize my dialogue without knowing my movements in the set. Of course, that was basically an excuse. Fortunately, with age, I have found nature slapping my lazy hands anyway. I have to take time to memorize dialogue now because otherwise it just won't happen.

I find the same true for dance steps. Because I come from an acting motivation now, my mind won't absorb the simple movement and combination of steps as it used to. My mind needs to ask "why?" This is not an endearing trait to choreographers. "Because I said so" is usually the answer.

The scene in *The Turning Point* where ballerina Leslie Browne is questioning the movement she's being given to execute is infuriating to the choreographer, who screams, "It is not up to you to question. Just dance! Don't think! If you think, you hurt yourself, you ruin the flow of the movement. Dancing is to be felt, not thought about."

I would ask how could I feel if I didn't know what I thought. It is the chicken-and-egg problem.

Suffice to say, if one wants to stay in show business, it is necessary to remember your words, your steps, your notes, your moves, *and* your feelings, which are attached to each.

Fosse was instrumental in reminding me before it was too late that I should never forget my hardworking stage days, where preparation was essential and maybe even everything.

The reviews on *Charity* were mixed. A number suggested there were too many Mount Rushmore close-ups of me and others that the milieu of the picture was too theatrical and not a realistic depiction of Times Square dance hall life.

I talked to Fosse from Mexico. I asked him how he felt.

"If it's a flop," he said, "I'll want to put my head in the oven. If it's a success, I'll want to keep it there."

The picture was a moderate success. People didn't care that much about dancing, and the technique of singing or dancing in the middle of a real street, once so fresh, suddenly had become too unbelievable.

Fosse took it hard, but he learned from it. I took it harder. It was the first big picture I had actually carried. My name was above the title. If it flopped, it would be my fault. Several articles appeared in which producers claimed I'd had my chance to move into real stardom, but I'd muffed it. I wanted to muff them. I still remember the ones who said that, a kind of enemy's list of the memory. I went on to do other things and so, ultimately, did Bob. The next musical he made was a period piece, *Cabaret,* which, because it had a European (German) background, lent itself to theatrical expression. He won an Academy Award as best director for the movie version, and Liza Minnelli and many other people associated with it won too.

Fosse was declared the new genius in town, not only for musicals, but for drama as well.

Then he did *Lenny,* the true story of Lenny Bruce. He was attracted to it because he believed Lenny Bruce had a God-given, constitutionally guaranteed right to have as filthy an act as he deemed funny. He saw Bruce as a comedy performer with great courage. He was most intrigued by Lenny's lifestyle—the drugs and women—but he sparked particularly to the performing style Bruce used to convey his convictions.

Fosse had a hard time with Dustin Hoffman in the starring role. I suppose that wasn't news. Dustin is a visceral performer who has his own very definite ideas as to how characters should be played. But he wasn't basically a *performer* in Bob's sense of the word. He was an actor. And Bruce *was* a performer, meaning, he performed as himself, not as another character.

Fosse was determined to exercise his own First Amendment right to free expression as he told the story of an individual who went down in comedy history straining the public's tolerance for free speech. Fosse was drawn to danger, to taking things to the edge. He didn't intend to be controversial. It was more of a quiet confrontation with his own need to rebel. He knew he strained the seams of the fabric of social acceptability. He was, I believe, trying to figure himself out.

With *Lenny* a hit and several new Broadway shows beckoning him to return to New York, he decided to invent a deeper struggle for himself.

He began working on a drama about husband and wife relationships. The man and woman were about my age.

I read an early draft of the script and thought it could be wonderful with Fosse's guidance.

Things had not been going that well for me. After *Charity* and a couple more films, *Desperate Characters* and *The Possession of Joel Delaney,* plus a disastrous foray into TV with *Shirley's World,* I began to wonder what I was doing in the business. I spent over a year working for George McGovern and he lost too. I was badly in need of help.

I returned to the man who had found me in the first place . . . Fosse.

We met at Elaine's in New York for dinner. We talked about the script and about what I wanted to do with my work from now on. I asked him if he would consider me for the picture.

"No," he said. "You're too famous."

"Too famous?" I asked. "But I'm an actress who happens to be famous because I've done a lot of pictures."

"I know," he said.

"But Bob," I went on, "do you think I'm right for the part?"

"Oh yeah," he answered. "That's not the problem. People know you too well from all the years, that's all."

"That's all?" I asked. I started to sob, right there in Elaine's. "I can't believe you," I said. "You're telling me I'm right for the part. You know I'd be good, but you won't use me because I'm too well-known?"

"Forgive me," he said. I was beginning to detest his "forgive me" routine.

I left Elaine's embarrassed and worried about my future.

A few weeks after our dinner, Bob had a heart attack.

He had been working hard on the Broadway musical *Chicago,* starring Gwen Verdon and Chita Rivera. The word around was that *Chicago* was his gift to Gwen for not being overly faithful to her. He was nervous and smoking like a California fire.

When he was ready to receive visitors, I went to the hospital. He looked so pale and fragile in his hospital robe. So drawn and sad.

"Forgive me if I cry," he said. "The nurses tell me that depression is a natural reaction after a heart bypass operation."

I said that I understood.

"I was watching a terrible review of Stanley Donen's picture *The Little Prince* on TV right after I came out of the anesthesia. It made me so angry because of how it hurt Stanley that I had another heart attack right here in the hospital."

Bob started to cry. "Forgive me," he said. Tears slid down his face.

I watched him with a feeling I had never had for anyone in show business. A mixture of pure compassion, appreciation, love, and helplessness. I realized how deeply I cared about him.

We talked for a while.

"I had a strange dream under the anesthetic," he said. "More like a vision or a real picture."

"What was it?" I asked. He never shared such things, as a rule.

"I was dying," he said. "And my daughter, Nicole, came to me. I was trying to explain what dying felt like. I found myself doing it to rhythm. I was dying to rhythm. I sang a rhythmic song to her called 'Every Time My Heart Beats.' I saw the number about dying as clear as a bell. And I thought to myself, Even as I'm dying, I'm working. I'm trying to figure out how to make it into a musical."

As soon as he described his dream to me, I saw a musical. A musical about his life, his contradictions, his addictions, his loves, his insecurities.

"Why don't you make a musical out of your death?" I asked.

"What?" he said.

"Yeah," I said. "I mean, when you've been through what you've been through and you have a dream of dying to a musical number, you must be ready for a new kind of musical experience."

"What do you think it means?" he asked.

"Oh, probably something like you want to be in complete control of choreographing your own demise so it will be done right. So it'd get great reviews."

"Yeah," said Bob. "Yeah. Control my own death. Then I could have myself do whatever I want; the other people too."

He began to snap his fingers to the rhythm he said he

had heard in his hallucinatory dream. His eyes took on that familiar rehearsal hall glint, his shoulders hunched, and he lurched out of bed. It was as though he had no concept of how ill he was except for his depression.

A nurse bolted into the room.

"Mr. Fosse," she said. "Please get back in the bed or you'll have *another* heart attack."

"Yeah," said Bob. "Yeah." He crawled back under the sheets. His eyes brimmed over with tears again. "Forgive me," he said. "Thanks for coming."

I gathered my things and left. On the way out I ran into Gwen.

"How is he?" she asked.

"He seems okay," I answered. "He's real depressed. Madder than shit over that review of *The Little Prince* on TV."

"Yes," said Gwen. "He loves Stanley Donen. Remember he started with him in Hollywood. He somehow identifies with him. When Stanley gets bad reviews, Bob feels *he*'s gotten bad reviews."

"And," I added, "maybe he even sees himself as the Little Prince."

Gwen laughed.

"He does look like him," I said. "But Bob plays that other part, the snake in the tree, doesn't he?" I asked.

Gwen rolled her eyes. "Oh yes," she said. "Oh yes."

"Well," I said. "I hope he's okay. He means a lot to me. I probably wouldn't be where I am, wherever that is, if it weren't for him."

"I know," she said. "I remember it all very well. Even the fact that you wanted to understudy me, but you went on for Carol instead. I remember."

THAT NIGHT I LAY DOWN AND CRIED ABOUT FOSSE. I HAD a premonition that he was going to die. I didn't want to lose him and I was afraid he didn't understand what risks he was taking with his life. I cried for hours, wanting to help in some way. So, with the man I was living with—Pete Hamill, a brilliant journalist, novelist, and screenplay writer—I sat down and we hammered out a synopsis of a musical using Fosse's heart attack as the centerpiece for the comedy and dramatic action. We worked on it for a week. After Fosse left the hospital, we sent it to him. Weeks went by, and we never heard anything.

A few months later I heard he was making phone calls to people, imploring them to be honest and share with him their genuine opinion of what they thought of him.

When his request brought compliments, he refused to accept them. "I want degrading, scathing opinions of me," he'd say. "Tell me the worst thing you can think of."

Everyone knew that such an investigative approach meant Bob was getting ready to do something about his life.

When Fosse called Fred Ebb, who wrote the lyrics to *Chicago* and many other Broadway hits, he insisted that Freddie be excruciatingly honest about his opinion of him.

Freddie complied. He told Bob he had used him as the model and inspiration for the song "All That Jazz" from *Chicago*. He told him that the lyrics depicting a sleight-of-hand trickster who basically had no talent and relied on "all that jazz" to get by in life were indeed about him—Bob Fosse.

Fosse thanked him, not the least perturbed or anguished over his coworker's opinion of him because apparently, as we'd soon learn, he'd just been given the title for the new musical he was going to do about his heart attack! *All That Jazz*.

• • •

AFTER A FEW WEEKS I GOT MY CALL FROM BOB.

"Hello, Shirley?" he said. "This is Bobby Fosse."

"Oh, hi," I said. "How are you doing? How are you feeling?"

"Good," he said. "Really good. I'm working on a new musical called *All That Jazz*. It's about me and my experience when I had my heart attack."

"Oh," I said. "You're doing a musical about your heart attack?"

"Yeah. Great idea, huh?"

"It sure is. Sounds vaguely familiar to me." I waited a beat, thinking he would cop to it. But he didn't. He plowed right ahead, undaunted.

"So," he went on. "The guy is me. He has a heart attack and he dies. And it's a musical." Bob laughed like the *Peanuts* character he saw himself as. "And I want you to play Gwen."

"Gwen?" I asked. "Why can't Gwen play Gwen?"

"Because," he said, "you'd be better. She's not a movie actress and there's no one else who could be as authentic as Gwen."

I thought, This is my chance. I took it. "But, Bob," I said. "Don't you think I'm too well-known as *me* to play Gwen? Don't you think I'm too famous as me?"

He hesitated, vaguely realizing that I was rubbing something in.

"Too famous?" he asked.

"Yeah."

"Well, you're famous for being a dancer from Broadway and you'd be authentic."

"So you say the picture is authentic and that's why you want me to play Gwen?"

"Yeah," he answered, "it's a true story. I mean, I'm

telling the nitty-gritty truth in this thing, about me and my life and what people really think of me.''

"But the guy dies," I protested. "You say the guy is you, but you're not dead. How can you say that's authentic?''

Bob hesitated for a moment. "Okay," he said. "I promise I'll be dead by the first preview.''

I choked. He was probably not far off the truth.

I said I couldn't dance that well anymore and didn't want to spend the time and effort dieting and going to class. It was a relatively small part. He made me promise to see him a few weeks later when I'd be in New York.

I met him at my apartment in New York a few weeks later. He had never been there. I had pictures of friends and people I knew from all over the world on my table. Bob spotted a picture of Fidel Castro and me. From that moment on, all he wanted to know was whether I had had an affair with Fidel or not.

He knew I wasn't going to play Gwen in the picture. He also knew that I *knew* his love life and sexual proclivities were complicated and tangled. If he could find a way to smoke out some juicy details of my personal life, they might come in handy for him later, either in real life or on the screen.

The picture turned out to be the crowning achievement of Bob's career. It was an excruciatingly honest delineation of how he saw himself. To me it was American Ibsen, a Yankee Greek tragedy.

He lived through the first preview, which relieved me no end.

Time passed, and when I decided to do my first stage show I went to Bob for recommendations and help. He was wonderful. He suggested people and spun ideas for me.

I went on a killer regimen to get myself back into

dancing shape—lost twenty-five pounds, did yoga, jogged five miles a day, went back to class, took singing lessons again, and in general prepared myself for a return to the stage and *performer intention.*

Gwen offered to preside over my anguished hours of debating whether I could still cut it. She reminded me that knowing who you are in a one-woman show is more important than anything else. You can dance well, sing well, and act well, but if you're not comfortable being who you are, the audience won't be comfortable.

New styles of dancing had come along since I had last indulged myself. She pointed out TV programs that would bring me up to date.

Hour after hour she'd choreograph me, put me through my paces, and see to it that I was doing the correct spot training in the gym. She recommended Alan Johnson as my choreographer, and he worked out so well that we've worked together ever since. Gwen was invaluable to me.

She was in the audience when I opened my first date in Vegas, at the MGM Grand. She supported, applauded, and gave me strength and good notes.

Fosse was in the audience when I opened at the Palace in New York. He came backstage with his own notes, helpful and correct. I should take out the forced jokes. I should talk less. Keep in the comedy number I was debating about. Get a new opening costume. Otherwise . . . I complied with everything he suggested. He was the best.

He was generous, nervous, and hauntingly depressed as he smoked away. I wasn't concerned, though, because depression was the state he was most familiar with. I did wonder how deep depression could go without getting really serious.

I saw him a few times after that. Then the end came.

He collapsed of a heart attack on the street a few blocks from my old dancing school in Washington, D.C. Gwen was with him. They were doing repairs on the national company's production of *Sweet Charity*. He lay on the curb as Gwen and others tried to help him. I wished I could have been there. He died on the street that was his "home."

I thought of how the destinies of the three of us had overlapped. How many times I had walked that very street, going to and from dancing school. I feel I owe my beginnings to Fosse because he was the first to acknowledge me. He died doing *Sweet Charity,* which had launched him in Hollywood because I had acknowledged him, and in the arms of the woman I very nearly understudied on Broadway; had I done so, it probably would have prevented my becoming what I am today. The three of us understood pain. We had been trained with pain as an instructor, and although we never had prolonged discussions on the subject, we also understood how much attitude and consciousness were necessary in transforming pain. In our creative expressions we each had had to work with our consciousness and attitudes in order to find some kind of harmony on the other side.

Each of us, I believe, was playing an integral part in the others' lives, and I believe that was destined also. Fosse and Gwen were probably in my life somehow before any of us came dancing into this world.

# 9

# SHOWBIZ POLITICS

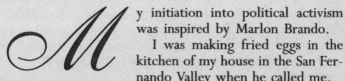y initiation into political activism was inspired by Marlon Brando.

I was making fried eggs in the kitchen of my house in the San Fernando Valley when he called me.

I had been in Hollywood a few years and was still learning the ropes. When I picked up the phone and heard his soft, yet insistent voice say, "Hello, this is Marlon Brando," I knew it was really him because of his famous tonal quality and the pauses between his words. He had a way, even over the phone, of drawing you into his decision as to what words to use. Immediately I felt responsible for fulfilling whatever request he might have for me.

"I'm calling about the proposed execution of Caryl Chessman in Sacramento," he explained. "I'm very much opposed to capital punishment. It's cruel and inhuman punishment, I'm sure you agree."

I didn't know what to say. I'd never thought about it really. But it seemed right to be against it.

"I guess so," I said.

"Yes," continued Marlon, "Mr. Steve Allen and I are going to Sacramento to protest to Governor Pat Brown. We want to stop this execution and we want you to accompany us."

"Me?" I asked.

"Yes," he answered.

"But, Mr. Brando, I don't know anything about this. I've read about it, but that's all."

As though he didn't really hear me, Marlon continued.

"Your presence in Sacramento will be a gesture in living up to your responsibilities as a human being."

I hesitated. Why should anyone care what I thought of capital punishment? Why did I matter? Why did Marlon Brando *think* I mattered?

"But," I said, "why me?"

He took a moment before he delivered his next pronouncement.

"You are a new and budding star," he said to me. "Young people will be looking up to you. You carry no other baggage with you, and if you don't take up this challenge, it will haunt you for the rest of your life."

I looked at my fried eggs. They were charcoal.

I thought of *On the Waterfront* and Brando's plea for the dockworkers' union and how Lee J. Cobb had beaten him up.

"Well," I said reluctantly, "okay. Just tell me what you want me to do."

"Thank you," he said, "I'll do that. And," he went

on, "we missed you on the Selma march for civil rights. This will make up for it."

The Selma march? Yes, I had seen that on television, but I had not felt I should be there . . . Marlon had a way of making you feel guilty over things that had never occurred to you.

We talked for a while longer, and when I hung up I realized that something had happened to me. Marlon had made me think about my responsibility as a human being and a citizen for the first time. It was a complicated realization. I was sort of a new celebrity, and I was shy about expressing myself, not only because I was not well enough informed about issues, but also because I dreaded being accused of grandstanding for publicity.

It's not that I hadn't been educated about social caring. I had. But my awareness had been more historical.

I had come from a Mason-Dixon-line family, which means that we lived on the line that separated the North from the South. My father was from a small town, Front Royal, Virginia, and my mother was a Canadian who became a naturalized citizen of the United States. When Mother went through her citizenship studies, my brother and I went through what we could understand of it with her. Thus, our early lives were imbued with a rudimentary understanding of political, social, and individual freedom in our country.

Our family lived in Richmond, the capital of Virginia, home of nine U.S. presidents; not an insignificant historical environment to grow up in. We learned about the Civil War from the land we played on, and during vacations, historical sites such as Williamsburg, Vicksburg, Bull Run, Yorktown, and Gettysburg were places where we shuffled through fall leaves and watched fireflies on summer nights.

We became somewhat interested in the power, meaning, and manipulation of politics because both of our parents seemed interested. They both adored Franklin Delano Roosevelt. We always listened to his fireside chats on the old radio in our living room, while Daddy smoked his pipe and Mother tried to learn more about being an American. Two events are seared into my memory.

One Sunday morning in December 1941 we gathered around the radio. I was dancing to "the music goes round and round and it comes out here." I was seven years old and I remember wearing long floppy socks to keep my feet warm. Suddenly the music stopped and an announcer came on to say that President Roosevelt would speak to the nation. He began to talk. I remember wondering what "infamy" meant when he said, "This is a day that will live in infamy" and went on to announce something about the Japanese attacking Pearl Harbor. I remember my parents cried and I couldn't understand why. I knew it must be important because it was the first time I had heard the word "war" and it meant something bad.

The second event took place one afternoon a few years later. Warren and I climbed the steps on our back porch. We had just returned from the neighborhood movie house. Mother met us at the back door, ashen and crying. "President Roosevelt just died," she cried. "Oh, what will happen to us now?" She said she had worked hard to become an American, and he had been her president during that process. She said he had made her feel that she mattered, that she had a good heart, and because he was paralyzed from polio and couldn't walk, she loved him. She said most people loved him because he made people feel.

When Dad sat in front of the television set until "The Star-spangled Banner" signed off for the night and tears flowed down his cheeks, I wondered why. It wasn't until my teenage years that I began to understand the emotions of patriotism. I have never understood where they came from, but sometimes the pride of being an American was overwhelming. My chest would seize up as if it might burst. I wondered if other people felt that way about their countries.

I remember how concerned Daddy was about "communists." When one of the Canadian members of Mother's side of the family showed decided "communist leanings," Daddy invited her to Washington, D.C., so he could show her the citadel of freedom. For days we toured the Lincoln Memorial, the Washington Monument, the White House, Capitol Building, and Supreme Court.

Mother was as informed as Daddy because she had to be. Their emotional involvement was contagious and has informed my own patriotic attitudes ever since. I can't say that I was knowledgeable about the specifics of political issues. My attitude was less defined than that, and infinitely sentimental. But the sentiment is what moved me.

A leader who knew how to talk to the people became fascinating to me. If he spoke from his heart, like Roosevelt, I deeply believed that he meant what he said.

During my teenage years, I slowly began to realize that really fine politicians were good performers. They knew how to communicate their feelings. If they did it well, my parents liked them, trusted them, and voted for them. Later, when we sat in front of the new thing called television, we talked about people's expressions and whether they were telling the truth or not. Television was a platform from which anyone able to "come across" might take a position and be influential and effective. Daddy said the days of decisions made in smoke-filled rooms were over. A person who could make a clear and decisive point on television was a natural influencer, and he or she didn't necessarily need to know anything about politics. He predicted political campaigns would shift their focus to the TV screen, and politicians would be called upon to succeed as performers.

We would be able to see a politician floundering if he was weak in his communicative skills, but the people who were able to break through the screen into the living room would become major new influences. In this sense, performers and politicians were alike. They communicated to people about themselves, and those who communicated from the heart and soul were the ones who really got through.

So Marlon and Steve Allen and I went to Sacramento to see Governor Brown. Steve didn't have quite the talent for making you feel guilty that Marlon did. But he made up for it with his pragmatic intelligence. Steve was a true intellectual with a library full of books he knew by heart. He had even written some of them.

Governor Brown received us graciously. He ushered us into the dark, cold governor's mansion in the state capital. Years later I could understand why his son, Jerry, would opt for sleeping on the floor in a warm apartment in Laurel Canyon when he became governor.

Governor Brown listened to us and was pleased that actors would be so genuinely involved with social issues. (Later, though, when he ran against Ronald Reagan, he said, "Don't forget an actor killed Lincoln.")

But on that day we found him open to discussion about stopping the impending execution. He said he would think about it.

Unbeknownst to us, a large press contingent had gathered on the steps of the mansion. There were reporters from all over the world to interview these three showbiz people who claimed to have such sympathy for a convicted kidnapper—sex offender.

At the same time, other politicians entered Governor Brown's office. They wanted to meet the contingent from Hollywood.

I had never seen stars and politicians interact before. Here was Brando, the finest actor-activist in the country, and Steve Allen, whose *Tonight* was an influential must on TV, and me, a budding novice at everything. There were state senators, the speaker of the assembly, congresspeople, and so on. The politicians eyed us and vice versa, each enamored of the influence and power of the other. Marlon and Steve exuded great confidence in their fame, but they also seemed unctuous and yet at the same time patronizing. The politicians were agape at the possibility of using either Steve or Marlon to advance their causes. *We* wanted to learn how *they* "did it."

After a while it became obvious that we would all have to handle the press outside. The politicians didn't want to miss being seen with us, yet they knew the issue of capital punishment was volatile. The press could slant the story any way it wanted. Already I was learning that the press was everybody's natural predator. Above all, we would have to mold, sculpt, circumnavigate, outwit, and tactically maneuver their opinion of us. It would be my first lesson in broken field running with the press, because the real issue was not what we politicians and performers were saying. The issue was how the press perceived us. They could make or break public opinion about us simply by what they chose to accentuate or eliminate. They also, however, were in competition with each other, which, on the one hand, helped fairness prevail, and on the other made "the story" more important than the truth.

We walked outside and the flashbulbs bombarded us. I

had never experienced that before, particularly not in a political context. I was frightened and unprepared. I hardly knew who I was, much less what I thought about social or political issues. The three of us went to a bank of microphones. The politicians surrounded us. The reporters didn't wait for anyone to make a statement. They started yelling questions at us immediately, which were all about whether we were using our celebrity to influence a social issue.

There it was, the one question I felt vulnerable about. I hated the idea of abusing my privilege. Of course, I felt I had the right and even the duty to take a position on something I felt strongly about, but when they asked us if we were doing it for publicity, I got intimidated.

Steve and Marlon spoke of the cruelty of capital punishment and how state-institutionalized killing never stopped crime. They spoke eloquently of the necessity to uphold the civil and human rights of a person even if it was not popular.

Then the press asked me why I was there. How my answer came to me I don't know. I guess it was part of the on-the-job training. I said, "We artists owe it to our country to do what we can to prevent ourselves from looking barbaric to the rest of the world."

That was my initiation into spontaneous response to questions from the fourth estate. I learned something else that was very important that day. As I watched Steve and Marlon interact with the politicians and the press, I realized it was the performers who possessed the more important currency of communication. That was the currency of acting. They knew how to *act* sincere, humble, insecure, brave, modest, and concerned about capital punishment. The politician knew about facts. I remembered what my dad had observed twenty years before. If you really mean it, the public *and* the press will get it.

Marlon and Steve lit the flame of my political consciousness in Sacramento, which, to this day, although tempered somewhat, has never gone out. It has never failed to amaze me that not only does the press ask my opinion of nuclear testing, presidential campaigns, and the Chinese revolution, but *I* actually tell them and *they* print it.

I had been educated to have an opinion in our free society, but never to feel that it mattered.

I was basically a human being with an artistic ambition and not much time for anything else. I was sequestered within the confines of my own self-imposed discipline, and although I had a surface awareness of a sociopolitical world operating around me, I knew next to nothing about the specifics either of how it operated or what difference a simple caring human being could make.

I'm ashamed to say that I was never really aware of the most ghastly period in our modern political history . . . the McCarthy period. I'd see the hearings on television when I came home from school for a moment before heading off to dancing class and rehearsals. But it never occurred to me that the very fabric of our political freedom was being torn with the House Un-American Activities Committee.

I didn't know what my parents thought of that McCarthy person either. I knew he had something to do with hating communists and, of course, Mother and Father hated communists, so I never gave his ranting and raving much thought. I guess our household was fairly typical. I heard that some Hollywood stars were involved, and I remember Gary Cooper saying that he never would have made *High Noon* if he'd realized it was a communist picture. That confused me because I thought *High Noon* was a great Western, so I really couldn't understand what he was talking about. Soon after, I read that Patricia Neal, who was supposed to be his mistress, had become very upset with him because he had said those things to the committee.

And I remember Lucille Ball, who was my favorite on television, saying that she wasn't then and never had been a member of the Communist party. I couldn't imagine why anyone would think that my beloved Lucy could be a communist.

No, I had no sophistication as to what was really happening during those times. In my late teens and early twenties, I was leading an insular life in ballet and musical comedy, trying to become something in New York. It wasn't until I met my husband, Steve, who was twelve years older than I, that I began to understand there was a complex political world to be navigated and understood and that in some ways it touched each of us. Slowly I learned the tragedy of it all . . . the people who informed on their best friends so they could keep their jobs, the ones who took the Fifth Amendment and trapped themselves without realizing it. As I learned more and more about the enforced betrayals and read books and listened to the fear in people's voices even after it was essentially over, I felt ashamed that I had not somehow instinctively perceived how cruel and un-American McCarthy had been. Later, when I understood, I took his violation personally. He had besmirched what America stood for.

After the wreckage, Hollywood began to find its conscience and its duty to uphold political freedom. Now that they had been personally touched by politics, people who had previously been insulated in their craft began to become more involved with the world around them.

I began to learn more about modern politics from Steve; it was he who taught me that the McCarthy period had been possible because of other events that had preceded it.

Steve also told me his father had fought in the Abraham Lincoln Brigade during the Spanish Civil War, which was a testing ground for fascist technology and weapons. He argued that if America had joined in the Spanish loyalist cause against the fascist forces of Franco, which were aligned with Hitler, we could have intimidated Hitler enough to squelch his takeover of Europe, and thus avoid the Second World War. But we didn't because we were so isolationist. History, then, was a continuum, a stream of events with a cause-and-effect relationship, and if we didn't understand the past, then we wouldn't understand the future.

Steve also told me of his own passion to enlist in the paratroopers and how strongly antifascist he was. He told me his own war stories of fighting in the South Pacific and being among the first troops to enter Hiroshima after the bomb. He told me of the small girl he had adopted because she had lost her parents. He named her Sachiko. He said she died from radiation sickness, and if he ever had a child of his own, he would call her Sachi. I was learning what a personal experience politics and history could be.

My political attitude began to evolve in earnest. I took Marlon's suggestion and analyzed my own feelings about the civil rights movement. I went into the Deep South, worked with John Lewis, James Foreman, and SNCC. I stayed with black families and saw for myself the injustice of segregation. I experienced white cops stopping my car and searching me because I had "niggers" in the backseat. I experienced the Ku Klux Klan burning a cross on the front lawn of the family I stayed with. In many ways I was attempting to work out the contradictory prejudices of my own father, who spoke so lovingly of "those nice

Negroes'' when he liked them and "niggers" when he didn't. I remembered feeling that in the North, a black person could go as high as he wished, but shouldn't come too close. In the South, a black person could come as close as he wished, but shouldn't go too high.

I was brought up by a black maid, Dora, alongside her little boy. My memories were never of conflict, but rather of integration. That's why I felt comfortable traveling alone in areas of Mississippi where no other white person would go. My involvement with the civil rights movement became an issue of personal clarification. It didn't feel political to me. It was a matter of humaneness and personal sensitivity. That's why it held such power for me. And then came Vietnam. My political involvement became total. I became "radicalized," as they called it then—politicized on a personal level. I'm not really sure why. I just couldn't abide the idea that America was the self-appointed policeman of the world, killing people in order to make the planet safe for democracy. It felt like another form of fascism to me; why couldn't we just let Vietnam alone?

But when George McGovern made his famous Vietnam speech on the floor of the Senate and said, "No longer should we send young men to die for old men's ideas," I got involved with wanting to do something about it.

Frank Sinatra and the Clan had supported Jack Kennedy for president. I had first met Jack when he was a senator. He drove me home from a party one night in his rented convertible. He stopped on Mulholland Drive and for a moment I thought I might have to finesse my way out of becoming another one of his conquests. But no, he only wanted to talk. Very nice, a bit presumptuous, and open about Hollywood being a place to sow his seeds of fun and future fund-raising. I, on the other hand, was for Adlai Stevenson. I had become a real liberal and felt that Stevenson represented what I believed more than Jack did. I had arguments with Frank about this. He said Jack knew how to use power and Stevenson didn't. He said it took greater courage to go for Jack because he was more political, which might be more suspect, but was more effective. In the end, it didn't matter. Jack Kennedy became our president and I came to love him as so many did, although I wasn't really included in the inner circle. I witnessed the rupture between the President and Sinatra based on Frank's association with the Mob. I couldn't blame the Kennedys. Frank never spoke to any of them again and it was soon after that he became a Republican.

When Kennedy died, I was as devastated as everyone else. I felt that a light had gone out of our lives. I stopped being interested in politics and retreated from any involvement. Then Bobby declared. I got interested again. I knew people who were with him in West Virginia when he broke down and cried at the poverty he saw. His friends told me he had made a fundamental transition in his political values. They said he essentially had always viewed himself as the black sheep in the Kennedy clan. Because he was smaller than the others, he identified with the underdog. He said he wanted to dedicate his life to taming the savagery we each held within us and he wanted to seek a newer world where everyone would be equal. My friends said they were astonished at his growing sensitivity since his brother's death, and I liked what I heard.

Of course, my father was right. I became a bleeding-heart liberal and would work for any candidate who evinced the same affliction.

I became a Robert Kennedy delegate from California. That meant I often passed the weekends with him and the Kennedy clan when they came to Palm Springs, where they had a home. There was croquet on the lawn, barbecued hamburgers, lots of political gossip, dancing in the local clubs at night, and of course the flirting sexual games, some of which were consummated and some not. I was one of the nots.

One night I was sleeping in a guest room when someone crowded into bed with me. I couldn't tell who it was, and when I said forget it and rolled over, he left. Anonymous sex was not one of my things. I liked Bobby, though. Yes, I knew he was politically ruthless in many ways, but that just assuaged my sensitivity about being a bleeding-heart liberal. Besides, I thought he would be more effective than Jack, particularly in wiping out crime.

Bobby and I talked a lot. I asked him about his background and feelings within his family. He told me a story I've never forgotten and have never really understood.

He said it was common knowledge that the family was driven to be competitive in athletics, but no one really knew the price exacted by his father, Joe Kennedy, if he thought they hadn't tried hard enough to excel.

One of their favorite sports was skiing. Bobby said he loved to ski, but he was always afraid to reach the bottom, because if he wasn't bleeding or scarred in some way, his father would send him up the mountain again until he had evidence that Bobby had tried hard enough to do it right. I was shocked by the story, but as time passed I realized he was continually doing a different version of the same thing.

He'd stand in front of open windows, unprotected, in a kind of provocative dare. He seemed to want to defy fate and win.

He made an appearance on *Meet the Press* a week or two before the California primary wearing a yarmulke and talking about jets for Israel as though he was Jewish himself, when the whole world knew his was the largest Catholic political family in America. To me, his appearance was inflammatory, and again I thought of how drawn he was to attracting danger to himself. I was somehow always afraid for him. I remember feeling he shouldn't go out in crowds even though Rosie Grier and Rafer Johnson were there to protect him. He aroused a messianic emotional response from crowds as though he was their last best hope. And I said just that when I introduced him for his appearance at the Sports Arena. When he walked out, he seemed so boyish, so slight, so dependent on others. It must have infuriated his enemies, who knew how relentless he could really be.

And then it was over. He had won the California primary. When a journalist friend called me in New York at 2:30 A.M., woke me up, and gave me the news that Bobby had been shot, I couldn't believe it. Another Kennedy? What was going on? Where could I or anyone else who desired change put our trust, our efforts, our hopes for the future? Was there an international conspiracy? Had we really become the Wild West?

The assassination of both Kennedys and Martin Luther King pierced the liberal patriotic vision that I had grown up with. Who was there now? Whom could I believe in?

After Bobby was assassinated, George McGovern called me. I remembered Bobby telling me that George McGovern was not just a decent man in the Senate; he was the only decent man there.

George said someone had to pick up the mantle of the Kennedy legacy and take it even further. He said he was going to be the one. He would lead the Kennedy delegation to the convention.

That was 1968 in Chicago. My introduction to the

politics of American fascism rolled into gear. Joe McCarthy was nothing compared with this.

A journalist friend of mine arrived in Chicago earlier than the rest of us. He called me in alarm.

"It's a police state here," he said. "Armed guards everywhere, snipers on the roofs. It's like Mayor Daley is spoiling for a fight."

I took what he said with a grain of salt and proceeded to continue my education about convention rules, etc.

Then I arrived in Chicago myself. The mood was like I imagined a militaristic banana republic to be. My friend was right. There were surly cops everywhere, trying to provoke arguments. Cops looked down from every rooftop with their rifles aimed at civilians below. Why?

I sat next to Rosie and Rafer in my delegation. They were there to keep Bobby's legacy alive. I had a small, portable TV set in my purse which Rosie and Rafer perched on a platform close to us so that everyone could see.

Because of that TV set, we saw what was happening in downtown Chicago, and the cop goons on the convention floor did not like that one bit. They knew the TV belonged to me, so they took to standing in front of me as I sat on my chair. They literally shoved their crotches in my face until Rosie and Rafer stood up, towered over them, and glared into their faces. Then they'd attempt to remove my set from its perch. Again Rosie and Rafer rose in intimidation.

The history of the '68 convention is well documented, but from my point of view it was a time that marked the distinction between the humane practice of democracy and its opposite. Violence within our borders was institutionalized. I remembered what Khrushchev had said when he visited the *Can-Can* set. He said he and the

Russians wouldn't need to lift a finger, because America would bury itself.

Many of my friends in the anti-Vietnam movement still bear the physical wounds inflicted by the Chicago police. The police riot became a new form of blunting protest; the media would duly theatricalize it in order to ensure ratings. Politics and show business became inextricably intertwined. Hubert Humphrey won the nomination and George McGovern retreated to run another day.

AFTER THE CONVENTION, I MOVED TO NEW YORK. MY interests and pursuits centered around the investigation of Richard Nixon's duplicitous policy in Southeast Asia as well as at home. Nixon personally made me sick. I hated the way he smiled when he was reporting carnage. He seemed afraid of democracy and had the furtive look of a person who thinks of himself as a victim. I didn't like his family either. I felt Pat Nixon had been molded by her husband. She seemed like a waxen figure who might melt under a really bright light. The daughters scared me because I hated the spectacle of female fascists. One expected this from men, some of them anyway, but young women? Oh my.

When Nixon got on the air and talked about how he was handling Vietnam—"Peace is at hand" and all that—I couldn't bear his duplicity, his lies. I couldn't understand how Charlton Heston and other people I respected could support him.

Then came the antiwar march on Washington. The shattering of the public's confidence in government policies had inspired a bold skepticism on the part of everyone who thought beyond pursuit of their daily bread. People from all strata of society were willing to come to Washington and openly question not only our government's policies, but also its truthfulness. Nixon was so distrusted, there were open calls for his impeachment. I had grown up respecting authority, but I was rapidly learning that the authorities didn't command my respect or anyone else's any longer.

When I saw our attorney general, John Mitchell, jail some three thousand people just for peacefully addressing their grievances, I knew I had to do something.

I had such distrust of Nixon and other politicians that I and others like me began to court more prominence in public. There was growing anger and anxiety within the artistic community. The press saw it. That gave them an opportunity for scintillating copy, so they began to elicit our opinions more and more. We, flattered that our thoughts and feelings were solicited at all, began to pontificate. Sometimes we made sense. Sometimes we were outrageously uninformed. The phenomenon of celebrity pundits was driven by press demands. We supplied that demand.

Opposition to the Vietnam War drew many Hollywood stars out into the open. Stars who had never been outspoken before. The politicians saw our willingness to be heard and solicited our help. Our political visibility increased.

When George McGovern decided to run for president in 1972 against Richard Nixon, there was no decision for me to make. . . . I dropped all my movie projects and went to work for him. A gentle preacher type was better than a crook. I invited him to my home in Encino, California, to meet liberals who would probably be considered a privileged elite, but were nevertheless effective. They were interested in helping with women's issues, civil rights, antiwar activities, and environmental change. McGovern was appealing to them because he was from a small-state background. He exuded integrity and high moral values.

He was not given much of a chance at the outset of his campaign, so he hoped stars who believed in him would attract the press. He believed we gave him a certain credibility, and we believed that helping to initiate a grass-roots campaign gave us credibility. We wanted to be respected for involving our hearts and minds in affairs other than artistic and moneymaking ones, and McGovern wanted to be respected for being a candidate who could attract us because of his moral fiber.

My first year campaigning with McGovern put me in touch for the first time with the soul and sweat of some real American people I would never otherwise have met. I visited living rooms, spoke at union rallies and fundraisers, joked and tried to be charming at ladies' lunches, and commiserated with the disillusioned on college campuses. Seven days a week and almost twenty-four hours a day, I talked for and about McGovern. Sometimes I couldn't remember what city I was in. But I loved it. I learned about Americans. I learned about presenting political views to small-town TV stations and I learned that there was a way for a celebrity to communicate without seeming to be out of touch with real life. The faces of the people I was communicating with were so open. I could see all my films in their eyes when they first gathered around me. I was a celebrity in their midst. But it didn't take long for me to rediscover the person I had been before Hollywood. I went back to my roots as an American who cared just like them. I too was a person just trying to love her country and make sense out of life. These wonderful people with whom I communicated were helping me simply to be myself again.

I was very lonely at times because I lived in strange hotels, never seeing much daylight. I was up at six A.M.

to do TV all day, and with the living-room meetings at night, I rarely went to bed before two A.M. I found myself talking about military spending, the tax system, problem cities, the necessity of having quality people on the Supreme Court, the intricacies of the abortion issue, and, of course, all aspects of the Vietnam War. I had come a long way from Sacramento and Marlon Brando. I learned by the questions people asked me. I would make late-night phone calls to experts so that I could answer questions with more facts and deeper knowledge, and for me, the campaigning was about one man—McGovern. Nixon should not be reelected. McGovern should.

I saw what a responsibility I had toward the man I was campaigning for as well as toward the public. Because I was a celebrity, people listened to me. I was a dream merchant. I was what they often longed to be. To them I had risen from their ranks to taste the nectar of success and fame and money. They were interested in what I knew and what I'd seen, and now I wanted to give something back to the people who had helped make me what I was. I wanted to help them see an alternative to corrupt government. I wanted to feel my chest burst with pride over being an American again just like I had as a teenager.

During this period, Harry Reasoner did a sarcastic piece on *60 Minutes* debasing artists' involvement in the political arena. I tried to call him, but he wasn't available. So I wrote a piece for the op-ed page of *The New York Times*. It said in part:

> Large numbers of Americans seem to understand now that it is the responsibility of everyone, including artists, to search for humane solutions of society's problems. Somehow they sense that artists can be both champions and prophets of social change

because they are so inextricably involved with the full range of human life. Politics that are void of the insight of art, its compassion, humor and laughter—are doomed to sterility and abstractions.

The show-business community is among the most generous and giving of any in this country. Millions of dollars were raised by artists giving concerts and doing fundraisers. Even Richard Nixon's dirty tricksters couldn't dampen our enthusiasm. They systematically cut my telephone wires and threw garbage at the front door of my New York City apartment, out of which I was running the Women's Advisory Committee and organizing concerts at Madison Square Garden. Nixon and his crowd were political gangsters. They didn't believe in or even understand democracy. They mocked and ridiculed those who not only desired change, but were idealistic enough to believe it was possible.

While people were dying in Vietnam and racial tensions festered here at home, while the sexual revolution took root and experimentation with drugs infected our young, Nixon and company seemed to operate with total unawareness of the demoralization and cynicism that were building. To me it was especially frightening to think of Nixon appointing more Supreme Court justices. McGovern, at least, had a soul. And he was a moral leader. The leadership he provided would be truthful, at least.

At one point near the end of the campaign, McGovern turned to me and said, "If Nixon gets reelected, I would not want to live in this country." I was glad no one else heard him.

If George McGovern had gotten elected in 1972, I would have given up performing, fame, Hollywood, and the good life to work for his administration. I would probably have asked to be a part of something to do with the issue of overpopulation in the world. I would have had hope and women would have had more equal roles in the decision making processes of our government much sooner. Our leaders, who were overgrown boys playing war games, would have had to come up with solutions for problems and conflicts. If McGovern had won, all of us would have lived in greater harmony and health and the world would now be a more humane place.

But with the humiliating defeat of McGovern and the reelection of Nixon, I found myself disillusioned, no longer wanting to be part of the political activism on the home front. Instead I found myself interested in foreign policy and foreign leaders. How did they feel about themselves and us? How did they see human rights and democracy? What did they think of the future of communism and much more?

I took a woman's delegation to China soon after Kissinger had been there. I put together a group of twelve women, including a camera crew. We were from all different sociopolitical points of view and shared the desire to see the world's newest revolution.

China made us reevaluate everything. We filmed ourselves going through culture shock, aware for the first time that there were other ways to live, other political structures, other viewpoints on love, sex, death, and money—even animals. I was never so homesick for animals as I was when I was in China. The Chinese way of relating to animals, particularly to dogs, was cold and detached. A dog was as liable to end up on your plate as it was to tag along wagging its tail. We filmed people peering into our faces, fascinated by our round eyes and various colors of skin.

We filmed a woman having a cesarean birth who was

awake and talking to us. She had one acupuncture needle in each ankle and experienced no pain.

Most of the delegation got sick with a Chinese strain of pneumonia. The hospital care was excellent, sensitive and kind. Each person learned something individual during this experience. Overall they realized that some of the ancient Chinese techniques of healing were far more advanced than our Western drug treatment.

What we saw in ourselves as American women was the paramount value of our trip. We couldn't possibly assess the objective truth about the new Chinese human experiment in three or four weeks. But we could assess what it did to us and how it helped to clarify our individual attitudes to our own lives.

We were impressed by China, but we had the feeling all the time we were there that the Chinese people were tolerated by their leaders, like unknowing children. That Mao was the patriarch and was to be obeyed out of a benevolent respect for one's elders; that the state knew best for its people, who were still suffering from their "bitter past."

The past *was* bitter, no doubt about that. Everywhere we went someone gave a heartfelt speech about the pain of it. And I also felt that what they had today, regardless of its limitations and the lack of freedom, was comparatively better. The people seemed reasonably content and fairly well fed. The medical system was more than adequate, the educational system oppressive with its indoctrination, yet they were learning to read and write. Women enjoyed a status of greater equality; at least wife beating was outlawed and infanticide of girl babies was a crime. Possession of dope was a capital offense punishable by death; divorce, a matter for local courts to decide; self-criticism a part of the fabric of collective life. The communes were extremely harsh, but those who were forced to labor there reported that they learned a great deal from it. Husbands and wives were separated for years at a time in order to contribute their talent and energy to the cause of the New China, the New Revolution. Everyone was involved in the spirit of a new dawn, and when foreigners like those in our delegation came to visit, the people we encountered were anxious to share what they were doing with their new energy of meaning.

All of us on the delegation learned more about ourselves, as well as about this strange and restricted new world. We began to look at our attitudes toward materialism and possessions and money a little differently. Unita Blackwell, a black activist from Mississippi, told me one day that she was reevaluating what she wanted, as a repressed person, for herself and her people. She said she used to want a bigger share of the white man's pie. Now she was suspicious that the pie itself had made the white man sick.

While we were in China our own government had begun to crumble. Every now and then we'd run into an American journalist who'd keep us informed about Nixon and Watergate and the unfolding American political drama.

The Chinese were not surprised at Nixon's corruption. They said they always knew who they were dealing with. In fact, from their point of view there was very little difference between Nixon and McGovern! But they were concerned that they had cast their lot with Nixon in opening their borders. They knew he was "a son of a dog," but he was *their* "son of a dog" and they were not happy at the impeachment talk.

I ruminated over the year and a half I had spent with McGovern. I remembered what he'd said about not wanting to live in a country where Nixon was president. Did our nation need to go through this trauma of shameful revelations in order to understand what the calamity of Nixon's political landslide meant? I felt morally vindicated for all my high-toned preaching. I tried to get a Massachusetts license plate that said, "*We* voted for McGovern." No longer did I feel like a naive idealist, a Hollywood dilettante.

For Nixon to put me and many other artists on his famous enemies list, claiming we were anti-American and dangerous, made me laugh. It also made me madly enthusiastic. Of course it was an acute violation of our human and civil rights, but it proved once and for all that many of us actors, actresses, and performers were important, authentic and influential enough to be afraid of. I wrote to Harry Reasoner asking his opinion, but he never acknowledged my letter.

After Nixon resigned and Gerald Ford came and went, the politics of hope reentered our lives with Jimmy Carter.

I had met Carter on the McGovern campaign. (I also met and worked with a young Democrat named Bill Clinton during those days.) Carter carried his own bag when he campaigned as a political outsider who could bring real change to Washington. Even though he had been governor of Georgia, his personality was not that of an established politician.

He was unassuming, witty, very friendly and affable, and had the gleam of the spiritual missionary in his eyes. His wife, Rosalynn, was smart, kind, and hospitable, with a keen overview of almost every situation. She was a real partner to Jimmy, proud of how much she and her husband had done for the equality of black and white in Georgia.

During the campaign and after Carter's election, I was afforded their southern hospitality at the White House. I was amused by brother Billy, by faith-healer

Ruth, and most of all by Miss Lillian, the president's mother. I also got to know some of the servants who had been there for years. They showed me around when I asked questions about Richard Nixon's occupancy. A butler ushered me into one of the historical sitting rooms and pointed to some round burn marks on the antique carpet.

"Nixon used to sit in this chair totally naked," said the butler, "drinking scotch from a bottle and smoking cigars and dropping the ashes on the carpet." He said Nixon was drunk a lot and was, to put it mildly, "quite primitive."

But things were different now. The Carters were genteel, regular, and fun, particularly Miss Lillian.

Miss Lillian loved the spotlight. It brought out her theatrical instincts. *Because* she was the president's mother, she became even more eccentric. Miss Lillian could have been a model matron in a Tennessee Williams play (preferably a comedy). She was more direct than the sun's glare. She would gaze through to the very soul of you and then make a quip that spoke to something you felt was a secret. She was breathtakingly honest about the President. "He says he never tells a lie," she said. "That's a lie. You know kids. They are always lying, particularly Jimmy. He knows how to make it sound good. He says I had a born-again experience with the Peace Corps in India. Well, I had a good trip, but it didn't change my life."

Miss Lillian had a disarming way of telling the truth as she saw it without really hurting anyone. I liked being around her because she reminded me of the down-home people of my childhood. The people who could spin tales on the back porch long after dark. She was real even though she knew she was an entertainment. She was spry and would take guff from no one. She often stayed with me at my home in Malibu and forced me to go to baseball games, where she cheered, jeered, and leered at the players. She loved the L.A. Dodgers, and once in the dugout she ate so much caviar she became really sick. I called my doctor, and before he realized he was treating the President's mother, he suggested she form her own vaudeville act with other "Golden Girl types," as we'd later call them, just to inspire the Gray Panthers of senior citizenry.

President Carter would call every night to check on his mom and express his "pride" in our having such fun "just being ourselves."

I liked and enjoyed the Carters a great deal. They were simple, highly intelligent, and deeply spiritual human beings. In fact, I thought Jimmy Carter saw himself as an American Gandhi whose moral responsibility was to walk among his people, counseling them on what he called their "malaise."

The people surrounding Carter in the White House were something else again. Tim Kraft was a quiet but thorough chief of staff who loved Dean Martin. I endeared myself to him when I got him and his party tickets to see Dean and Frank at the Westchester Premiere Theater. Tim had no idea that the guys with cauliflower ears walking up and down the aisles—including a priest who wore a diamond cross covering his vestments that would have been the envy of Bulgari in Rome—were later to be indicted for racketeering.

Hamilton Jordan was the raucous playboy of the Carter crowd. I attended a party in Beverly Hills with him once. It was rather boring, to my mind, but when I opened the morning paper, I'd have thought a dope orgy had taken place. I saw nothing of the sort of thing that was reported by the paper. Namely, cocaine and wild women. A few people went to the bathroom quite frequently, but the "wild women" were somewhere else. Jordan had a way of attracting such headlines. He was shrewd and politically well aware, but since he had power, he was going to use it to have some good-ol'-boy fun. He *was* fun, but sometimes at his own risk.

The Carter crowd in the White House loved being around movie stars just as everybody else did. Since they were liberal Democrats, they found themselves meeting liberal performers. The connection between politicians and performers was in full swing again. This time they were younger: Linda Ronstadt, Chevy Chase, and others.

We held the premiere of *The Turning Point* at the Kennedy Center in Washington, D.C. The Carter family were guests of honor.

Soon after that, I went to Hamilton to tell him that Herbert Ross, the director of *The Turning Point,* the Twentieth-Century Fox brass, and I had been invited to Cuba to present the film in Havana. Alicia Alonso, the prima ballerina assoluta, was an old friend of Herbert's wife, the great ballerina Nora Kaye, and was still residing in Havana. She longed to be reacquainted with American ballet, so Nora would come with us.

Hamilton gave us his and the administration's blessing, and because I wanted to shoot a live-TV-musical special from the Riviera nightclub in Havana, he offered to be of any help he could.

It was a breath of fresh air finally to have a Democratic administration, one more open to person-to-person exchanges between political adversaries.

Our group from Hollywood made our rendezvous in New York, and after many complications relating to traveling to a country the United States didn't recognize diplomatically, we left for Havana.

By then I had traveled to many communist countries—Russia, Czechoslovakia, Romania, East Germany,

Poland, and mainland China. As soon as we landed in Cuba, I could see that with all its dreadful drawbacks, the Cuban revolution was the sexy one. There were margaritas on Varadero Beach, laughter and teasing in the streets, and much raucous Latin humor in the nightclubs. A delegation from Russia and Romania was visiting Havana when we were there. We saw them everywhere and observed their behavior. They were very stiff and formal. To them the Latin American temperament didn't compute. They sat in restaurants and nightclubs unable to comprehend how good communists could be having so much fun. Part of the emotional commitment to Soviet-style communism must have been to give up good times. I know there were thousands of artists, writers, and poets in jail under Castro, but it was not so well-known then as it is now. The men and women who represented the communism of Eastern Europe were dark-spirited, dour, somber, and inflexible. They couldn't even see their way to getting drunk, which was something they had no problem with at home.

The great treat of this visit for me was meeting Alicia Alonso and her ballet company. She was magnificently regal and humorous, yet she was almost completely blind. She showed us around her school, negotiating her steps with intuitive precision. She told us that sometimes she even performed. I couldn't imagine what it was like for her to dance without eyesight. How did she judge space? She was so proud of her allegiance to the revolution and said she operated with complete freedom. I had loved her dancing since my childhood. I had heard of her involvement with the revolution when I grew more aware. She was a dancer's dancer, so I asked her how she felt about artists' political involvement. She told me a story. She said years ago someone from the press had expressed astonishment that she, as one of the world's great ballerinas, would become politically active. "How do you have time to acquaint yourself with political revolution?" he asked. "And why are you even aware of it?" She answered, "Why, where do you expect me to dance then, on the moon?"

We spent a whole day with Alonso. Just to watch her and Nora Kaye interact was the fulfillment of a childhood dancing-school dream.

Then we all went over to the Cuban Film Commission, saw some of their recent films, and met with actors, painters, and poets. People in the arts are the same all over the world. We feel we know each other regardless of our cultural and political differences. We know we see the world differently, and because of this, we often feel isolated from the mainstream and connected with one another. Of course we didn't expect any open criticism of Castro, but we all had the feeling that these artists felt commissioned with the responsibility of furthering the revolution any way they could.

The consensus seemed to be that Fidel Castro had raised the level of literacy to 90 percent or higher and that economic times were hard because of the American embargo on their goods. Yet there was laughter and joking and drinking and fun between us. The weather was rainy and heavy waves surged over the retaining walls along the Havana coastline. I had not thought of Havana as having problems and attributes similar to Malibu.

We walked along the beach, ogling Cuban women in bikinis, remarking among ourselves, "These are communists?" There were beachcombers displaying magic tricks and vendors serving margaritas. We ran into many Canadian visitors because their government had a more liberal policy toward communist countries. I thought of my father and his abhorrence of communism, his fear that my mother's relative in Canada had "communist tendencies." I wouldn't have wanted to live under such a system, of course, but that didn't make the people who believed in it evil.

*The Turning Point* opened to an enthusiastic response. The people and the critics appreciated the opening immensely, but in general felt that the story was more of a soap opera than it should have been. We had lengthy discussions with members of the film union about the content of the story.

Some people couldn't understand why the characters in the picture had a problem with adultery. They argued that monogamy was not part of human nature and not expected in marriage. Others strongly felt that the woman I played, a ballet dancer who gave up dance to have a husband and children, could have been married and pursued a career with no problem. In their society, they said, such a dilemma would have been unbelievable because everyone was equal, everyone desired to work. I told them that American women were suffering from exhaustion in attempting to be homemakers and work in the marketplace simultaneously. I asked if their men helped with the children and the housework. They rolled their eyes and shook their heads. But they said, "We make it work. We have the energy."

I wondered.

I also wondered how they reconciled communism, the Catholic faith, and the African influence that underpinned the entire culture. They said their revolution embraced these aspects of life. This was so different from what I had seen in Eastern Europe, Russia, and China. Then I met the man responsible for it all and began to see why Cuba was different.

Our movie group was ushered into a waiting room in the offices of Fidel Castro. Settling into comfortable chairs with our soft drinks, we waited and chatted. We had been there for about forty-five minutes when an aide came and asked for me. I identified myself and he said Castro wanted to see me . . . alone. I looked at Herb and Nora. They winked, nodded, and gestured for me to go.

I was led by a uniformed attendant down a wide hallway. At the end of it was a thick double door. It opened just as I arrived, and as if on cue, there stood Fidel Castro.

I looked up into his face. He was very tall. His familiar beard was well groomed and his eyes alive with interest.

I put out my hand. He shook it and greeted me in Spanish. His translator did so simultaneously. Then he moved and gestured for me to follow him to a chair. I watched him walk and was struck by how effeminate his body movement was . . . the sound of his voice . . . his involuntary way of being. I never expected such a feminine essence in Fidel Castro. I expected a macho revolutionary and a swaggering leader of men. I had heard that he would suggest sweeping me up into his Jeep for a jaunt through sugarcane. Barbara Walters had told me to beware. This didn't seem to be the case.

We sat down. Before I knew it, he had launched into one of the famous Castro monologues interspersed with questions about everything American from instant orange juice to the Kennedys. I longed to ask him if Sam Giancana had ever personally lit a cigar for him.

He told me of his trip to Manhattan when Eisenhower was president. He said he had had to stay in Harlem because he wasn't recognized as a head of state. He used his hands a great deal when he spoke. His fingers were long and expressive.

He spoke at length about *"los niños,"* the children of Cuba, and what their literacy meant to the future success of his revolution. He spoke of poets and artists and theatrical people and how they contributed to a revolution. I asked him why so many were in jail. A revolution needed inspiration, not demolition, he said. When I spoke of freedom of expression, he said that was for the American Revolution because ours took place so long ago. His revolution was not completed yet.

He spoke of the problems of cities, and traffic, and space. He said he was fascinated by the skyscrapers he had seen in Manhattan and wondered how they had been built. He asked me about the theater in New York and whether I did live theater as well as movies. I said yes and then told him I wanted to do a live-TV show from the Riviera nightclub in Havana. I said I wanted to contribute to a better understanding of our two cultures. He thought about it awhile and nodded yes. Then he said "Good" in English. I wondered how much English he really spoke. I asked him if it was true that he had been an extra in the original *Ten Commandments* directed by Cecil B. DeMille. I said there was a rumor that he was one of the spear carriers, and there was a photograph to prove it. He thought a moment and said he had never seen the picture.

I decided not to press the issue.

We talked for about three and a half hours. I was concerned for Herb and Nora and *The Turning Point* party, who waited patiently down the hall. Fidel knew they were there but he was clearly on *"mañana"* time, enjoying himself and looking for a way to be remembered diplomatically to Jimmy Carter. I admired his uniform and told him military duds were all the rage in the States. He clocked that fact and summoned the rest of my party.

They entered, still cheerful and thankfully not at all resentful of the time they had waited. Fidel asked them about our film and the ways of Hollywood, and declared how essential it was for us to have a people-to-people bridge between countries of differing political perspective.

He was charming, hospitable, talkative, and generous in seeing to whatever needs we might have.

We left him with humorous warnings not to pirate our picture. We wanted the people of Cuba to see it, but we didn't want him to steal it! He laughed, knowing full well, as did we, that he would do it anyway.

After a dinner of excited chat about meeting Castro, I went to my hotel room to get some rest. At about 11:30 there was a knock on the door. I opened it. There stood Fidel, alone except for his translator. He had a bag of gifts in one hand and one of his uniforms in the other.

"You admired this," he said. "I brought you one." He handed me the uniform and asked if he could come in. I thought of Barbara Walters, but I ushered him in anyway.

We sat together on my sofa. His translator became the invisible woman.

Fidel pulled a box from his bag. It was hand-carved. He opened it to reveal Cuban cigars. "Your Mr. Hamilton Jordan smokes these," he said, "and perhaps after dinner even your president would like one."

I lifted one of the cigars and smelled its aroma. I could see why they were a frequently smuggled item.

"Thank you," I said. "I will personally give these to Mr. Jordan and President Carter."

"Now," said Fidel, taking out another longer, thinner box. "This is for your Mr. Brzezinski."

"Oh?" I said.

"Yes," said Fidel. "It's a peace pipe. I would like to smoke the pipe of peace with him, particularly as it relates to our role in Angola. It's difficult to say these things officially, but you are a people-to-people bridge. Please give him this pipe and offer my gesture of peace.''

Fidel gently opened the gift wrapping and showed me the pipe. It looked exactly like what he said.

"I will take this back with me," I said. "Thank you. I'm going to see them as soon as I return."

Fidel then extracted a huge glass box from his bag. There was a stuffed bird mounted inside.

"This is a dove," he said. "It's a dove of peace. It's my gift to you. It's Canadian. I know your mother was Canadian. We have many Canadians here. Also, I know of your work with Mr. McGovern. I know of your feelings about the Vietnam War. I know of your efforts for peace; therefore, I want you to have this dove."

He handed me the big glass box. Why was he doing all of this? I wondered. Wasn't there another emissary available? Were we just the right people to act as unofficial ambassadors in the diplomatic world because everybody liked movie stars? Were we famous enough to command attention, but not quite authentic enough to be taken seriously?

I had delivered messages from Helmut Schmidt of Germany to President Carter prior to the Paris conference, from Willy Brandt to Pierre Trudeau, from Olof Palme of Sweden to the antiwar movement in America. It was as though personally delivered messages from famous artists who "cared" enabled political leaders to test the waters of future discussions. Were we, as Castro said, "bridges" to opposing worlds?

Castro stood up, walked around my room, and asked me if I'd enjoyed myself in Cuba. I said I had particularly liked the bands and the old-fashioned nightclubs. He then talked for another hour about the necessity to understand that his was a poor country and that he wanted friendship with the United States. He longed for the embargo to be discontinued and suggested that there were very good deals for American business in Cuba, and he added, ''I will do whatever I can to provide access and equipment if you do your TV show from Havana.''

I listened, wondering which artist might be suffering in a Havana jail for writing a book or painting a picture that challenged some of his revolutionary dictates. Then I thought of John Mitchell's corruption and Spiro Agnew's lawbreaking and Richard Nixon's bombing of Cambodia. I thought of the declining rate of literacy in America and the dope dumped on our streets, somehow undetected by federal authorities. I thought of the kickbacks and the Mafia and the criminal activity committed in the name of capitalism.

All life seemed to be a choice of second best, leaving us with the age-old conflict of whether the future was worth the sacrifice of the present. I wondered what continued to motivate Castro. Apparently he had to sleep in a different place every night. What was it that gave his destiny meaning year after year? Was it possible to identify so much with your people that you came to think of the two as one—the De Gaulle *is* France syndrome? Was that what drove Castro? In his mind, Castro was Cuba? And vice versa. Maybe that was what it took to be a revolutionary leader.

I watched him as he sipped some water and delivered his sermons, his observations and aspirations for his people, as though I was an audience more important than any other. He was captivating and obsessed at the same time. He was gentle, yet deliberate. His energy never dissipated. He paced and cajoled and entertained and preached. In these moments the destiny of Cuba seemed to be cradled in his arms. I wondered how long that would last. I wondered what would happen to Cuba when he died.

When he left, I hung his uniform in my closet.

When the maid came in to clean the next morning, she found it. She looked at me and then back at it. Had her leader sold out to an American movie star or had the movie star succumbed to the charms of the sugarcane fields? She smiled and left.

When I returned to Washington, I took the presents to the White House. I carried them in a large tote bag.

My limo drove through the gate and let me off close to the Rose Garden.

I walked through the door, impressed that security had been so subtle.

I first went to Hamilton's office. He wasn't in. So I moved over to Brzezinski, the national security adviser. I had called to say I was coming. Zbigniew invited me in. He asked how my trip to Cuba had gone. I told him fine.

We sat in the sitting area of his office, chatting until Hamilton came in. He asked about Cuba too.

"I have something for you," I said.

"Yeah, what?" said Hamilton.

"A present from Castro." I pulled out the box of cigars.

Zbigniew jumped up. "You have a present from that murderer with you and you got past security?"

I looked at him in shock. "Well, yes," I said. "I thought those metal detectors at the entrance were enough to tell us there's nothing dangerous here."

"Nothing dangerous?" said Zbigniew. "There could be a bomb in that box."

"A bomb?" I asked. "How would it know when to go off? I had it on my lap coming from Havana."

"What have you got there?" said Hamilton, ignoring Zbigniew's alarm. "Did he send me cigars, I hope?"

"Yes," I said. "And the box is beautiful. It's hand-carved."

"We have to disarm this box," said Zbigniew, becoming more and more agitated.

"There's no bomb in this box," I said.

"And how do you know?" he questioned.

"Just let me have a cigar," said Hamilton. "Never mind the bomb."

"I will not be responsible for what happens when you open that box," said Zbigniew.

"*Okay,*" said Hamilton. "I will." Then he jokingly backed away from it. "You open it," he said to me.

I looked at both of them. Zbigniew was, by now, up against the wall and Hamilton was having a sadistic good time.

I unwrapped the ribbon from the box and went to open it. I lifted the top tentatively about one inch. Nothing happened. My confidence increasing, I lifted the top all the way open. Suddenly a sharp, shrill alarm went off. I jumped back from the box and gasped. Could Zbigniew have been right? I looked over at him. He was smiling maliciously. I looked at Hamilton. He was chewing his gum and shrugging. He pointed to a computer-run safety device on the shelf.

"That thing monitors the President's movements," he said. "When he leaves the Oval Office, it goes off. That tells us where he is."

Zbigniew continued to be tight-jawed and paranoid. Hamilton dove into the box of cigars, extracting one, and lit it. It did *not* blow up in his face, which was duly noted by Brzezinski. Tim Kraft came in.

"Are there Cuban cigars in here?" he asked. I offered him one, saying they were from Castro.

"Great," he said. "I've always had to smuggle mine in from Switzerland."

While the President's men smoked their cigars, I pulled out Castro's present to Brzezinski.

"This is for you," I said. "He wanted you to have it."

"What is it?" Zbigniew asked.

"Well," I said, "maybe you should open it and I'll tell you what he said."

There was an outer box housing the inner box for the large peace pipe.

I slid the outer box off and handed it to Brzezinski. He picked it up gingerly. "This would make a good coffin for my daughter's dog," he said.

I blanched. What was wrong with this man?

I then handed him the peace pipe, which he extracted and held up.

"Fidel says he wants to smoke the pipe of peace with you," I said.

Brzezinski turned it over, then threw it down on the table.

"I'll smoke this thing with him when every last Cuban soldier is out of Angola and not a minute before!"

I looked over at Tim and Hamilton. Cigar smoke curled around their heads. They shrugged.

Brzezinski left his office. Tim and Hamilton wandered away. I stood looking around. Was this the way it was done?

I gazed around at the office of the man who was commissioned with the task of effecting peace in the world.

The shelves were decorated with replicas of nuclear missiles and high-tech rocket launchers. Brzezinski had proudly shown me these toys on a previous occasion as an example of how we would keep the peace for the free world. The free world? Free from what? And free from whom?

Hamilton's secretary came in and broke my reverie of confusion.

"Mr. Jordan would like to see you in his office," she said.

"Oh, sure," I answered.

I walked from Brzezinski's office, seriously skeptical about the artistic-performer-as-bridge concept, and into Hamilton's office.

He invited me to sit down in front of his desk. The desk from which momentous advice concerning the entire planet would be given.

"So, did you get to the Riviera nightclub down there?" asked Hamilton.

"Yes. We did. It was great," I answered. "A little old-fashioned, but great."

"Pretty showgirls?" Hamilton asked as he winked.

"Yes, as a matter of fact, except they all dressed like Carmen Miranda."

"Yeah?" he asked.

"Yeah," I answered.

"So," he continued, "are you going to do a TV show from there?"

"I hope so," I answered. "Fidel said he'd do anything he could to help facilitate it. He'd give us crews and equipment . . . everything. He wants America to see that Cuba isn't as bad as the propaganda."

"Great," said Hamilton. "I love this idea of your doing a show down there. So would the President. You know what? We'll get Miss Lillian to do a time step with you on the stage. She loves show business."

"Do you really mean it?" I asked.

"Why sure," said Hamilton. "Jimmy would love his mother to do it and you know she would."

I was elated. Later I ran the idea by Tim Kraft and Brzezinski. They seemed to love it.

I returned to California, talked to the network, who okayed the idea, and sent an advance team to Cuba. They spent a week or so arranging what was necessary for a live broadcast from Havana.

Our creative team set to work doing research so our songs, comedy, and patter would be authentic. We were certain we had the earmarks of a classic musical show broadcast from a communist country ninety miles away.

Then the network called. They had changed their minds. It was too big a risk. I asked what the risk was. They said "the whole thing." I called the White House and spoke to Hamilton. "What happened?" I asked. "Did you guys express concern?"

"No," said Hamilton. "You know we loved the idea."

"Did Brzezinski do something?"

"Who knows with him?" answered Hamilton.

There it was. Passing the buck, going with the philosophy of "when in doubt, don't."

So our show never happened. A small failure in the scheme of things, but I felt it could have made a difference. I didn't know whether the Carter administration had been done in by the network or the network had been pressured by someone within the administration. Who had time to wade through that morass? I laughed. Yeah, everybody sure loved show business. Too bad the leaders of the free world didn't take the humanity of the rest of the world as seriously as we in show business did. Maybe we were bridges, but when would the politicians and powers-that-be venture across?

# 10

# "WOMEN'S PICTURES"

*I* have been blessed with doing some really good "women's pictures." That is to say, films whose subjects and casts appeal to a woman's point of view. I'm not sure what that definition means, though, because the public is not as compartmentalized in its thinking as we often perceive it to be. If pictures with women are termed women's pictures, why are pictures with men just pictures?

The term "women's picture" never really came up in Hollywood until the middle of the seventies, when women were being redefined in our culture as a result of the success of the women's movement. Until then, pictures about women's lives starring Joan Crawford, Lana Turner, and Bette Davis were pictures for everybody. Those heroines of yesteryear must have made actresses feel they could play anything. There were love stories, family stories, stories of human values, and stories with socially redeeming messages of hope. The stories usually revolved around the female character because they were about feelings. The women were the leavening influence, the inspiration, the anchor. Or, conversely, they were caught in the conflict of ambition, jealousy, love triangles, bad marriages, backstreet affairs, mother-child troubles, or coping with a crumbling world. . . . Feelings. . . . Life.

Nobody is really sure what changed or why. We only know that now the average habitual moviegoer is between eleven and seventeen years old. They prefer action pictures, which are typically inhabited by men. With the advent of high-tech screen techniques, many of these action pictures have developed into showcases for special effects, usually peopled by men who either portray buddies to each other or enact the slave/master role in a story about the triumph of good over evil or vice versa.

When action pictures, science fiction, crime dramas, and stories of sexual perversity prevail, there is not much room for women unless we play dominatrices or outer-planetary dark goddesses. Violent action accelerates and men are required to resolve it.

Why do we need so many pictures like this? Because they reflect what's happening in our society? The violence and deterioration of values? Of course, but there's more. I call it millennium consciousness. The human race recognizes that the end of a millennium is about to occur and this causes profound anxiety. We feel we can't keep up with the changes—they're all happening too fast. This causes deterioration, until finally we sense, on a visceral level, that we must reach inside ourselves and find some centeredness and peace in order to express what has been suppressed and get on with the badly needed transformation of our consciousness.

In many ways our modern culture has inflicted a kind of velvet control over our inherited, unresolved conflicts. We live with an overlay of civility, but often it's only that—a surface. The violence, sexual perversity, racial hostility, anger at poverty, and revolt to experience human freedom are real. On some level we human beings intuit that we still function as if we lived in a jungle. We need to confront our unconscious jungle brains, and understand how they make us behave, before we can begin to feel the new energy of the millennium shift, the jump to a higher spiritual consciousness, and resonate to it.

Movies and television can help us do that, but instead they mainly *reflect* the violence and confusion that is occurring. Our industry is not living up to its responsibility to inspire and nurture the best in ourselves and our audiences. Art has a way of tapping into the subconscious of human life, which lately we've not felt we had the right to look at. Somehow in the last ten years, looking and feeling deeply has been considered self-indulgent, embarrassing. Films can help relieve this embarrassment. The films of the forties and fifties did just that. They were more conversant with human emotion and, because of that, starred more women—Bette Davis, Joan Crawford, Myrna Loy, Rita Hayworth, Loretta Young, Joan Fontaine, Olivia de Havilland, and so many others. In the sixties came the Vietnam War and with it the violence we witnessed every night on the seven o'clock news.

The more we observed the violence—bodies floating down the Mekong River, children burning with napalm—the more distanced we became from our own feelings. The more distanced we became, the less we found the examination of feeling even palatable. Add to that the technological advancements in communication, and there simply wasn't enough time to keep abreast of it all. We became inundated with events and happenings outside of our own lives, which left precious little time to absorb and process what occurred *inside* our lives. The faster information traveled the less communication there was between human beings.

Slowly but surely, we have abdicated the recognition of our own deep feelings and, more precisely, the spiritual feminine in ourselves. Its presence on the screen, unless it is etched with comic relief or car chases, is usually unacceptable, it makes us squirm and wriggle. We are afraid of oversentimentality, of seeming unintellectual. Yet we *know* that the feminine side of ourselves is nurturing, we *know* our feminine side is intuitive. We know our feminine side is mostly, and at its best, patient and nonjudgmental. *And* our feminine side recognizes that we cannot go on as we are and expect to have a loving and peaceful world. Still, our feminine aspects are not considered commercial. They are not considered politically viable. They are not considered qualities of leadership.

We are afraid that these qualities will not excite audiences, will not elicit cheers and spark competitive rooting. We are afraid and embarrassed because the feminine is more internal, more attuned to a silent knowingness, more connected to the deep core of why we're here and where we're going. We feel, but we are unacquainted with our intuition. We don't acknowledge the quiet recognition of the God spark within us.

All of the above, in my opinion, is why writers, producers, and studio heads are confused and bereft of ideas where the feminine is concerned. They are afraid to empathize with what feminine feels like. Yet pictures like *Terms of Endearment, Driving Miss Daisy, Fried Green Tomatoes, Steel Magnolias, The Piano* and *Little Women* are successful enough to warrant the production of more like them. So why more movies with women are not produced is a question no one seems able to answer, unless of course it is *because* female profitability is unacceptable. Women in equal economic control would expose everyone's emotional attitudes about women, including those of the female executives who currently make decisions on a playing field controlled by men and according to the cultural dictates of the moment. If more "women's pictures" were made and successful, the field on which Hollywood plays its game would change completely. No longer would women be relegated to decorative cages to be toyed and played with according to the whims of men. And more important than anything, if more women were in economic control, the men would have to face their fear and anxiety at being subservient to the female authority figure again. In other words, it would be a "mama" problem all over again.

The women's movement has tended to amplify this problem, which before was subtly swept under the rug. But the battle between the sexes is exposed full-blown now, and the men and women who commit money to develop projects would rather avoid the "mama" subject than stigmatize themselves by revealing their ignorance of their feelings about their own mothers. In fact, they use politically correct attitudes to obfuscate their deeper conflicts with mama.

Therefore, we have, it seems to me, a crisis of feminine, mother-earth spirituality versus masculine commerciality in *both men and women*. Or more to the point, humanity versus money.

We seem to be shirking the recognition of the missing feminine, mothering parts of ourselves, in favor of focusing on what will keep us afloat in a world of masculine intellectual materialism. But it doesn't keep us afloat. We are drowning and we know it. Instead of fighting to keep from drowning, we could surrender to the flow of the water and float. But this "law of reversed effort" is suspect. It does not command respect. It is considered weak and untenable, flimsy and emotional. More than anything, it is considered to have no strength, no stamina, no bite, no power. It is a vegetarian concept in a flesh-eating environment.

The notion of "let go and let God" is a spiritual, feminine, mothering fantasy that engenders nervous laughter and rolling eyes. It is too *allowing*.

Yet whenever a man has taken his masculine endeavors to the max, he returns to the serenity and peace of his female counterpart for sustenance, love, hope, and nurturing. He knows in his heart that the world out there is unbalanced and he knows why. The first person he knew and depended upon was his mother. She was allowing. The last person will be the female in his life, because she is allowing. He will want her as he goes to meet his maker. That is one of the few times he really recognizes her and, in so doing, realizes how he has denied the female in himself. Why does it take death to come to terms with such a spiritual truth?

Human beings have always had a general belief in the doctrine of the wholeness of the world, a spiritual belief that we have an ethical purpose for being alive. The purpose supposes a recognition of God within and without us. We live on Mother Earth and reflect Father Sky. The duality makes the power of One. It has always been considered a holy teaching, a philosophical tradition taught to young people as a preparation for their future life—the equal recognition of the masculine and feminine. This has been so in primitive tribes as well as in highly developed civilizations.

In our present civilization, this spiritual background has gone astray. Our Christian doctrine has lost its way. It is religious, but it is no longer spiritual. We have lost our balance because of it. We are drifting without orientation. Our lives are losing meaning because we ignore and negate the spiritual meaning.

In a world that believes we all swim in shark-infested waters, are there no alternatives to masculine solutions?

I believe there are. If we all, including feminists, more fully acknowledged that we have been bereft of the spiritual feminine for far too long, there would be less violence, anger, and hostility in the world.

With that recognition, our culture would be soothed. Our films and television would reflect the resulting serenity and we, I hope, would begin our transformation into the new millennium with a consciousness of stability, balance, harmony, and "allowance." We would return to what we were meant to be—the Power of One.

THE FEMININE POWER AND LONGEVITY OF SEVERAL FEMALE stars gives the hope and security that we are not lost. They continue to shed their light in my own small universe. They have influenced me deeply and I treasure their friendship.

Liza Minnelli is the one I've known since she was a baby. At the end of each shooting day on *Some Came Running* after we returned to Hollywood from location, I'd stop by Vincente's house to see Liza—she was about ten. She'd don a party dress with exquisite trimmings and proceed to dance and sing for me. She'd tell me about her games, her school, her ideas for plays and musicals. Liza was the image of her father, but her talent was Judy's. She questioned me about the shoot, my wardrobe, why my hair was dyed for the part, whether I fell in love with my leading men, and whether I enjoyed being a star. I could see that her intentions for her life were clear. Yet there she was alone with her nanny, playing show business with a twenty-four-year-old who was grappling with the same questions.

Over the years, Liza has become the one I go to for advice regarding the world of the stage. How do I handle two shows a night at an altitude of 7,500 feet? Who is the best new lyricist? Does Donna Karan do show clothes? What about that theater in Mexico City? Should I have an intermission? Who is a good drummer? Should I go self-contained or hire an orchestra in each place? On and on. She is a professional par excellence. She is giving, she is wily and shrewd, and she is nearly always right. She has been through personal pain and knows she is in constant rehab. I want her to write her autobiography so that others can know what is possible in themselves. She is an exemplary survivor.

BARBRA STREISAND IS ONE OF THE ''REAL'' ONES. IN EVERY way; sometimes too real. She is a universe of her own because she relates that way. To me, that is her most precious characteristic. Her directness and her sometimes harsh candor are the very spine of her honest personality. To be sure, her honesty is specifically *her* truth, but it is usually laced with such blazing insight that she redefines truth.

Barbra and I were born on the same day, April 24, seven years apart. She has fascinated me since I first saw her in her debut at the Coconut Grove when she was eighteen and I was twenty-five. I remember she was late going on because her hair wasn't dry. When she finally appeared in a navy blouse and miniskirt, I knew I was looking at and hearing a talent that was a gift from God. I can see why she is obsessed with sculpting perfection in her life. She begins with something perfect—her voice. Yet she is often insecure with the world that surrounds her because she would like to see it in perfect terms.

Though her feet are firmly planted on the ground, she is in a continual cosmic search for the meaning of self. Such a trait is consistent with the sign of Taurus.

She is attracted to sensual specifics that most people overlook; for example, she will notice a new perfume you're wearing or whether one of your teeth has been capped. She will detect a spice in an exotic dish, or the particular energy of an individual as his mood changes.

She has a need to express her appreciation of beauty in the environment that surrounds her. And though she sometimes finds herself maddeningly conflicted, she deeply desires harmony.

She is very sensitive to the opinions of others while seeming to fly in the face of public opinion.

She feels compelled to express perfection as she sees it and can become depressed if she feels others are not living up to their own potential.

She enjoys collecting "things" because she has done without.

I have seen her argue over the cost of a set of tiles for her home while at the same time she can forfeit millions of dollars because the cameras might disturb the view of her live audience in Vegas.

I have seen her put her audience before herself several times. She is also frightened of them, but only because she is nervous she won't be perfect. Forgetting her lyrics is a major nightmare for her.

She is a film director par excellence. I would trust her completely to direct me in anything she wished. She has taste, humor, and an exceptional sense of timing. Sometimes she goes for portrait perfection to the extreme, but at my age that would be a plus.

And as a friend she is unceasingly interesting and challenging. She is a sponge when it comes to learning, possessing a Talmudic trait to better herself, and her questions are deep and probing, usually motivated by her obsession with detail.

Our talks are satisfying and always an equal interchange.

Regardless of where we are in the world, we will either talk or be together on our birthday. She is sentimental that way and we are family.

She is a woman I feel attached to, and I love her and appreciate what she does with her life. She is an inspiration to me because whatever baggage she carries around with her as a Taurus is the baggage I carry myself.

May she shine forever because then I and others like us can see ourselves.

ELIZABETH TAYLOR IS NOW AND ALWAYS HAS BEEN, AS long as I've known her, completely aboveboard about who she is, and who she is not.

Even when she reigned supreme as Hollywood's exquisite misty-eyed temptress, she talked of quitting "it" before "it" quit her. She is funny and cynical about having lived the life of a supreme celebrity as early as she could remember.

In the old days, she would traipse into my small beach apartment, a few lavender dresses slung over her arm for going out to dinner later, and play with my boxer dog, Caesar. He was not house-trained, and whenever he made a mess it was Elizabeth who cleaned it up. Every man I knew was in love with her, more than prepared to drive their cars off of cliffs if she spurned them. I watched in awe as she wove her lovely illusionary spell, yet remained real at the same time. She spoke openly about her personal life, never seeming to be concerned whether her secrets would be safe. Her vulnerability was her strongest protection because she had a nose for whom she could trust.

While making *Around the World in Eighty Days,* I had the privilege of watching the beginning of her relationship with Mike Todd. The day Elizabeth met him, she told me she had felt like the mongoose charmed by the cobra. "I know I'm going to marry him," she said. "It's beyond my control." I wondered how that felt.

The two of them courted each other with flirtatious phone calls. They were a combination for combustion. She was divorcing Michael Wilding, who became too sweet and dependable to be exciting. I watched with such personal curiosity how she would handle the possibility of a new life with an unpredictable, modern-day P. T. Barnum. I was observing her in relation to my own marriage to Steve Parker. How difficult was it for her to leave Michael? He was kind, reliable, and the father of her sons. But the physical attraction had gone out of her marriage. Would that happen to me? I wondered. How did you survive in Hollywood without a husband who was a support system? I remember the day Mike Todd died in a plane crash. The *Lucky Liz,* his plane was called. At the last moment Elizabeth decided not to take the trip because of the flu.

When I heard the news, I rushed to her house. She was sitting up in bed, paralyzed with grief, being attended to by Sydney Guilaroff, hairstylist at Metro, who lovingly tried to ease her pain with vodka and orange juice.

Her desolation was so raw and intense, it curdled her face into agony. I'll never forget her anguish at God. "Why? Why?" she sobbed. "Why did God take him?" Indeed, I thought. She *had* needed Mike. I couldn't understand it either.

With the tragedies in her life and the accumulation of health problems she later came to "overneed" prescription drugs. She told me of her personal horror with prescription drug addiction and her desire (along with some others) to sue the AMA for malpractice because they willingly enabled her addiction.

But when Elizabeth was clean, she was a joy to behold. The primordial pleasure she derived simply from tucking into a mountainous cheeseburger with the works, or barbecued ribs and potato salad, or Chasen's chili was a lesson in basics. But when she dieted, her silver-screen discipline prevailed. Nothing would induce her to compromise her determination to starve herself. And when she was ill, she was so tragically beautiful, seeming to accept adversity as her destiny. When her violet eyes glisten with sadness, I remember the pain she has experienced, which informs the empathy she has for those who can't help themselves. She is a woman who never had a childhood. She has never been unfamous. She was and is a goddess of the primitive, salt from the soil, the original earth mother whom the gods from the sky found fair. She is a milkmaid, a Jewish mother, and queen of the jewels.

But when she lost Mike, it affected me deeply. Didn't you need a person who was there only for you? A person, a friend, a support system you knew you could depend upon as the Hollywood currents swirled treacherously around you? Yes, you think you do until suddenly they are not there anymore, for whatever reason. That is when you reach down into the untapped core of yourself and find what you are made of. That was to be my own experience some years later.

NOWHERE WAS THE EFFECTIVE POWER OF WOMEN MORE evident than on the set of *Steel Magnolias*. The crew (mostly men) stood back in awe as they watched the women work out their creative problems with sensitivity and a minimum of turbulence. The actresses were there for each other at every insecure turn in the road. We were a bonded team.

We all had houses (it was a long shoot in Natchitoches, Louisiana) and we'd intermingle for hours. My house was next door to Julia Roberts's on Sibley Lake. Julia was new, had only done a few pictures, but the moment she walked into the rehearsal room it was obvious she was a born movie star. Initially Meg Ryan had been cast as Sally Field's diabetic daughter, but when a conflict of schedules eliminated her, Julia stepped in. Her cheekbones, her smile, her tall, thin, eye-catching body, and her raucous laughter were meant for stardom. On top of that she was nice. A small-town girl from Smyrna, Georgia, she seemed to feel destined for the screen. Her big brother, Eric Roberts, was already established in films. It was Julia's turn now and she embraced it completely. *Steel Magnolias* made her an instant movie star.

It wasn't so much her charisma, her carriage or command, that made her magnetic. It was the way she filled the spaces between her words and movements. Her facial expressions were immediately in sync with her feelings. The immediacy was so involving, it was hard to look at anyone else for fear of missing an electrifying moment of raw expression.

As I watched her work in front of the cameras, I realized she believed everything was truly happening to her. It wasn't acting, exactly. She went through real discomfort during her diabetic collapse. She was dizzy and sick with anxiety. And when she was dying in the hospital bed, she was terrified that her own death could be imminent. She said she felt herself slipping away and expressed her concern to those of us she was close to.

When an audience senses that an actor is dangerously real, they are riveted. They are experiencing "It."

When Julia shook with fright at the return of her abusive husband in *Sleeping with the Enemy,* it was to a large extent real too. She trembled in terror, and often after the director yelled "cut" she found it difficult to come out of the emotion. The audience knows when emotion is that authentic and responds by investing their trust in such a star.

The director, Herb Ross, with whom I had also worked in *The Turning Point,* regarded Julia as another of his "baby ballerinas." That is to say, he wished to have a ballet master's control over his new discoveries. He wanted her to dye her hair, have her beauty marks removed, and never eat more than a thousand calories a day. He claimed he could detect the effects of an extra Saltine cracker on an actress's face. Julia stood up to Herbert's well-meaning dictates very well. Some suggestions—the weight, the hair color—she accepted, but the beauty marks around her eyes remained.

We older actresses—Sally Field, Olympia Dukakis, and I—had dealt with our own versions of a meticulous Herb Ross. We watched proudly as Julia put his judgments in proper perspective. She was a bit intimidated by our experience and our survival mechanisms and knew it was necessary to develop her own if she was going to be a long-distance runner.

I watched her write poetry and get up in the spotlight of the Bodacious Night Club on Highway 34, seize the microphone, and sing her heart out. I was not surprised when she married Lyle Lovett. He is a live performer with excellent values, who gives an authentically personal slant to the poetry of his music. When Julia became the first authentic, charismatic female movie star in years, the rest of us cheered. We had recognized it first and like to take a little credit in helping her along.

Olympia and I paired off right away. Aside from the

fact that we were the comedy duo in *Steel Magnolias,* she was also involved with her cousin Michael Dukakis's bid for the presidency and had a little theater of her own back in New Jersey that she ran with her husband. We had much to discuss and more than much to laugh about. I liked to kid her that though we were contemporaries, she could still play my mother.

Sally Field had little Sam, her infant son, with her on location. His nanny handled him during the day, but all Sally's nonworking hours were spent with Sam.

Sally is an actress of incredible range and enviable technique. She has been in the business since she was a kid and knows what it's like to weather transitions of aging, sometime failure, and love affairs relating to work. She also has a practical, down-to-earth approach to life in Hollywood: her family comes first.

Dolly Parton spent most of her time writing songs and catching up on her music. For an inexperienced actress, she was amazing in her ability to cry on cue and know not only her dialogue but everybody else's. The temperature was 112 degrees in the shade and we were shooting Christmas scenes. There was Dolly with her high heels, thick wigs, and whatever else it took to turn her out, cool as a breeze, unperturbed by the physical discomfort. I've never seen Dolly without her wig; I don't know that anyone has. She came to the set made up and ready to work while the rest of us struggled with our reflected early-morning images in the mirrors of the makeup trailer.

When anyone flew off the handle or was cruel to someone else, Dolly would say, "He's suffering from not being enlightened." She kept her fabulous figure with a simple procedure. She took a plate full of food, then divided the food into three sections, one for her and two for the guardian angels that she said sat on her shoulders. She never touched their food because they needed nourishment in order to protect her. So deep was her belief in this procedure that it enabled her to retain her figure.

Daryl Hannah was a tall, lean, fairy-tale earth spirit. Sweet beyond words, kind and considerate out of the ordinary, she never ate much and was deeply involved with environmental concerns and the Contra-Sandinista wars in South America. She was living a tearing relationship with Jackson Browne at the time and very much respected his views on the world.

Daryl had her huge dog with her and rode horses whenever she could. She came from a wealthy family, but operated as though she had nothing, searching for flea-market bargains. She dressed as though she were a poignant refugee until the moment when she was called upon to be a glamorous star. Then the transformation was startling. Her underfed figure was suddenly poured into a gold lamé, skintight, sequined dress cut far above the knees, revealing exquisite legs, no hips, and a wasp waist. Huge chandelier earrings hung from her ears. Her hair was done in golden ringlets. Whenever all of us went out together, particularly when we attended premieres of our movie, Daryl was the one we waited for—not Dolly—not Julia—not me—not Sally or Olympia. She would undulate her way through the waiting paparazzi, turning their heads as though the rest of us were novices when it came to glamour. She always apologized for her tardiness, but fascinated us at the same time by describing how her anxious insecurity dissipated as she transformed herself into a movie queen.

So our gang of wonder women met, worked, and lived together. We cried, laughed, and teased together. I don't remember a moment of jealousy, envy, or proprietary behavior. In fact, each of us was more concerned for the others than we were for ourselves.

Herbert said our interpersonal security system was so balanced because we each loved and were satisfied with our parts. I think it was more, much more than that.

We knew we were part of a new feminine sensibility that was as efficient as that of men, but operated with a compassion and intuition that was much more effective. The crew noticed it right away. At first they wondered if we'd disintegrate from within, running afoul of the usual creative conflicts and differences. When we didn't, they began to truly study our ways. They saw how we came to each other's aid when one of us was in trouble with a scene. Sometimes we'd ask the director to leave us alone while we collectively rushed in to help our own. We covered for each other, we cooked for each other, we joked with each other, and we respected each other's privacy. It was an experience not unlike what people saw on the screen when the movie came out, only we weren't just in character, we were being ourselves.

The same thing happened when I made *Used People*. Our director was a young woman from England, Beeban Kidron. She had directed *Oranges Are Not the Only Fruit* for the BBC and won an award for it. She was as meticulous and caring as any man I'd worked with, but somehow I felt more comfortable in allowing myself to be opened and orchestrated by her. She sat right under the camera, witnessing every tear and nuance. I never felt invaded or exploited. Though she was younger than my daughter and had almost no experience, I trusted her opinion.

The creative impulses of women are different from those of men. They are more fluid, more flexible, more tentative, sometimes more difficult to understand and more in need of clarification. But women take the journey of depth and tend to do it together. Men tend to take the journey of efficiency and tend to accomplish it separately.

The actresses on *Used People*—Kathy Bates, Jessica Tandy, and Marcia Gay Harden—formed the same trusting bond that I experienced in making *Steel Magnolias*. We shared our lives, our loves, and our fears. For three months in Toronto, Canada, we were out of touch with the familiar stimuli of our lives. So we became friendly with each other. Again I marveled at the success of the female sensibility. Beeban had stamina that put the male crew to shame. Their respect for her was unlimited, and we actresses found it a new experience to strive to please a woman director. She was specific and almost always correct in her criticisms and objections. With a male director an actress harks back to pleasing Daddy. With a woman, somehow it is more of an equal endeavor.

Sometimes a member of the crew would challenge Beeban in a personally macho way. She was polite, but held steadfast to what she wanted.

Marcello Mastroianni, the male star of the film, adored being surrounded by women. Marcello is a debonair charmer who hated to rehearse, worked hard on his English, and essentially lived to have his five-course Italian meal regardless of what time we finished working. He discovered a homestyle Italian restaurant that would stay open for him until all hours. They served his favorite wine and had busts of beautiful women on the walls. Marcello had reached a point in his life where he desired only good company, good food and wine, and with luck a good script. Now and then he and I would talk deeply and personally about the loves in our lives, and how such relationships dovetailed with our work. We laughed about the time he and Faye Dunaway, who believed they were being successfully discreet, ran into Robert Mitchum and me on a London street. We believed *we* were being successfully discreet. And so the conversation led to the dilemma of falling in love with one's costar.

"One must love one's costar," said Marcello. "Otherwise how will the audience believe it?"

# 11
# MEN I HAVE LOVED
# . . . TO STAR WITH

have made over forty films, and therefore worked with over forty sets of co-stars. The kaleidoscope of their talents, their personalities, their senses of humor, their serious concerns, their wives, children, lovers, agents, and even parole officers definitely makes the real world civilianlike.

Learning to honor, appreciate, understand, revere, and even fall in love with a few of my leading men taught me more about myself than my marriage with Steve did. These relationships were often more intense and sometimes more intimate. When you make a film, you are confined to a certain set of personality combinations every day from five A.M. to nine P.M. for at least three months. And that's just while the film is shooting. The preshoot rehearsals and the postproduction (dubbing, reshoots, and publicity) round out to four or five months. If you don't fall in love, hate, or frustration, you must be dead. To make a film is a real commitment to yourself and the people around you. Out of that you learn how little you really know about yourself.

As in the mirroring effect of all relationships, I've seen so much of myself in each of the people I've worked with. Sometimes that was quite painful and I'm sure they've seen themselves in me. I don't know how to do them honest justice except to give a thumbnail sketch of how I spontaneously remember them.

DAVID NIVEN (*AROUND THE WORLD IN EIGHTY DAYS*) WAS WITTY and an excellent technician in both comedy and drama. But he intimidated me. When I arrived on location for *Eighty Days,* he was bitingly sarcastic about my being cast as a Hindu princess. I guess Mike Todd hadn't told him he wanted a *campy* Hindu princess. Mike, in his inimitable way, had uncovered some iconoclastic research that convinced him that the highest-caste Hindus had blue eyes and freckles. My red hair was perhaps going too far, however, so he made me dye it black.

Niven bought none of this, and for quite a few days treated me like an unwanted guest at a garden party. I was so new in the business, so eager to please, and feeling so lonely on location in the mountains of Durango, Colorado, that he really hurt my feelings. I never told him. I somehow needed to brave my way through it, and by ten o'clock every morning, after the Hindu makeup, hair, and costume were in place, I would have an attack of diarrhea. By the time I walked onto the set, I did not have the confidence to be imaginatively campy. I had a terrible time and in many ways blamed his standoffish, detached, droll Englishness for my insecurities.

I know he had no respect for me until the picture was

John Forsythe in *The Trouble with Harry*: Maybe he'll be my first and *last* leading man. Copyright © by Universal City Studios, Inc. Courtesy of MCA Publishing Rights, A Division of MCA Inc.

*Around the World in Eighty Days* with (left to right) Robert Newton, Cantinflas, and David Niven: This was Mike Todd's idea of camp.

*Hot Spell*: I don't know where the tears came from, but Shirley Booth said she was impressed.

*The Sheepman*: Glenn Ford let his horse christen my hat.

*The Children's Hour*: James Garner broke me up continually while we shot this scene. *Below*: I adored Audrey Hepburn and I miss her.

Jack Lemmon: The nicest man in Hollywood.

*Irma LaDouce*: Billy Wilder asked us to take exactly seventeen seconds out of this scene. Jack looked at the clock, and we did.

George C. Scott and Art Carney in *The Yellow Rolls Royce*: I had to introduce myself to both of them every day.

I brought Michael Caine to Hollywood—and then disguised myself for *Gambit*. Archive Photos

*Woman Times Seven*: This was the night Danny Kaye walked into our set and swept me away. Vittorio De Sica allowed it.

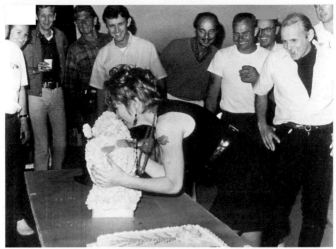

*Sweet Charity*: *Above*, Fosse actually took a break for birthday cake. (Makeup man Frank Westmore is the one with glasses.) *Below*, with Chita Rivera (left) and Paula Kelly (right). I just made sure I got out of their way.

The 1968 Democratic Convention: I was watching downtown-Chicago violence on my TV set.

1972: I am still proud to have worked for McGovern.

At a fund-raiser for Bella Abzug, with Elizabeth Taylor.

Fidel Castro later gave me one of his uniforms.

*Two Mules for Sister Sara* with Clint Eastwood: I loved Clint even though he was a Republican. Photofest

*Being There* with Peter Sellers: I wish Peter had told me we were having an affair. Archive Photos

*Above*, with Anthony Hopkins in *A Change of Seasons*: This was before we resolved our feelings for each other. *Below, Loving Couples*, with James Coburn: I had to go on a diet to fit into this dress.

*Terms of Endearment*: Starring and sparring with Debra Winger.

Photofest

Every take with Jack Nicholson was different and lovingly devilish.

Archive Photos

With Jack and Jim Brooks: It was all worth it!

*Steel Magnolias*: Olympia Dukakis and I became good friends
because we recognized ourselves in our characters.

*Postcards from the Edge*: Meryl Streep is the best in the world
to me. But Dennis Quaid isn't bad either.

With Marcello Mastroianni in *Used People*: "I don't understand your accent" became part of my character.

*Guarding Tess*: Nicolas Cage took my suggestions and then made me laugh.

Still on the stage after forty years and forty movies.

over and he saw that perhaps I might make it in the business after all.

When we starred together in *Ask Any Girl* some years later, his attitude had changed and so had mine. I had more confidence, and he let me see more of himself.

He had a beautiful wife named Hyördis, a tall and striking Swede. When she drank, she was quite free-wheeling with other men.

"Why don't you simply present your entire package, then?" David said to her one evening at dinner when she was embarrassingly flirtatious. He was hurt, and *she* was sarcastic and detached. I remember thinking I should look for the deeper understanding in everybody.

We went on to do our love scene the next day and David never missed his marks, was always in his light, was letter-perfect in his lines, but he never looked me in the eye. I could see why Hyördis tried to provoke him—not that that ever threw him off center. Years later, when I saw his performance in *Separate Tables,* I was ashamed I hadn't recognized the depth he was capable of as an actor.

JOHN FORSYTHE (*THE TROUBLE WITH HARRY*) WAS KINDLY and patriarchal to me. I was quite green about life, play, and work. John never had a problem with any of these three. In fact, nothing seemed to bother him.

John and I had love scenes together, but they were fey, in the spirit of the movie. I watched him through adolescent eyes (I was barely past nineteen) as he seemed to pursue a friendly relationship with a woman who ran a farm in the mountains of Vermont. I didn't know nor did I ask what the real nature of their relationship was. I remember wondering for the first time about faithfulness and monogamy in the movie business. Hitchcock wouldn't allow husbands on the set, and Steve and I had just gotten married. I wondered, were you expected to be solitary while on location if you were married? The crew didn't appear to be. In fact, there seemed to be an unwritten freedom clause in the location contract. Whatever happened happened. I felt immature and unsophisticated as I watched what went on around me. In reality, I was judgmental. I thought that people who flagrantly threw their marriage vows aside just because they were away from home were cheats. Oh boy, did I have a lot to learn.

John, on the other hand, was gracefully tolerant of everything. Later, I could see how he peacefully rode the waves of ten years of *Dynasty*. I loved seeing him become a white-haired, suave TV megastar, and he communicated his pride in me too. He wrote me a fan letter after I really hit it big. It was sweet, loving, and fatherly. But it never reached me. A secretary at the studio intercepted it, answered it, and sent him back a black-and-white glossy photo of me, signing it *Sincerely, Shirley MacLaine*. John brought the photo with him when he visited me backstage once in Las Vegas. I was mortified, but he smiled that knowing, understanding smile, just like a tolerant guardian. He was my first leading man, and as such was so tender with me.

GLENN FORD (*THE SHEEPMAN*) DECIDED I SHOULD LEARN TO smoke a cigar. I did and threw up. Then he put my cowboy hat under his horse to "christen" it.

Glenn *definitely* looked into my eyes, and told me his life story with women. I was fascinated, but frankly much more interested in the news that the ghost of Rudolph Valentino inhabited the house he lived in with Eleanor Powell. He said Valentino would sometimes move the furniture around and put on music that he had loved to tango to. Glenn loved the presence . . . Eleanor didn't. When I told him that Eleanor was my father's favorite star and dancer, Glenn was not amused. He was competitive with Eleanor. He hadn't resolved their split. But Glenn was a darling man with a dry sense of humor. We became good friends, though not as good as he'd have had some people think.

JAMES GARNER, WITH WHOM I MADE *THE CHILDREN'S HOUR,* is perhaps, except for Dean, the wittiest and funniest of all the men I have worked with. Our picture together was somber, but my sides ached at his off-camera comedic turns of phrase.

Jim seemed quite happily married in a way that allowed him to make delicious fun of his family life. In fact, his comedy took priority over everything else. Audrey Hepburn and I had to develop a certain disciplined resistance to his humor or we couldn't have settled into our serious onscreen friendship.

Audrey had a nobility of spirit and a sense of fawnlike fun that touches my heart to this day when I think of her. She possessed qualities of such rare richness that her penchant for perfectionism seemed simply a trifle. I used to wish I could have her style and talent for fashion. I felt gawky and unkempt around her, and I told her so. She said not to worry, she would teach me how to dress if I would teach her how to cuss. We made a deal that neither of us lived up to!

Jim Garner's day was made when he could break the two of us up in the middle of a dramatic bloodletting. (I have never understood why Jim didn't have his own comedy talk show.) Our director, William Wyler, feigned deafness whenever he saw Jim take control of our attention with his comedy. To him, we were childlike pretenders who were not tending to business.

•   •   •

JACK LEMMON, MY DARLING JACK, (*THE APARTMENT, IRMA La Douce*) is the epitome of what it means to be a nice person. He was always prepared, yet mischievously open for a good laugh. His genius was so riveting that I would often come in on my days off or stay late at night just to watch him cast his comic spell before the camera. I wished Billy Wilder would pay as much attention to my talent as he did to Jack's. But the attention had its downside too. Billy was so enamored of Jack that he pressed him to do take after take just to see what would happen. Jack, being the cooperative professional, complied, often to his own detriment. The later takes were forced, and often those were the ones Billy printed. I, on the other hand, only had to do it three or four times because frankly I don't think Billy thought I was capable of much more, but at least I stayed fresh.

Jack is a miracle of longevity. His staying power becomes more and more evident. He has a sad, befuddled quality that makes his talent for both comedy and drama so enduring. I remember the morning he got an Academy Award nomination for *Days of Wine and Roses*—I wanted so much to be recognized one day for having the talent to do both comedy and drama equally well, like Jack. His ego never overrode his nervous need to be better. I used to watch him at the end of every day holding a mug of martinis in his fist. He is a dear man who forever worried that he might not pass muster. I loved him for it because I knew how he felt. When I close my eyes today and see him holler "Magic Time" in my memory, I'm reminded yet again that he is the master of magic himself and a *real* friend. We have been looking for another film to do together. Hopefully we will find a good script before the magic is gone forever!

•     •     •

My OTHER JACK——JACK NICHOLSON——IS THE MAN WHOSE career I personally admire most. He has had the courage to remain in a perpetual state of experimentation, purposely flying in the face of what is expected and acceptable. When I saw his film *Five Easy Pieces,* long before I met him, I felt he was single-handedly ushering in a new style of acting, a brand-new spontaneity that seemed to indicate he was performing without a script. In fact, his performance in that film gave me a new lease on what I believed possible. I was an actress who fell in between the old, formal school of acting and the new school, which demanded the spontaneity of the decision making process.

When I learned that Jack's famous chicken-salad-sandwich scene in *Five Easy Pieces* was actually scripted, I realized that the intimidation of improvisation was not necessary. It was only a question of realistic tone. And when I finally worked with him in *Terms,* I saw how much of himself he was willing to throw away in order to risk the fullness of the unexperienced *now.* Each take with Jack was purposefully different. He reveled in perpetrating the unexpected. Planned response to Nicholson was not a good move—better to leave yourself open. Homework was better left at home. He challenged me to take a chance and not plan my moves or feelings. If he had a frog in his throat, he'd never mutter "cut" and stop the scene. He'd use it, play with it, and ultimately make it seem that the scene was written that way. If you could go along with his freedom, you'd be as good as he was.

There's a story about Jack that only contributes to my admiration for him.

He had a very small part years ago in *Ensign Pulver,* which Josh Logan directed. Logan was famous for needing a whipping boy to vent his anger and anxiety on. Nicholson fit the bill for some reason.

In front of the cast and crew, Logan attacked Nicholson one day, decrying Jack's talent, his physical appearance, and how he photographed. He finished the verbal lashing by suggesting that Jack seriously consider going into some other line of work because acting was definitely not a profession for which he possessed even a modicum of talent.

Jack said nothing. At lunch, a friend of his (who told me the story) approached Jack, asking how he felt and what he was going to do about Logan's harsh advice.

"I'm going to try harder," answered Jack.

He went on to do the now famous Roger Corman horror flicks and little by little learned to individualize his talent until he became one of the premiere actors of his generation.

I was impressed by Jack's stick-to-itiveness.

I think Jack sees life as basically absurd. He seems to be without vanity. He loved showing his middle-aged stomach in our picture and still manages to view himself as a devilishly dangerous sex object. Frankly, I'd like to see him play a woman. What a lesson in the art of controlled outrageousness that would be! She would probably be the woman I'd like to be one day. I thought Jack's best performances, however, were in *One Flew over the Cuckoo's Nest* and *Hoffa*. Never was there a greater range evident in an actor's talent. I was sitting next to him when he received his Lifetime Achievement Award from the American Film Institute. "I don't know what to say when I get up there," he said to me. "I've had every comedy writer in town up to the house, but none of that is me. I don't know. Why are they giving me this thing anyway?"

I was touched by Jack's feeling of undeservability. He

never liked to speak in public. Like many actors, he needed the camouflage of a character. When we went around the country accepting our awards for *Terms,* he was never comfortable, and on this AFI night nothing had changed. I sensed that his 1994 golf-club assault on a car that had cut him off was born out of anxiety over the Lifetime Achievement Award. He told me he felt deeply embarrassed and unworthy. His mouth trembled and his hands shook. When he finally rose to make his speech, something in him released his feelings. There were tears in his eyes. He stopped for a long moment, looked around the room, and actually said, "From now on I might fall in love with myself!"

He had allowed himself to reach the heart of the matter . . . his opinion of himself, which touched everybody in the room. He taught all of us that night that it was okay to be hesitant, to be publicly unaware, and finally to acknowledge that we all loved him.

RICHARD HARRIS (*WRESTLING ERNEST HEMINGWAY*) LIVES UP TO his reputation as a bombastic Irishman given to highflown, grand, eloquent stories. His bounce and vigor, his ornate emotional complexity belie a nature that is shrewdly involved with survival. He is great fun to be with until something triggers an insecurity. Then one understands the stormy Irish soul beneath. We had a love scene that involved his character's admission that he was impotent. It was a sensitive evening's shoot. I was playing an independent older woman who was nevertheless lonely and sexually frustrated. All sorts of jumbled thoughts went through my mind as I finally had the chance to play a love scene that involved senior citizens with juice. Flanks of sexy younger women darted across my brain. Would the public *want* to see gray-haired elders enact their conflicts? I couldn't remember having seen a real love scene between people over forty in years. Was this even in bad taste?

Richard was having his own doubts about this issue, which for an actor playing an impotent man I could only speculate upon.

He procrastinated and wouldn't come to the set.

I began to get tired. It was three o'clock in the morning and he had already had a run-in with the director.

I waited patiently as long as I could and then, with total insensitivity, I yelled, "Richard, get your butt in here so we can get this mutha and go home."

Reluctantly he slouched onto the set and tried his best. He was really quite wonderful even when he was over the top, but he had lost the belief in himself.

It took us another few hours and about ten more takes to wrap for the evening. Our relationship was not the same after that; neither of us felt good about our behavior.

To me, ROBERT DUVALL (*HEMINGWAY*) IS THE BEST ACTOR IN the world. To work closely with him, feel his artistry—and yet be engaged in a conversation about something as mundane as how to make corn bread right up until "action" is called—is to be in the presence of the true muse at work. He doesn't burden others with his presentation. He is singularly without self-indulgence. His curiosity, appreciation, and interest in others are what inform his work. He is self-questioning, with an aptitude for melting into the crowd, a tendency to forgo his own identity while remaining aware and sensitive to how he is affecting others. His genuine guilt at having hurt someone during a heated moment of conflict was very important to witness. He is the finest actor we have and one of the most unassuming.

Robert was playing a Cuban in *Wrestling Ernest Hem-*

*ingway,* and while we were rehearsing he took me to dinner at the home of a Cuban he had met in Florida. Robert melded into the man's family, watching and observing every move. I couldn't quite do that. I was still the movie star, and slightly apart. I longed to be able to abdicate my persona. Duvall was a little crazy in that he *had* to become Cuban. And when he rose from the table and began to tango (he's an expert at that too) I saw a Valentino in our midst. I watched his body and footwork become his entire focus. His eyes became possessed with the dance and its sexual intent. I had never imagined him this way.

I was witnessing a true artist—a human being capable of removing himself from himself. I wanted to be able to do that. I wondered if becoming dislocated from your central identity was necessary to accomplish such a transition. If so, I knew I didn't yet have the courage to get out of my own way and allow it to occur.

IN NICOLAS CAGE (*GUARDING TESS*), I EXPECTED AN UN-kempt, brooding, complicated, dark-spirited young man who was part of some cult even I had never heard of. This was the impression I had of him from *Moonstruck* and *Raising Arizona.* Instead I found a clean-cut, intent, and very respectful person who took his work and talent seriously and was more than fun off the set.

I watched him wonder if he could tease me without getting admonished. I was, after all, someone he had been looking at on the screen since he was a baby. I still thought of myself as thirty, of course, but I unhappily saw him relate to me as a motion-picture maven of maturity. I wanted to have fun and let him see that I wasn't some overrespected, ancient icon.

He got the message, and I was so grateful that he finally began to handle me with the same sense of unremitting play that he displayed with people his own age. As a matter of fact, I think he eventually saw me as somewhat more playful and less mature than his eighteen-year-old girlfriend! That made me feel so good, happy, and comfortable. The day he said, "You really have a crush on me, don't you?" I wanted to kiss him, but not for the reasons he might think.

GENE HACKMAN (*POSTCARDS FROM THE EDGE*) IS AN ACTOR I've always found romantically attractive. In fact, I told him so. Some years ago, at a party, he walked into a room and came over to me. There was a captivating sexuality about the way he did it. Sometimes a man's walk speaks volumes more than his words, and a woman's words speak more than her actions. I would have changed that if he'd have made the slightest suggestion.

PAUL NEWMAN (*WHAT A WAY TO GO*) IS A REALLY PLEASANT, but reticent friend. In real life, I've always had the feeling he wished he were somewhere else . . . racing cars probably. He enjoys speed and defying gravity. I watched him drink nearly a case of beer a day, do hundreds of push-ups and sit-ups, and after a steam bath, look as lean and trim as if he had been on a fast. Paul was a method actor back then with questions like "I need to know whether my character makes love with his boots on or not." When I suggested he probably made love *to* his boots, we got the scene.

Paul was one of the first actors to display political acumen and courage in his campaign for Gene McCarthy in 1972. He debated Charlton Heston on the evils of nuclear testing and won. He became a stable and well-informed voice for the moderate left of the Democratic party. I admire his social conscience, but more, I have deep respect for his graceful approach to aging, the longevity of his career, and the solidity of his marriage. He is a man who has defied all of the pitfalls of Hollywood.

RICHARD ATTENBOROUGH, NOW LORD ATTENBOROUGH (*The Bliss of Mrs. Blossom*), is a man of true gentility and style. His talents extend far beyond acting, and when we worked together in 1966, his mind and heart were already occupied with a picture he would ultimately direct, *Gandhi*. He wanted me to play Margaret Bourke-White. He was obsessed with putting the life of Gandhi on screen and talked continually about it. I wondered if I would ever feel that much committed passion for a project. He was turned down for twenty years by every studio in town, and when he finally got the money to realize his vision, I was too old to play the part. Candice Bergen did it. In Attenborough's (Dickie as we all called him) work, I saw a way to artfully entertain people while giving them a sociopolitical perspective on life.

As an Englishman who admits to guilt and responsibility for so much of his country's past, he is ennobling and not afraid of seeming sentimental in his unabashed liberal point of view. He seems to want to wipe the slate clean and put the past right.

When I saw *Cry Freedom,* I wept at his unrelenting courage, and when he failed with *A Chorus Line,* I learned that he needed to comprehend the authenticity of a given group of people more thoroughly in order for their universality to be felt by an audience.

How could he as an Englishman ever hope to get into the universe of a gypsy from Manhattan? Even Fosse would have had trouble—which he knew, by the way, because he turned the picture down. But Dickie, bless his soul, saw dancers as a metaphor for all human beings.

•　　•　　•

MICHAEL CAINE (*GAMBIT*) WAS A COCKNEY ACTOR; I HAD liked him in *The Ipcress File*. He tickled me with his dry, sardonic wit, and I asked him if he'd come to America and star with me in *Gambit*.

He came all right and cut a swath through the single girls in Hollywood like a rocket with no resistance.

He'd report for work after a hard night's play, stagger into his trailer, blast his Beatles records up to hyperspace, and try to get some sleep. Michael was funny about his Hollywood escapades. He was most confused by American panty hose. He couldn't figure a way to get into them, around them, or through them. I suggested he hang himself with them.

Michael is the actor who works more than any other in our business. He takes a part and finds a laugh at every corner. I'm so glad he never forgot his humble beginnings because that memory is the reason for the audience's continued identification with him. I will always feel proprietary about him because I brought him to America.

WORKING WITH PETER SELLERS ON *BEING THERE* STRETCHED even my imagination.

It began on Valentine's Day when we were on location in Asheville, North Carolina. I received five dozen red roses from an anonymous person, but I knew they were from Peter. We adored working together and enjoyed a common interest in metaphysics, numerology, past lives, and astrology. However, Peter could operate on the cusp of reality rather than in the full center of it. For example, the day after I received his roses I thanked him profusely, but he refused to acknowledge that they were from him. Taken aback, I called every possible man in my life to thank him, and found all of them to be honest and apologetic. Peter still refused to acknowledge his sweet gesture. Nor would he ever accept my invitation to lunch or dinner or anything personal for that matter. He did, however, tell me in detail of his love affairs with Sophia Loren and Liza Minnelli. I wondered about his lack of discretion but sometimes found his reenactments very funny.

A few months after our location, when filming was complete, I ran into a very prominent producer and his wife who asked me with a wink whether I had enjoyed my time with Peter. I didn't understand the innuendo and simply said our relationship had been a little detached personally but fine.

"What do you mean, detached?" she pried. "Come on, we know you and Peter had a fling."

My mind raced.

"A fling?" I asked. "He wouldn't even have a meal off the set with me."

The producer shook his head in disbelief. "Oh," he said. "Peter used to tell me many things about the joys of the love affair he was having with you. In fact, I've been in his presence when he was whispering sweet nothings to you on the telephone."

I couldn't believe what I was hearing.

"Then he was whispering to a dial tone," I said. I explained about the roses, the refused lunch and dinner invitations, and his total immersion in the character of Chauncey Gardiner in the film.

The producer nodded his head knowingly.

"I see," he said. "Don't you?"

"See what?" I asked.

"Well," he went on, "Peter had fantasized a reality with you that would have been shattered had there been personal and real contact off the set. He needed the reality of life to be separate from his fantasy."

It made sense. Sometime later I ran into Sophia. She

told me the same thing had happened with her. "I know the men I've slept with," she said. "And Peter, bless his phantasmagorical mind, was not one of them."

The relationship with Liza seemed to be true, however.

I remember our last day's shoot together. We were sitting in the backseat mock-up of a limousine. Peter had been to a numerologist the night before. Looking into my eyes, he told me that the numerologist had warned him that his wife's numbers didn't match his own numbers. Peter was clearly most concerned about this information. I didn't realize then what was really happening in his head.

Within the next few weeks, he divorced his wife. Later, when I realized the fantasy he'd harbored about me, I felt somewhat responsible.

Peter was an actor extraordinaire. He inhabited his various characters in such a deep way that, I now believe, they came from his past life experience and inhabited him.

GEORGE C. SCOTT (*THE YELLOW ROLLS-ROYCE*) WAS ADDICTED to chess. Perhaps he was using it as inspiration for his character (a gangster)—I don't know. I couldn't find out because he never talked. We starred together for a few months and never exchanged more than a "good morning," if that. He was very much in character, impeccable with his lines, but he talked only to his makeup man. George would wander over to him after every camera setup to complete the chess move he must have decided in his mind during our take.

George and I have become friendly since our picture together, and he doesn't even remember that we worked together really, which proves to me once again that a working relationship and a personal one do not necessarily overlap or coincide in any way. An actor's emotions are not grounded or even sound-minded when he or she is working. It's as though they belong to the character rather than to the actor. Often actors or actresses can look back at their behavior on a film and deny their actions. Their memories are faulty because they were, in effect, operating from an altered perception of reality.

I FOUND THE SAME TO BE TRUE WITH ANTHONY HOPKINS. We did a film together called *A Change of Seasons*. He was insecure about playing comedy. Hopkins couldn't find a comedy rhythm that satisfied him in the picture and came to me for help.

I found myself harking back to the lessons of energy I learned from Fosse. I tried to be sensitive to Tony's needs, fully cognizant of what an extraordinary actor he was (and is).

We talked for a long time, and when he left my trailer I thought we had found an important level of professional communication. But I must have read something wrong; there was something in him I missed. Perhaps I was "too" helpful in my suggestions for comedy to a brilliant dramatic actor. I was confused and sad to see that Tony retreated and basically didn't talk to me for five weeks. When we did our scenes together, the director had to interpret what we wished to say to each other. Our relationship became tense and subtly hostile. I didn't like Tony and he didn't like me. He thought I was aggressive, opinionated, insensitive, and in general obnoxious. I felt the same way about him.

We played a husband and wife who had a silent war going on between them as each pursued an extramarital affair, so our real-life behavior was not without merit, yet this way of living inside a character is, as I've said, a technique I find difficult to work with or sustain. It feels self-indulgent to me. That is my problem, of course, not that of my partners, who might find it necessary and contributive to work that way. Perhaps it means I don't commit totally to the project. Whereas some actors are willing to give their lives over in totality, I insist on holding on to my center and my ego so that I know who I am after six o'clock.

I spoke to Dickie Attenborough about Hopkins, wondering if the problem was something I misunderstood in the English character and culture.

"No," he said, "when I directed him in *Magic,* he was brilliant, but the same thing happened, wouldn't talk to me for weeks. But he'll come to you one morning on bended knee and ask your forgiveness. He's really *okay,* you know."

I appreciated that conversation, and just as he predicted, about halfway through the film Tony came to me with tears in his eyes and apologized. I accepted, apologized myself for not understanding, and we were fine. He said he didn't know why he broke communication and I believed him. Tony's personality was so multidimensional that sometimes he must have gotten lost in his various moods. I didn't understand that completely because I'm not capable of giving my own dimensionality full range as an actor. I'm not as good an actor as Hopkins. Perhaps that is why I was so judgmental of his acting approach. But to me, personal, real-life communication was the top priority. I didn't feel that the end justified the means. The process of the experience was supposed to be where the learning lay. But I couldn't figure out what I was meant to learn from what was happening.

I'd glance over at Hopkins, sitting in a chair, eyes closed, deep within himself, either preparing for a scene or literally existing somewhere else. He had not talked to me for weeks. The crew shouted orders around him, the makeup person touched up his face, hair and wardrobe people fiddled with strands and lint, and Tony never moved. He was focused within on something beyond my comprehension, and as much as it irritated me, I was awed by it. I wanted to understand what was going on, but even with his apology I felt shut out. When the film ended and we parted, so much was unresolved for me. I wondered if he felt the same way. There was nothing I could do to force an understanding. I'd have to accept things as they were.

Then, years later, I saw Tony's frightening performance as Hannibal Lecter in *Silence of the Lambs*. I thought back to our experience together. His capacity to scale the ranges of human behavior was unparalleled. I dreamed of him that night. The next day we were on the same plane together. We acknowledged each other but didn't talk. Two days later, we were placed next to each other at an awards luncheon in California. We posed for pictures together, whispering that the photographers had no idea how phony our smiles were.

We spoke in general terms about movies, acting, our film together, a few old times . . . but we said nothing that addressed our problems together, nothing of substance. I still felt unsatisfied, but I was glad we were finally getting along. He was elusive yet pleasant and so was I.

A few years after that, I was at a party in Hollywood. Out of the corner of my eye I saw Tony moving around graciously and happily from guest to guest. I couldn't take my eyes off him. I knew I needed to speak to him . . . to tell him how extraordinary his work had been in *Remains of the Day* and *Shadowlands*.

Without thinking, I walked up to him, touched his

arm, and told him how much I admired not only his recent work on the screen but his blazing honesty in the interviews he had been giving. He had talked so candidly about his drinking days and the discomfort he realized he had caused others. I congratulated him also on the freedom he seemed to have achieved in his soul, which left him open to portray his screen and stage characters with no inhibiting restrictions or blockages. His eyes filled with gratitude and appreciation. He took my hands. "Yes," he said, "I'm different now than I was during the time with you." His expression was deep yet filled with a kind of reverent joy.

"What happened?" I asked. "You've found something. Do you mind my asking what it is?"

He reared his head back and laughed. The laugh was completely unaffected, as though no agenda was hidden underneath it. I remembered seeing the Dalai Lama laugh like that. I couldn't understand the total freedom in that musical sound and sparkling smile. It was the "laugh of the charismatic" that I had read about. The laugh that surpasses all logical reason and seems to come from some divine source.

"Look," said Tony, taking one of my hands in his. "You know how I have suffered from my insecurities and anxieties, anger, rage, and so on." I nodded.

"And," he went on, "I stopped drinking and joined AA and got into the twelve-step program. I seemed to search futilely for what they called my higher power, but I couldn't find it. I was miserable, continually upset with myself and everyone else, even though I had a support system and I was sober."

Tony hesitated. "You won't think I'm crazy?" he asked.

"Me?" I answered. "You're asking me if *I'll* think an experience of yours is crazy? Hardly."

He relaxed and proceeded to tell me about an experience he had had during a five-day break from shooting on location in Colorado. He had gotten in his car and driven north. He said he didn't know where he was going and didn't care.

Soon he found himself at Bear Lake. He sat beside the lake, wondering what life was all about, when suddenly he looked up.

"It was incredible," he said. "There were two hawks flying overhead. Suddenly they weren't moving. They stopped in midair. In fact, time stopped. Nothing moved."

As he spoke he seemed to be reliving the experience so intently that I could see the lake, the hawks, the sky, the stop-frame of time.

"Then," he said, "it happened. A feeling of complete knowingness came over me. I was everything around me. Everything around me was me. I understood emotionally and spiritually for the first time what it was like to feel one with everything. It lasted no longer than a few seconds, but it was so profoundly moving that I knew my life was altered forever."

Tony looked into my eyes, wondering at my reaction. I felt my eyes fill with tears. "I wish that would happen to me," I said. "I understand it intellectually, but I've never experienced it emotionally."

"Yes," he said. "I know you've been searching for that. Maybe you're searching too hard."

He was right. My search could be so relentless that I might walk right by what I had found.

"Did it stay with you?" I asked.

Tony laughed that laugh again. "At first," he said, "I thought, Well, I've had a mystical experience, that's all. It'll be over in a few hours. But no. First I broke down and sobbed, then I laughed for an hour, then I cried again. I *was* everything and I felt everything. Then a voice inside of me said, 'Now get on with it. You've found this. Get on with your life.' I guess I got on with it, and now I laugh most of the time.''

Tony and I stood looking into each other's eyes. I was completely happy being with him in the bustling midst of that party. I didn't want those moments to be over. I didn't want to leave him. I didn't want either one of us to move on to other guests.

With a connection that moved us both, we embraced, pulled apart, then embraced again. This was the man I had found so impossible. What an ironic laugh on me.

"I surrendered," he said. "I know now that my life is not up to me anymore. It's up to the God in me."

I gazed at him. I had never heard an actor talk like that, much less an English actor. They are usually so intellectually oriented, so ready to scoff at anything spiritual. But this man was different. Because he had been difficult, he had come to a new understanding. Because he had felt the depth of despair, he could embrace its opposite.

We stood there together for a magical half hour. We had not only resolved our differences but had come to the understanding that all alone, we each had been looking for the same thing. I had perhaps not been as difficult, but I wasn't going as deep either. Out of his "difficultness" he had found the answer.

Before we parted that night, I asked him how he had found working with Debra Winger in *Shadowlands*.

He reared back and laughed again. "Oh yes," he said. "Her. Well, of course, we English won't put up with behavior that is not about the work."

"So?" I asked. "How did you handle her?"

"I laughed," he said. "I just laughed whenever she

was impossible. And I guess I liked her. Perhaps because I understood. She was *okay* really. Yes, I liked her.''

So Tony Hopkins (Hannibal Lecter, repressed butler, guarded Welsh intellectual) gave me my most important lesson in creativity. It all comes from God, regardless of how ragged its expression.

I WAS IN PARIS SHOOTING *WOMAN TIMES SEVEN* WITH VITtorio de Sica directing and male costars who were legendary: Vittorio Gassman, Michael Caine, Philippe Noiret, Lex Barker, Alan Arkin, Rossano Brazzi, and Patrick Wymark.

We were shooting at night, on the street, when Danny Kaye walked right into the shot. I had never worked with him. But I remembered him as the standoffish, funny genius on the Paramount lot when I worked there with Dean and Jerry and Shirley Booth.

In the way that show-business people have of ignoring social decorum when we see each other in public places, Danny walked right by the other actors, made his way toward me, and proceeded to gather me up in his arms and emit a stream of French double talk that completely disrupted the shooting, enchanted De Sica and the crew, and alleviated my anxiety about a scene I wasn't too fond of anyway.

He was wearing a combat jacket, his famous custom-made space shoes, and a funny hat. His blue eyes sparkled with wit and mischief, and I was captivated.

After the night work he took me to his favorite cheese-and-wine shop and I returned to my hotel at dawn. We had talked for four hours.

He showed me parts of Paris I never knew were there, and as he was leaving to return to New York, he asked me if I would be his copilot across the Atlantic! I said I had to work the next night. He told me he wanted to cook me a Chinese dinner in his favorite restaurant in lower Manhattan and he'd have me back in Paris in time for my night call the next day.

I did it and I told no one. Danny and I flew across the Atlantic in his Learjet. He let me take the controls. I was in heaven, literally. Flying so high with some guy in the sky was enough to write a song about. It was romantic, professionally mischievous—we were not allowed to fly because of insurance concerns—and my idea of liberation.

We landed in New York, where a car met us and took us to Chinatown. When Danny arrived, it was like the return of Sun Yat-sen or something. All the cooks left the kitchen and he took over.

The dinner was incredible, terminating with fortune cookies that said, *Woman who fly upside down when making picture have crack-up.* We ate for hours, visited some nightspots, and without sleeping, he flew me back to Paris. It was a globe-hopping spontaneous romantic dream. Everything Danny did was bigger than life and more expertly expressed than most mere mortals could ever hope to achieve.

Yet he had been born David Daniel Kaminski in Brooklyn. He showed me the house he grew up in. It was a mundane beige-yellow box squeezed in between others like it.

From this he had invented himself, the phenomenon that was Danny Kaye.

That was when I began to understand on a deep level how necessary the golden threads of fame and identity could be.

To suggest that Danny Kaye would ever do anything to jeopardize the monument that his wife, Sylvia, and he had carved for themselves in the halls of human history would be ridiculous. I was beginning to see what prisoners of fame and self-invention we could become. It was even more than that. When you become a Danny Kaye, you are profoundly attached to the component parts that have helped create your identity. Your wife, your material, your coworkers, your support systems are necessary to sustain your success. Your charismatic identity is so firmly fixed in the firmament that change of any kind would threaten a swift descent.

I could see why Danny Kaye needed to sustain the support systems that guaranteed the continuance of his gifts. I began to understand why these megastar talents always put themselves first and foremost in the mix of human intercourse. I could really understand why a Danny or a Frank Sinatra took for granted that they were star suns around whom everyone else *should* orbit. It was their moment in the universe to shine brighter than the others, and I felt they *should* be protected so they could live up to their destinies. They were not John Q. Public. This time around they were meant to be special.

I could even see that it would be sacrilege if any one of these star suns denied his or her luminosity for the sake of marriage, or children, or a relationship. Frankly, I don't think such sacrifices would last long anyway. Star suns are meant to shine and provide light for others. They are not *like* others. Something in their souls is willing and indeed determined to live out such a destiny regardless of the personal price, a price the rest of us are not willing to pay. Husbands and wives and children must adjust to their needs and self-centeredness. Perhaps, in some other time and place, these stars would receive luminosity from those who do not shine now.

Many people felt Danny Kaye was aloof—cold, tyrannical, and insensitive. I did not experience that. On the contrary. Perhaps he was personally unfulfilled, whatever that means. But aren't we all? I think Danny and I saw that in each other. Most other women he knew had obligations and responsibilities that fulfilled their need for security and a contract for the future. I was free and unencumbered, willing to go anywhere and do anything for a lark. Barbecued ribs in Texas or a cheese fondue in Switzerland was a reason to build a trip around. I felt I had my own Ali Baba magic carpet and Danny was the captain of space travel.

But more than anything, Danny loved conducting a symphony orchestra. "It is a feeling of complete and total power," he'd say. "They do what I want because of a flick of my wrist or a nod of my curly head. . . . Power."

Perhaps that was the feeling he was reaching for . . . the feeling of power that would protect him from helplessness.

Contrary to most opinion, I felt that Danny allowed his insecurities to be seen, at least to me he did. Because of those insecurities, he was aware of the sensibilities of others, and because of that he sometimes acted like an autocrat. He was forever counseling others who were in trouble either physically or mentally, but he insisted that they obey his suggestions completely. Because of his medical expertise (he was known to have actually performed surgical operations because of his extensive knowledge of the human body and his dexterous fingers) many people did exactly what he recommended regardless of how autocratic his behavior was.

Danny Kaye knew he was a slave-driving perfectionist, compelled to isolate himself in the cocoon of his own genius as he drove those around him to be as brilliant as he. His wife, Sylvia, who wrote all his material and oversaw his life, was the landlady of his territory. She knew about our love affair, I'm sure, and lovingly included me in their lives. She understood that Danny was a master manipulator and that part of his fundamental brilliance was his towering talent to tell tall tales! He told me he had learned all he knew about sex in China—a concubine had educated him, he said. I have to assume she taught him how to cook too, because his Chinese dinners, chopped, cut, prepared, tossed, and served by Danny in his Chinese kitchen at home, were prized invitations in Hollywood. I used to love to go there when Betty Comden and Adolph Green, Gene Kelly, and Judy Garland would gather around the piano and sing new material. If the rest of us liked it, it stayed in whatever show or movie they were making. If not—not.

Yes, Danny was dazzling, but to me he was a flawed and often lonely friend who longed for understanding, awareness, and ever-widening avenues to express himself. He invented complicated new dishes at my house until my own cook refused to allow him in "her" kitchen anymore. One dish in particular was my favorite, chicken baked with peaches. It was succulent and sweet. I remember watching his fingers as he concocted something adventurous. They were sensitive, graceful tentacles searching for the perfection he longed to mold, sculpt, and paint.

While Danny "overincluded" me in the circle of friends in his home, which often made me uncomfortable around Sylvia, it was my problem, not hers. It was also true that he wished us to spend a great deal of time with Laurence Olivier, who was inferred to be one of his lovers. I know nothing of that. I only know that we spent many happy times together. When we decided to part, we wept.

"I am desolate at saying good-bye to anything or anyone I have ever loved," he said.

I understood then that whoever and whatever had

helped him achieve his radiance in the world would be a permanent fixture in his heart. He might never acknowledge them directly. His way of thanking them would be to go on in much the same way he always had until his light in the sky dimmed from above, not from within.

## 12

# STARRING IN
# REEL LOVE

here is a moment just before start-
ing a film that is more electrically
charged than any other. It is not the
first take on the first day or the last
take on the last day. It is the mo-
ment when the male star meets the female star. It drips
with voyeuristic interest. The director, producer, wardrobe and makeup people, and writer observe, as though
invisible, the chemistry that may or may not explode
between the two.

In real life, when two attractive people meet the moment is not so charged with titillating expectation. They
just meet, and the moment passes—usually.

But people in films carry another aura around with
them. A $35-million film can depend on the chemistry
between two people who will be spending every waking
hour together for at least three or four months.

The meeting usually happens in the producer's office, or sometimes in a rehearsal room, or if you're lucky, at dinner, where you can be alone and talk about the survival wars and the personal prices that have added up. There is an admiration for your partner because you know something of what he has been through too. At ground zero level you know that both of you live to be loved or you wouldn't be stars. You are simultaneously adult survivors and needy children. Civilians don't live with such striking contradictions. That's why they are different.

We actors are acutely aware that the professional people in Hollywood who have seen it all in movies are basically still civilians. They sit behind the camera and scrutinize us "beautiful people" who are commissioned to play out their romantic dreams. But we don't feel beautiful. On the contrary. We are anxious beyond words and terrified that we won't live up to the expectations of not only the producer and company, but of the person we will be playing with as well. We know we possess something that other people feel is charismatic, a kind of indefinable chemical secret. But we don't know what that secret is. When the producer and director and others watch us meet, we know that they feel they will never be like us, never feel what we feel, never be adored as we are. *But* we also know that they are secure that they will never tremble at the hazards of laying themselves open to critical and public ridicule. So we understand the trade-off is that they are there to protect those of us who do lay ourselves bare. They are there to appreciate and sometimes envy us. But they are also there because we are doing "it" for them.

And so the "god and goddess" of the screen meet.

Immediately there is some kind of interaction. It is never a neutral meeting because stars wouldn't be stars unless there was an intense, irresistible energy flowing. Immediately there is an unspoken dance of territorial imperative, a kind of subtle power stakeout. You evaluate experience both professional and personal. You admire, you estimate, you appraise, and you assess your partner against predetermined judgments. You try to be objective. You have seen most of his work, so you discreetly compare what you've seen with what you see in front of you. And while all of this is going on you know you are a woman and he is a man. You are human, with unconscious and involuntary yearnings. You are not yet really involved with the script, but your belief in the love story lurks at every moment beneath the surface of this first meeting.

Sometimes you find you are playing opposite a man you cannot bear to be around, but that is rare—very rare. Hollywood's legendary conflicts such as Jeanette MacDonald–Nelson Eddy and Tony Curtis–Marilyn Monroe do occur, but the contrary is usually the case. The leading lady and leading man often find themselves swept up in a centripetal force too strong to deny and too sweet to give up. Everything surrounding them conspires to bring them together.

First there is the script. You believe what you have read or you wouldn't be in the film. Second, when acting is superb, it is real. You have to *mean* it when you say I love you. You know that simplicity is the key to any scene, any dialogue, any interaction.

That might be when it actually begins. I don't know. For me it was usually when my partner had acknowledged *me* in the love scene. I was never attracted to actors who fell prey to the seduction of the fantasy, seeing me as the character in the scene. To me that was adolescent and it left the real me out. I liked a partner who used the story as a catalyst to know himself better and as a result was able to see me.

There is much to be learned from the characters we play. They inspire us to know nooks and crannies of ourselves and discover how to face the unexplored. They act as mirrors, teaching us why we were drawn to them in the first place. There are, I have found, almost always aspects of ourselves that are yearning to be acknowledged and dealt with.

So to have a love affair on the screen requires an abstract courage that quite often becomes specific in real life. To deal with its power and turbulence can be professionally unsettling. There's the sleep problem. The energy required to get through the schedule of making a film is debilitating enough. But to "fall in love" and lose sleep over it is a manic experience. It's not just the lost hours of peaceful rest. It's the fragmentation of focus. It's the feeling of psychological dislocation. It is paramount to keep your center when working. Being "in love" is a bi-locational "frame of heart." You find yourself compelled to act your love impulses as *you* feel them rather than as the character feels them. This is not professional, nor is it good for the authenticity of the picture.

When you are in love with your costar, your deeper human honesty, the *real* you, sparkles and twinkles regardless of how dissimilar those qualities may be to the character's qualities. This is not good. If you're a first-time actress, it doesn't matter so much, but if it's incumbent upon you as an experienced actress to be "in" your character, you can't be besotted with your costar. It can be deeply discombobulating! To be in character does not mean being yourself.

Comparing notes with other actresses, I have found the most troubling aspects of a movie love affair to be not only disturbance of badly needed sleep, but the inevitable question of equal turf. A completely objective professional working relationship allows the personal requirements for equal time and space to be voiced ipso facto—no problems.

But when we as actresses go spiraling off into the love swirl with our partners, we tend to abdicate our hard-won female rights as costars. We tend to refrain from putting our feet down on a point of principle or artistic disagreement. We find ourselves so busy being attractive and decidedly "un-actressy, un-bossy, and un-smart" that as professionals we are not pleased with ourselves. We know the reputation we actresses have—overbearing, aggressive, competitive, unyielding, and focused on self. Therefore, when we are "in the love swirl," we revert to what our mothers or men in our lives have taught us about sustaining appeal. We become cute, shy, subservient. We make no demands. This is professionally stupid.

Actors are not above using this well-known response to their advantage, deliberately seducing actresses. It happens the other way around too. The idea is . . . make your costar fall in love with you and you end up with things your way.

To me this has always been obvious, and consequently a giant turnoff.

But when my costar finds me genuinely lovable and peers deep into the recesses of my soul in order to know more about me, I am a sucker for the love swirl.

We surrender vulnerability on so many levels when we act in a movie. We surrender our feelings, our barriers, and our self-protection. So do our partners. This is precisely why the potential for soul connection emerges. Perhaps we play roles less in the process of making a film than we do in real life. In movies, our emotional territory is always new and the role-playing is transient.

The difference between our work and other kinds of work is that we *allow* the manipulation of our emotions and feelings as a means to an artistic end. We throw up our hands in unconditional surrender and say, "Here I am. Use me, sculpt me, orchestrate me, but please love me."

Therefore, we become totally vulnerable as we witness our partner do the same. Nothing is more attractive. It is a raw, unadorned divesting of self. It is an indomitable act of trust. It is a perfect environmental breeding ground for Love.

The memories of love affairs sparked by screen romances are still with me, reignited into feeling by a song or the weather or a familiar smell. How volatile the terrain of romance was when I was young. How reckless and explorative was I, new in the movie kingdom. I thought I knew just what I wanted and who I was. I had my "feet on the ground," yet my head was "in the stars"—a metaphor of my mother's that, for some reason, she felt was an axiom to live by.

Only now do I realize how much loneliness contributed to my colorful life. Only now do I understand the power of romantic attraction born out of a feeling of isolation from myself.

Why was the loneliness so profound? I don't know. I had a reasonably loving and attentive childhood, which, on the face of it, should have prepared me for the "big time." But no one can be prepared, regardless of background, for the illusions that seduce and alter the logical well-grounded mind.

I have seen it over and over as the years pass, and only because I went through it do I understand the price such exquisite distortion can exact.

I watch young actors and actresses today—and even some middle-aged ones—struggling with what is real and what is not. It has been ever thus, I suppose, when one works and lives in the land of altered reality . . . Hollywood.

On a soundstage you create a life and environment of such real intensity that the outside world seems a hoax. On a soundstage you are attended and appreciated and, because of that security, are challenged to experience aspects of yourself that heretofore have gone unrealized. Because of the catering and coddling and cuddling, you never feel threatened or jeopardized to venture into areas where angels fear to tread. You feel invincible, free to recklessly abandon yourself to the fantasy of the moment and the relationship that has been prescribed for you in the script. You find yourself interrelating with the most attractive people in the world, people who have survived their own wars of unreality and stand opposite you emotionally triumphant—nothing can faze them anymore. This is a chemistry hard to resist.

And so you begin a work relationship that depends entirely upon the sharing of feeling. And when feelings are shared, there is a bonding. And with bonding there is involvement, and with involvement there is love. Thus the waters of reality become murky.

I have had these feelings more than once. It is difficult for marriages and other long-term relationships to survive the narcotic fantasies of movie relationships. The emotional illusion coupled with the separation demands of a location put a strain on a primary relationship that is difficult to withstand.

There you are, cradled together, sometimes on a foreign location, playing lovers because the script demands it, finding values that are peculiarly personal to enliven the onscreen chemistry, continuing to be together long after working hours are over because it's comforting. . . . All of these elements inevitably lead to a shared trust that is just right for what is required creatively. Then you begin to live your creative illusion and you see how fine is the line between your life and what you are creating on the screen. Your illusion carries you along until your feelings are beyond your control. The illusion has a life that is determined to be its own, and you are, in effect, its servant.

All of this was at work when I met Robert Mitchum and we did *Two for the Seesaw*.

Mitchum had been a childhood movie hero of mine, a broad-shouldered, barrel-chested, macho, gentle giant of a man who resorted to violence only when profoundly provoked. I loved those qualities in him. What I wasn't prepared for was how much of an underachiever he was. I was fascinated by a man who seemed to have no ambition, no dreams to fulfill, no drive to prove anything to anybody. It was a case of opposites attracting when he walked into the small office on the Goldwyn lot. I stood up and looked into his face. He shook my hand.

"Don't let me take up too much space," he said. "I'm basically a Bulgarian wrestler. I'm not right for this part."

"You're wonderful," I said. "I've admired you for so long—I think you'll be great."

He lit one of his Gitane filtered cigarettes and inhaled deeply. As yet he hadn't looked me full in the eyes. I wondered why. He pulled the cigarette out of his mouth as he exhaled the smoke, leaving a thin trace of white cigarette paper stuck to his lips. I watched, fascinated. Was he aware of it? He wasn't. He let it fade away naturally. I noticed his fingers and hands were well used. A small bone poked out of the top of one of his thumbs.

He walked across the room with a rolling swagger and sat down. Then he looked up at me.

"Hey," he said, "I've got a broken nose, and I can change a tire without help. I'm nothing but a goddamn mechanic. If I can be a movie star, anyone else can be a king. . . . But why you want me for this part is your problem."

The die was cast. I willingly fell into the role of rescuer, saving him from himself. It gave me something to do . . . unlock the great Mitchum so the world could witness what gold there was underneath.

Over the three years that our relationship flourished, I found him to be a complex mystery, multifaceted, ironically witty, shy to the point of detachment, and incapable of expressing what he personally desired. . . . Perfect . . . He became a project.

His intelligence was a trait he orchestrated cannily, doling out clues to it just at the moment he felt he was being taken advantage of unfairly.

But usually his modus operandi was to act as if life just kept happening to him. He felt no responsibility for anything, really. He said he was a lucky bum, basically a hobo who rode the rails as a kid, got himself arrested for vagrancy, and when he needed to work, did so by washing dishes or pounding sheet metal at the Lockheed plant. He said he'd been in jail three times, usually for some disturbance, nothing really serious, so he was technically an ex-con who had trouble traveling without permission.

He saw himself as a common stiff, born to be lonely, who should expect nothing from life except that the roof doesn't leak. He told me once, "When I awake in the morning and pee and it doesn't burn, I figure it's going to be a good day."

He called actors who primped in front of the mirror

"girls" and feigned disinterest in what might be a good script for him. He was more likely to go fishing with a stranger than to talk deals with a big producer.

He responded with humor and sarcasm when actresses spent other people's time primping in a mirror before a take. He had an appreciation for what the camera demanded, but was privately appalled at the makeup and powder applied to his face before a take. He would mutter under his breath that he felt like a primping asshole.

When we began to work together, I realized immediately it would be an experience like no other.

He made me feel that it was incumbent upon me to draw out his sensitivities and prove to him that it was safe to express them. He had a way of teasing me with just enough poetic artistry that I felt I'd be missing the adventure of a lifetime if I just did my job and walked away from what I intuitively knew was a deep and stormy fragility. All in all he was an exquisite challenge. And I went for it, in a big way. I think many other women before me had done the same, although he vehemently denied it. When I questioned him about his past relationships with women, he appeared vaguely stunned, as though the thought had never crossed his mind. He refused to relate to such a concept, almost as though such behavior occurred only among lesser mortals. He was an elitist and a commoner simultaneously. "Hell," he said, "I've never even known if a woman dug me. I'm just trying to get through the day. If they say I have an interesting walk or something, I just say, 'Shit, I'm only trying to hold my gut in.' " This was one of his favorite self-deprecating lines.

But he seemed to like and respect women, sometimes saying, "They are better men than me, Gunga Din." Robert was so obtuse and vague that I found myself addicted to the quest for clarity in our relationship. I would sometimes ask him what time it was just to have the thrill of a specific answer!

His favorite drinking story to promote romance (I suspect) was his escape from the chain gang. He has told it many times, in print, on television, and to me. It basically goes like this.

He described himself as a hobo, riding the rails and sleeping in trains whenever he got the chance. I could never quite get clear *why* he was living a life of such vagrancy. But at any rate, he got arrested for vagrancy and was sentenced to a chain gang in Georgia. He was shackled next to "some poor nigger" with whom he became friendly. He spoke with casual yet searing drama about the pain, the pus and infection the shackles caused him.

I would sit entranced by his explicit description of the humiliation of being chained to his bed at night. I didn't know whether to believe Robert or not. But when he went on to describe his bleeding and blistered ankles, how he tried to stuff cloth and old newspapers between his skin and the shackles, and how the guards caught him and said that the pain was part of the punishment, he had me—but good. I wanted to reassure him that this would never happen again. When he got to the part about his escape from the chain gang, I had the impression that I was hearing a well-rehearsed prose reading engineered to solicit sympathy and a kind of romantic horror in both men and women. The men would think he was a man's man and the women would desire to mother him. It really worked, and to this day I feel the story is true, if overdramatized.

Apparently the guards had taken pity on him, allowing him to do his chores without the chains. The image of Mitchum chained was surely enough to evoke pity in the most sadistic of prison guards, and he had an exquisite hangdog expression that worked in many situations.

Mitchum can lumber and stumble (his preferred body movement, I think) until you believe he's profoundly helpless. It's at such a moment that he makes the shrewd, unpredictable move. Right out from under you he can bolt, which is what he did—right into the dense Georgia woods. He described "feeling like a nigger being chased right before they lynched him." He ran zigzag so the bullets missed him. (I couldn't see Mitchum running fast, much less zigzagging.) But anyway, I sat mesmerized, as though I were in the woods with him. As though it were my *place* to be there with him. There I was crawling on my belly with him, my own legs leaking pus as I oozed my way through mud and gunk. Darkness descended. I heard crickets and owls. The full moon hung in the purple sky. I wondered if there were wolves in Georgia. We covered ourselves with dried leaves and twigs and branches and tried to sleep, wondering if the guards would accost us at sunup. "Nobody will come after us," said Robert, trying to whisper in his stentorian voice. "They'll just go after some other poor nigger to fill their quota on the chain gang."

When the sun came up, we found ourselves mired in a foul-smelling swamp with dozens of predatory water moccasins slithering around us. I could feel them on my skin. It made me shiver to the bone with fear. "Don't worry," said Robert, "they are as afraid of us as we are of them." We pulled ourselves up and began to walk knee-deep in the swamp. He said he wanted to get to a city to find a drugstore for medicine, but he didn't have any money, so he couldn't afford it anyway. My heart turned over again. The torture of infected wounds racked his body as he pressed on to avoid the authorities.

The memory of the shackles and the loneliness of incarceration kept him going. I was with him every step of the pain-riddled journey, fearing to be seen and recognized as we crossed the border into South Carolina. We slept in ditches and barns, stealing corn from the fields and fruit from the trees. The loneliness of the wilderness slowed us down and contributed to a dwindling faith in ourselves.

The mental isolation was hard on Robert because he was a young man who missed his family. He had only run away from home because it was the midst of the Depression (he was fourteen) and he wanted to make his own way in the world. "Instead I'm becoming acquainted with death," he mourned.

"I've always known," he went on, "that I would die at a very early age. I have pellagra—" a vitamin-deficiency disease, I learned "—and am wandering the American continent alone. My tongue is black from starvation and I know it is all my own doing. I must have been the dumbest of the dumb to precipitate this course of action."

He walked and grabbed rides on trains for close to a year. When he finally decided he'd had enough, he returned to his home to find that his family had moved. Persevering, he located them, and I was right next to him as he walked gently into the middle-class home, his leg swollen as big around as a tree stump where the wounds from the shackles had become poisoned with infection. His mother was glad to see him, but the family wanted to cut his leg off.

"I tried to tell myself that I had really lived life, but I cried myself to sleep out of loneliness. I still do.

"So, I drink as a preparation for death. When the great day comes it will just be one more hangover."

The first time I heard this story, my fate with him was sealed. I was from the South, where storytelling is an art. My father was my original educator in storytelling. Robert took the torch from him.

My mouth would hang open with compassion. Oh yes, how I wanted to be the person who would make Robert feel safe in the world. To me, his sleepy-eyed expression, his laconic drawl, and his undulating fullback way of walking belied the truth that he was a literate and painfully shy man whom I would draw out of himself for all the world to see.

So, from the beginning he was a man who triggered my interest because there was so much there to uncover, untangle, and understand.

I loved working with him too. He was considerate and kind, never late, and he always knew his lines as well as the lines of the other actors. He smoked his Gitane cigarettes, drank anything he could pour, and judged scripts by how many days he'd have off. Yet I believe he really cared and was too embarrassed to let anyone know.

Our director, Robert Wise, who was a lovely man and a fine director, witnessed our chemistry early on. Mitchum and I kidded around a lot, so much so that Wise took us aside and pleaded with us to take a little time and be serious before each take.

Robert and I had a way of telling jokes or laughing right up until the time Wise yelled "action," and we very much enjoyed making a sudden transition into the emotion required by the scene. But Wise couldn't adjust that fast. As a result, he felt isolated from the party.

Robert and I couldn't help ourselves. We were on a roll, attuned to one another's sense of the absurd and frankly insensitive to others in our environment. "Too swift for the pack," Robert would say.

We never spent any time together away from the set. Then, during a period when I had a few days off, I went to Hawaii to think and be alone. I was unreachable.

When I returned, Robert said, "When I didn't see you, I felt deprived. You are too much with me." From then on things changed.

The next day we shot a scene where he, in character, said, "You are a beautiful, beautiful girl." Even in black-and-white, I blushed so much they had to put an extra layer of makeup on me.

Soon he was driving me home from work, reciting poetry that he'd memorized. He put on a dazzling display of verbal pyrotechnics, which revealed to me an extensive knowledge of poetry and a state of consciousness deeper and more aware than his Neanderthal pose would indicate. We spent most of our work time together on the set or in each other's dressing rooms, and after hours there were long story-spinning sessions with other adoring listeners.

Sometimes he would drink too much as he recited by heart sonnets of Shakespeare.

Sometimes he'd gaze at the stars and barely acknowledge that I sat next to him in the car.

"I'm a caged lion with the soul of a poet," he said. "A poet with an ax."

Sometimes he'd buy a bag of pomegranates and bring them to me as though they were the crown jewels. He'd open them with his huge hands, turn them inside out, and separate the seeds from the fruit while he spun another story about his life.

The filming progressed, and day by day we and the crew became a family. In those days, stars could take the time for long comrades-in-arms coffee breaks, sitting around the camera, reminiscing about years gone by. It cemented the unity of the film family. Each person felt important and integral to the work. Robert, of course, identified more with the "working stiffs" than he did with the "above the line" personnel.

Crews are sensitive and sophisticated about creative behavior. They've *seen* it all and are *blind* to it all. Crew members can become like wallpaper, if necessary, melding into the woodwork yet surrounding the room with attention. They may gossip, but it's subtle.

They were aware of the relationship developing between Robert and me. They respected it. They allowed it without comment. They were included. There was nothing secretive or clandestine about it, and that was because our friendship was still growing.

It wasn't until after the picture that our deeper relationship really began. I called Steve to explain what was developing between Robert and me. I was a little afraid of it, and beginning to wonder how much longer I could wander around the romantic landscape without destroying the relationship I had with my husband. I didn't want to ruin Robert's marriage either. I wasn't sure where it was going between us, and I think I was looking for help from Steve. If he would come home, perhaps we could clarify our own relationship. But Steve said he was too busy. He chastised me for being adolescent and not understanding his need to establish an identity of his own. So Robert and I traveled together, meeting in places like New Orleans, Paris, New York, London, and even Africa. We loved bumming around. We got lost in the moment of wherever we were. Robert had no sense of time or purpose. The present was all there was. Then we'd part and there would be long stretches when we didn't see each other but kept in touch by phone, and the phone calls were like our travels, rambling, without a destination. His words haunt me still.

He said my face was "treacherously beautiful," like "some enchanted goblin's."

He said the glimmer of communication between us was probably "self-appreciation" because we recognized our own thoughts in each other. He talked about his "heavy rushes of feeling" and "dogged protestations in the limited lyric of mundane love."

Robert saw himself as a poet and I was an appreciator who worshiped his use of language, even though a lot of the time I didn't know what he was talking about.

There were times when we planned to meet and he never came. More than once I found myself in a hotel room or an arranged apartment somewhere in the world, waiting for him. These were the times I cursed him, but I cursed myself more for believing we could have a relationship that meant something. It made me ponder the reasons I found myself so involved with him at all. He was clearly not a man of usual values, or about whom you could make easy predictions. He was insular at the same time that he was so amusingly gregarious.

Then I began to realize that Robert, more than any other man I knew, was helping me investigate my unresolved feelings about my father. Of course, Dad had spun stories too, only his were tales of what he could have done rather than what he had done, and I hadn't realized it until I got to know Robert. Both had longed to wander the world, poking around in the way other people lived, finding adventures that would help them dismember their pasts. And both had deeply romantic natures.

My dad was from a small town in Virginia. He lived with both his parents, the stronger of whom was the mother.

Robert was from a small town in Connecticut. His family was fatherless until his mother married again.

I sensed that my father longed to venture as a "man" out beyond the perimeter of safety (he told me once he always wanted to run away and join a circus), and I saw in Robert the man who had fulfilled that dream.

And there were emotional areas so camouflaged in each man that I was compelled to salve their concern that exploring and exposing deep feelings would be too painful.

Every now and then Robert's true sorrow and pain would break through. Once I remember lolling in a bubble bath in a village outside of Paris. When I turned around, he was sitting in a chair, just gazing at me, silent tears sliding down his cheeks. He said it was because I was beautiful. But I could feel it was because he couldn't envision himself truly happy. Neither could my dad, so I was attracted very early to difficult, intelligent men to whom I thought I could bring happiness.

Robert taught me that that wasn't possible. Happiness resided—or did not reside—within a person. What a painful lesson.

Robert's manner of speaking was so obtuse and sometimes so esoteric that it constantly thwarted the clarity of feeling that I longed to hear. He was a master with rich language, seemingly calculated to impress; yet his thoughts wandered in many directions and he never much cared whether I or anyone else kept up with him. If I questioned him, he'd ignore me and continue down his path of thinking.

It would have been a thrill to hear a precise answer to just about anything.

Robert seemed to be alone, but in many ways he was dependent . . . on work, on recognition, on books, on booze, cigarettes, and a willing audience. The contradiction made him more and more interesting.

During our relationship, I was trying to draw my own conclusions about Hollywood when I read what he had told a reporter, Helen Lawrensen, from *Esquire*—one of the few reporters he agreed to talk to. Of Hollywood he said: "It is a dull, aching euphoria. . . . There is all this asinine waste of money. They decide they want to use a shot of a harvesting machine. So three guys go tearing around the country, stay at expensive hotels, get stoned, spend days taking color tests of the machine. They then decide it won't work. . . . [Hollywood] has no relation to real life, to real people. Oh, there are real people there, but they're in oil refineries and factories, not in movieland. Hollywood is Atlantis.''

A man after my own heart. But if Hollywood was Atlantis, Robert Mitchum was from Venus.

Once when we were in an apartment in New York, the dialogue between us had become so indecipherable that my mind closed in on me. He had a way of being so emotionally uncommitted in these exchanges that I felt like I was hanging bubbles on a clothesline. He had no strongly held personal opinions about anything. He was fine with that, lost in the maze of his meanderings. But I couldn't stand it anymore. I was so angry I opened the door, picked him up bodily, and threw him out into the hallway. I waited for some kind of appropriate response. He simply bowed and said, ''I'll tell him when he comes in.'' What did that mean? That was what he always said when he knew he could go no further.

He slunk away and decided that I had flung him out of my life. It didn't occur to him that taking some responsibility for his vagueness would help. No, he ''knew'' I was too good for him. Much later, I read a poem by Mitchum. The ''anguish of my solitude,'' he wrote, was ''sweet.''

I wrote him in despair as a result of his inverted sense of commitment to himself.

The fact that you don't need anything is in direct relation to what you already possess. But the fact that you don't *want* anything is a sad neglect of the

life you've been given. To want something enables
others to give to you. You must know I want to
give what is wanted. If you don't allow yourself to
want on the grounds that it is selfish . . . you
reduce yourself to a bum. To be a bum, and a good
one at that, is up to you. But must the rest of us
suffer the same existence because you are unself-
ishly selfish?

He demanded nothing. He had no desires, not in relation
to food, an evening out, or even an evening in. His attitude toward lovemaking was the same. He never took
the initiative. He enjoyed it certainly, he was sweet and
tender, but I never really knew what he wanted. Anything was okay. He was like that about his work too. He
never asked for anything. Not even good parts. He'd
take B pictures because he said "better me than some
other poor fool." And so he would intermittently ruin
his career yet another time, accepting roles in inferior
pictures until David Lean or Fred Zinnemann, who both
claimed he was one of the finest actors in America,
pleaded with him to be in their pictures. He said he was
ashamed of being an actor because people accorded him
more respect and fame and money than he merited. But
when his fine talent was proven once again, he'd sabotage it in a barroom brawl somewhere.

Once in a bar a man cracked Robert over the head
with a thick magazine. Robert looked around and
straightened, his chest expanding to its full breadth,
which was considerable.

"And what may I do for you?" asked Robert in his
mock-elegant eighteenth-century manner. I could sense
trouble.

The guy said, "I just wanted to see if you're really as
tough as you seem in the movies." He edged toward

Robert as though to provoke him. I remembered a friend of mine saying that Robert never knew his strength. He'd squash an alarm clock just by shutting it off.

"Sir," said Robert, "I'm a survivor of the Stone Age. I'm no hero."

That wasn't enough. Robert couldn't just shake his hand and be friendly and self-effacing. No, he had to be oblique and esoteric. So the man decided he wanted to talk about fighting. Robert bantered with him about prizefighting and the dangers of being big and strong. He was clearly talking about himself. The man asked Robert who he would least like to be in a fight with. Robert thought a moment.

"Frank Sinatra," he said.

"Why?" asked the man.

"Because," said Robert, "every time I'd knock him down, he'd get right back up until one of us would have to get killed."

That did it. The man walked away and left us.

Robert turned to me and said, "My problem is I look right in these dirty clothes."

Another time a guy hit Robert with a bar stool. Robert turned around and without a beat asked simply, "Why?"

The guy said, "I just had an impulse to hit you."

That really made Robert mad. He wanted a brainier explanation. The man's excuse was insulting to him. Robert picked the guy up and threw him into the alley behind the bar. Then he stuffed him into a garbage can—careful, by the way, not to really hurt him.

Barroom brawlers certainly weren't my type. But repressed violence did appeal to me. I began to see that Robert refused to articulate his feelings in order to avoid the violence he sensed in himself. He used liquor to quell it, of course, but sometimes it exploded.

Once we were driving at night and someone inadvertently cut him off. He took it personally and proceeded to ram the back of the man's car with our car for a mile or two. The man gaped in disbelief when he pulled over and saw Mitchum and me glide by. I was mortified. Robert just grinned, something like the grin he used in *Night of the Hunter*. It could send chills down your back. Was he so excellent as a perverted killer because he understood how close to the surface those characteristics were in himself? Was that why I found him so attractive? Jimmy Van Heusen used to say to me, "You don't like men who are nice to you. None of you women ever do. You all like guys who'll give you a hard time. Gives you something to be miserable about."

I see the truth in his words now. I and so many women I knew were psychologically unprepared for peace and harmony. We'd snatch unhappiness from the arms of contentment any chance we got. We were addicted to it, accustomed to it really. We saw our mothers as essentially unhappy and our fathers totally out of touch with their feelings—so what did we expect? It would take a master's degree in self-investigation to pull ourselves out of the morass of finding difficult men dangerously exciting. My education to that end continued.

After a particularly bad period of vague and convoluted communication between us, I fled to India. I needed to think and be in a country of ancient wisdom and patience. I sat in the palace of the Maharaja of Jaipur, writing Robert letters. I admonished him even as I tried to come to terms with myself. I hated him so. And I hated myself. I found myself conniving ways to do grave bodily harm to him and not get caught. My own violence, rawly expressed, astonished me! I would do anything, it seemed, to make him wake up, to make him real instead of a phantom hiding behind literary esoterica. I wanted to force him to scream and kick and demand. I wanted to hear about his dreams, what angered him, what truly terrified him. I wanted to hear about what he wanted from life, from his work, from me. I sat for days writing and remembering; the scenes are still fresh in my mind. Our trip to New Orleans where for three days we ate nothing but fresh oysters washed down with absinthe until I thought I would go blind. He literally became Cajun, and when we moved onto a barge on the bayou, he lay back, gazed at the stars, and became a fisherman, inviting some of them to join us. It was another world; a real one, somehow, but to me it felt like the twilight zone.

In Greenwich Village, he took me to hear Dave Brubeck and introduced me to musicians and music I had never heard of. When Sinatra heard I was hanging out with Robert, he told me Robert knew more about the history of music than any man he had ever known. He sang and wrote and recorded several songs that did very well.

I was with Mitchum the day that President Kennedy was assassinated and we spent the evening watching the replay over and over, wondering what life was all about. He spoke only of "the bastards grinding you down," never about the preciousness of our little time on earth.

And when I met him in East Africa, we'd sit out on the plains drinking vodka and ginger beer, commiserating with the whites who had been through Uhuru and the Mau-Mau experience. He loved watching the Masai tribespeople interrelate, particularly the women. He was offered the wives of many warriors as an act of proud generosity. I told him that was fine with me because the chief of the tribe had offered three hundred cattle to buy me.

I was so proud that I finally had the courage to leave

him and go off and live with a Masai tribe on my own, experiencing a deep harmony uniting man, animals, and nature. I was beginning to actually feel the meaning of all living beings being one. Robert's innate need for wandering, though a problem for me, was a trait I recognized in myself.

So I sat writing letters to him from India. I soon realized that he was a mirror image for my own lack of commitment. I was drawn to him not only because he was nearly twenty years older and a father image, but because through him I could learn how essential it was for me to inform others of what I wanted, needed, and was committed to in life.

Although Steve knew about my relationship with Robert, he never questioned my feelings. He didn't want to know.

Over the years my relationship with Robert wound down. That was inevitable. I was learning that life does not just happen to us. Nature and the universe abhor a vacuum. If I didn't design my destiny, scope out my future, dare to insist that my life was mine to mold and sculpt, then other forces, other people, other events would step in and do it for me.

Robert taught me by example that ambition needn't be ruthless, nor was the lack of it all that attractive. Because of the frustration he provoked in me, I decided I never wanted to do that to others.

My desires, my values, my plans, and my projections for myself became more definite. I would know what I wanted so that others in my life could know where they stood.

My dad, bless his soul, was never committed to belief in himself. He was like Robert in that they both had dreams, but lived more like sleepwalkers. I didn't want to be that way. Robert enabled me to wake up and take charge of my own ambition and dreams.

One night during the final days of our relationship, we were together when Robert had had a great deal to drink.

"I fear," he said, "that I punished you for daring to know me." He told me I had helped him to "sense, and see, and feel, freeing me to demand . . ."

Tears filled his eyes. He never finished the thought. What was it he wished to demand?

I knew what I would demand because of Robert. I would want more clarification of intention, meaning, and language. I would also never wait for a man in a hotel room for three days again.

# 13

# A MAN I LOVED
# . . . ON LOCATION

*S*ometimes real lovers in life have no chemistry on the screen. Sometimes chemistry between antagonists is what ignites the celluloid. There are many examples of the mysterious chemistry between screen stars. Taylor and Burton, Tracy and Hepburn, Gable and Lombard come to mind as real-life lovers whose chemistry translated to the screen. But for every one of them, there are pairings that don't work at all. And to add to the mystery, many costars who fall in love are married and deeply in love with their spouses. Screen pairing can ruin lives.

To me, one of the most fascinating and dangerous "scandalous pairings" was that of Yves Montand and Marilyn Monroe. They played out their combustion for the entire world to witness while making *Let's Make Love* together. Montand and his wife, Simone Signoret, were left-wing, basically communist, intellectuals. They admired Arthur Miller (then married to Monroe) and thus the stage was set for a tabloid parody that debased the original attraction of serious politics.

The set was the old Beverly Hills bungalow complex. The cast was the aforementioned four and the script was not to be believed.

Long story short—Montand and Monroe fell in lust and both of their spouses were written out of the screenplay.

Simone went back to Europe, where she played the wronged wife with dignity and understanding. Miller wrote *The Misfits,* which he hoped would rouse his wife to her senses.

Montand was so impressed with both his wife and Monroe's husband that he soon felt the "adventure," as he termed it to the press, had outlived its usefulness, whereupon he returned to Simone, leaving a backlash of bad feeling in America. Monroe continued to pursue him with limos and champagne. Montand waved away her "schoolgirl crush" and Signoret said she had never expected her husband's arms to remain empty when she was away.

Soon after that, Montand arrived in Tokyo to make *My Geisha* with me. I wondered if he would arrive alone. He did. I wondered how long he would remain that way, and whether I'd be the next "adventure."

Steve was producing the picture, which would be shot entirely on location all over Japan. I was extremely glad we would be working together. It would enable us to clarify our relationship at close proximity.

As Steve and I greeted Montand at the airport, he bent over and kissed my hand. Had he held on to it for a split second longer than necessary? I wasn't sure. I didn't know the language of hand kissing. He had the physical presence of an expert stage performer who understood the power of his own charisma. He didn't flirt or subtly flash his European charm. He didn't need to. He seemed fundamentally commanding in his humor and dignity as he spoke of his trip. I was impressed by the fact that he had conquered the world stage (he was a huge hit on Broadway), and seemed quite confident he could do the same on the silver screen.

The rest of our cast, Robert Cummings and Edward G. Robinson, and our director, Jack Cardiff, were deep in work. As usual for costars, it was important for Yves and me to get to know one another. I was nervous about it. We had lunch the following day. Since I was living with Steve and Sachi in our house in Shibuya, I met Montand at his hotel.

As we sat over lunch, he was businesslike and very concerned about his English, particularly because our picture was a romantic comedy. "I know the rhythm of the words must be expert," he said, "or the laughter won't be there." He spoke with slow formality. At that moment I couldn't have cared less about laughs. He had ordered sushi but didn't know how to use chopsticks. I took his chopsticks and placed them between his thumb and forefinger. His hands were warm. I wondered about his heart.

"So clever are these Japanese," he said. "I have heard so many of them speak this difficult language fluently. So clean and polite . . . an amazing culture. I think I take up too much space."

"What do you mean?" I asked, wondering what he was really thinking.

"Because I'm too tall."

With that, he took my elbow and eased me across the room, opened the door, and guided me out onto a crowded intersection. I felt as though I were in the arms of a master choreographer but didn't know the steps.

I tried to be debonair and offhanded when I said nervously, "So tell me about Marilyn, for goodness' sake. How was all that?"

He didn't blanch or give me any indication that I had invaded his privacy. He waved his hands in the air.

"It was an adventure," he said, echoing his comment to the press. "A sweet adventure."

"Simone was so dignified during the whole thing," I said, trying to make amends. "We all watched what she'd do when Marilyn's limo met your plane in New York and she was inside it with champagne."

Montand stopped and looked right through me. "Simone has great dignity," he said. "And Marilyn was insecure about her beauty, her acting, and herself."

Montand then took me over to a bench and motioned that we should sit down. "She was never late in the morning," he told me. "In fact she arrived hours before the rest. But after her beauty makeup and hairstyling, she felt unworthy of being a star. She felt she had not much talent and was ashamed. What people called her tardiness and temperament was really her humiliation. I tried to help her."

I felt so silly. My questions had been intrusive and insensitive. Sometimes when I was nervous I regarded celebrities in show business as though they weren't real, vulnerable human souls with needs and contradictions like the rest of the human race.

Montand went on to talk about Marilyn as though he had been her confidant and counselor as well as her lover.

Years later, I read his more in-depth account of his affair. He claimed in his book that if Simone had left him over Marilyn, he would have married her. He said their relationship had all the earmarks of a combination that was made to last, and that he and Marilyn had been moving toward a lasting commitment. Yet to me, on the bench that day, he reiterated that their affair was amusing and pleasant, but nothing serious.

The contradictions in him were confusing, and I found that unattractive, yet he seemed genuinely concerned that people be understood and dealt with compassionately. I didn't know how to handle him.

Fortunately I didn't need to worry about that for a while. The rest of the cast arrived on location and our little Hollywood movie family gradually became accustomed to the xenophobia of the Japanese culture. We were known to them because they loved our movies, but we remained *gaijins*—outsiders.

Edward G. Robinson and Robert Cummings had their wives with them, as did our English director, Jack Cardiff.

Because Steve knew Japan very well, he arranged sight-seeing excursions and made everyone as comfortable as possible as we moved to locations all over Japan, from Tokyo to Yokohama to Kyoto to Nara, Hiroshima, and Nagasaki, and back to Tokyo. But he was not around much.

The script by Norman Krasna, who had written *Let's Make Love* for Montand and Monroe, was based on *The Guardsman,* a French comedy of disguised identity. I played an American movie actress who disguises herself as a geisha in order to be with her director husband (Montand) on location in Japan.

A convincing makeup was the most difficult problem of our preproduction. How could Frank Westmore make me look Japanese without being obvious? The script simply said *she disguises herself as Japanese,* but no one told us how.

At first we used complicated prosthetic eyepieces, but every time I blinked or closed my eyes, the separation between my lids and the plastic was visible. It looked ridiculous, and the tests were awful. Being away on location, we didn't have the benefit of a prosthetic makeup laboratory, and the Japanese makeup people had obviously never run into this problem.

It seemed as though we might not have a picture. If the audience couldn't believe I was a geisha, how could my husband? We could disguise my height by choosing the correct camera angles. I could use brown contact lenses to cover the blue of my eyes. I could use rice makeup to cover my freckles. But how could I succeed in making the shape of my eyes Japanese? It was Westmore who cleverly solved the problem. He dug into his pockets and pulled out a few condoms. Because the rubber was soft and pliable, he cut out an almond shape and glued it to my eyelids. Applying makeup over the rubber disguised the lines of demarcation. I found that I could blink and even close my eyes without the camera picking up what we had used. Westmore made the supreme sacrifice . . . safe sex for his art.

While sitting long hours in the makeup chair, Montand and I went over our dialogue, rehearsing lines and studying our script together. In between rehearsals we spoke of life, had meals together, and in general got to know one another.

Actors and actresses share deep and personal secrets in the company of makeup and hair artists. Sometimes, when we are attracted to each other, it's easier to tell the truth in the presence of others. We know that they are discreet and nothing is repeated. In fact, the makeup trailer is where the *National Enquirer* should plant a microphone, except that almost no one in the trailer can be bought off. They know they'd never work again.

It was during makeup that Montand told me much about his life, that he was really an Italian and had been brought up in a poverty-stricken communist family. He told me about the Americans refusing him and his wife visas because they were seen as a threat to national security. I was touched and wondered if there was more to the story.

He spoke of his love for the theater and the quiet terror he felt before every stage performance as he anticipated instant public humiliation. There's nothing more attractive than a man who reveals his fear to me. Little things haunted him. A slight constriction in his voice, a small noncoordination of his hat and cane, the color of a band member's shirt. He spoke of his fright and his joy as if they were intertwined. He said he understood why Jacques Brel vomited before every show, and couldn't understand why Maurice Chevalier couldn't wait to get out there. He spoke of his identification with the underdog, his political consciousness, and why he still believed that the communist system would help people.

I told him of my middle-class American values, my ballet years, my love of spontaneous theater, my observations about moviemaking, and my growing left-wing beliefs.

We rehearsed together as he tried to explore the values underlying each scene. He was diligent, he worked hard, he was professional, and he was graceful to his coworkers. But soon I realized there was a subtext in his personal approach. He seemed to have a need to experience intimacy in complicated circumstances. He talked about close working relationships on a film leading inevitably to personal closeness, particularly on location. I wondered if he meant us. He gave me a nickname, Big Bird, because of my long-armed ''wing span,'' and I called him Montand-san. He laughed at all my jokes and was patient and coddling about my makeup problems. I found him irresistible. Yet I couldn't understand what my real feelings were. They were running ahead of me. I loved the provocative flirtation that I found myself indulging in, but I couldn't decipher how "close" we were really becoming. The relationship was mysterious and evasive and teasing and I lapped up every second of it.

I adored the way Montand treated my daughter, Sachi, who was then five. He would scoop her up into his arms and call her "princess." He had discussions with her about "getting up in the middle of the night when your parents are asleep to eat bread." He admired her party dress and told her she was beautiful.

He was relaxed and funny around the crew. He was also extremely comfortable with some of the gay men on the crew, which is always a test, an important criterion for me. A straight man who is threatened or put off by gay men suffers from something I can't reconcile. Montand didn't tease or flirt with them. On the contrary, he respected them and considered them equals in every way.

He was a serious actor, finding elements and dimensions in the script that had not been fleshed out, and he never stopped the improvement process.

Sometimes, because we shot all over Japan, Frank Westmore and I would board a train at six in the morning, and he was expected to apply the intricate prosthetic Japanese makeup while the train sped along at eighty miles an hour, lurching from side to side like an out-of-control speedboat. Montand sat watching the process, understanding the seriousness of what it would mean if my face was on sideways when it was projected sixty feet wide on the screen.

The sting of the dark brown contact lenses stuffed into

my eyes for hours, and the weight of the *katsura* (a high Japanese wig) gave me pounding headaches all day long. Montand brought me cold *shiburi* towels. The kimono's undergarments were wrapped so ceremoniously tight around me that I felt I couldn't breathe, my misery relieved every now and then by the comedy of going to the bathroom in my full regalia. It was a Marx Brothers sketch.

The Japanese toilets were placed in the floor. So I had to lift the many layers of the kimono above my knees in order to squat down on the floor. Since Japanese people are so much smaller than Westerners, the space in the cubicle is about half of what we need. I'd squat, but if I leaned forward in any way, I'd bump the top of my *katsura* against the wall in front of me and knock it askew. Once, when that happened, the force of it was so strong that one of my brown contacts popped out of my eye and plopped into the toilet. There was no way I could retrieve it because there was no room for me to turn around and find it. It was gone for good, and we had only one extra pair—in those days contacts were hard to make and very expensive.

Montand would tease me with a twinkle, understanding the absurdity of my playing a geisha in the first place, and call me his "Big Bird."

As rehearsals and shooting progressed, Steve was never around. He always seemed to be busy, which was understandable on one hand and guilt producing on the other—it left me time to freely know Montand better, but I was getting myself in deeper and deeper. We went to dinner, took Sachi for side trips, and in general, enjoyed being with each other. At that point, the relationship was completely platonic. He rarely spoke of either Simone or Marilyn and didn't seem to be interested in geisha houses or teahouse activity. He was focused entirely on me, yet in some subtle way I felt he was biding his time. I liked that.

I knew it would be relatively easy for me to have an intimate affair with Montand without causing much of a stir or upsetting the emotional balance of the cast and crew. I could see the crew was in and out of each other's hotel rooms all the time anyway. The hours were crazy, and intimacy just for R&R was a foregone conclusion.

Locations in those days, before AIDS, were a byword for sexual freedom. In the words of the witty actress Margaret Leighton, "When you're on the road, fucking doesn't count." As soon as the crews arrived on location, they bolted from their assigned rooms and acted like kids sprung from reform school. Early in my career, I was shocked. As time passed I became amused. Sometimes their antics were hilarious. Most of them had secure and long-term marriages, but monogamy was not the accepted rule of the day (God knows what their other halves were doing back home). It was a kind of experimental swapping of working partners for the duration of the film. The energy required came from a primordial need. The first six weeks of a shoot are fairly healthy. Loss of sleep, stress, and pressure from work are at a tolerable level. But heading into the seventh week and all the weeks thereafter, it's a miracle a film ever reaches fruition.

Perhaps love affairs provide an extra inspiration.

In the old days, the crews were mostly men, so they paired off with wardrobe, secretaries, and other women they "inherited" on the location site. Today, there are many more women to mingle with. I sometimes love to speculate who is with whom as I sit under the lights, seeming to go over my dialogue in my head, as if unaware of my surroundings. Crew members have a way of attending to their own chores with extreme concentration when they are truly diverted by a fling. Being basically a gossipy adolescent, sometimes I give in and have some fun with what I "see" going on; other times I do what they expect, which is to pull rank, be aloof, not concern myself with their "lower-echelon duties." In many ways the crew prefers that the star not notice them. That way they are outside our orbit—and vice versa. They do appreciate your calling them by name, but not so often that others might accuse them of currying favor.

The way to cause real trouble on a set is to have an affair with one of the crew when you're the star. "Class" crossover is usually verboten, but once, on location, I found myself attracted to one of the grips. He was a Latin with black eyes and hair and an all-knowing quality that covered up an inferiority complex.

The contradiction appealed to me, and before long we were living together.

I couldn't have been happier with him. His colleagues teased him, though, and eventually I learned a disappointing but necessary lesson: a man who doesn't feel he deserves you can be very cruel. After that I stayed on my side of "the line."

In a foreign location such as Japan, there was a significant chasm between the Western stars and the Japanese crew. Each of us had our own way of working and interrelating. The common language, though, was the understanding of light. A foreign crew is somehow incredulous that Americans, who have been in the movie business awhile, understand a key light from a fill light.

Technology is the common denominator, and the technology of light brought us together. Our Japanese crew knew that our director, Jack Cardiff, used to be England's finest cameraman. So our Japanese cinematographer was respectful and solicitous of any help Cardiff could provide.

Our days were composed of traveling, makeup, finding hidden value in the scenes, and contending with the various complaints of people who felt they weren't being given pecking-order respect. Sometimes the wives of our male stars were a bigger problem with their temperament than the stars themselves. Wives on location are continually searching for thrills to keep them occupied. They subconsciously feel left out of the emotional mix (they are) and need reassurance and attention to prove that they are as important as the people making the picture, which is also the truth.

Husbands of female stars rarely come to visit, and if they do it's not for long. It's too hard on the male ego, and besides, most of them have jobs themselves, which they can't leave. Moviemaking brings out everyone's need to be acknowledged. The continual waiting around promotes reflection as to what and who you are. That's why costars are moved to communicate with one another deeply. The *time* together conspires to inspire. That's what happened to both Montand and myself. We were having a good time, yet we were lonely and wanted more of each other. I felt reluctant because Steve was, after all, the producer of the picture, even though I rarely saw him and was beginning to wonder why he was always so busy. We were seeing no more of each other than when we had an ocean between us. When Montand wasn't with me, he was alone. I never saw him with a friend who might have alleviated this loneliness. I had my house and my daughter. I admired Montand for maintaining a disciplined centeredness. He told me he couldn't really sleep well, not only because the languages he dreamed in were jumbled—he was coping with both English and Japanese—but also because of his thoughts of me. He said he was a man in transition. I wasn't sure what he meant. He didn't elaborate. Perhaps it was a professional transition.

Because he had the experience of directing his own one-man show, Montand's awareness of filmmaking encompassed more than just acting.

He'd prowl around the set, touching cables and inspecting the cameras and lenses. He wanted to learn about the soundboard and how to make his voice different according to the distance between himself and the boom man.

He wanted to learn the rules of the game, how the machines worked. He didn't see himself as a mere actor; he couldn't because he had been trained, as part of his stagecraft, to learn and understand everyone's job and contribution.

Although he never had the tendency to place himself at the center of the movie operation, as he would have onstage, his concentration emanated outward, so that he was aware of much more than himself. He never felt the need to control what others were doing, but he was vitally interested in the artistic mechanics of it all.

Because he was a music-hall performer, he was used to being himself in his skin. He'd come on stage in his own selected costume, sing his own songs, having chosen his own musicians and controlled his own lights. To win over his audience he had to be certainly and centeredly himself.

Now he was in a strange milieu, using a foreign language in front of a camera. He knew he'd have to allow his character to take over his body, his heart and mind, and his responses would be the character's now. He jumped in with both feet and committed to his role completely. As the filming progressed and our relationship deepened I realized that Montand, being a romantic

Mediterranean man, would probably fall in love if his character fell in love. Was this what had happened with Marilyn and now was it happening with me? And was I responding with the same "in-character" impulses?

He was so forthcoming with his fears and anxieties, and I loved that. He was more of a sensitive Italian peasant than a French stage and screen star. His real self seemed to be a man of the streets with an exquisite sense of survival. Whenever we went anywhere, a luxury hotel for dinner, a theater, he'd immediately clock the emergency exit. He said it was because, as a man raised in poverty, his reflex was to escape quickly, if necessary. This applied not only to buildings, but to people.

He spoke of Simone as though she were a protector to him. She soothed him and admonished him for his own good. He depended on her, in a world of uncertain and unpredictable cruelty, to save him, yet he resented the fact that he relied on her so much, that she had made herself indispensable in his life. It was as though he would rebel against this matron-mother by exploring other women any way he wished.

His demeanor on the set was humorous and high-spirited. He was never moody or dark-spirited, as most people are sometimes. I wondered if there was a hidden reservoir of secret contempt and coldness that he covered with likability and a well-developed personal charisma. Certainly there was something profound in him that was withheld. This was one area Simone must have understood. I couldn't.

Our roving band of filmmakers moved all over Japan. The scenery provided a backdrop for our personal story as well as for the film. The schedule began to affect us. We never slept more than a few hours a night. Then Frank Westmore had his heart attack and was hospitalized. I was stricken. What would I do without him? His protégé stepped in, proud that he had learned from one of the great masters. I visited Frank a few times, but felt I couldn't hold up production. The early-morning make-ups on the wobbly trains continued with the young Japanese makeup artists now included in the circle that witnessed the intensity growing between Montand and me. Finally, in a hotel in Nara, while the rest of the exhausted company collapsed, Montand and I went to our respective rooms after dinner. Soon there was a knock on my door.

I opened it to find him standing in the hallway, his arms dangling at his sides, looking lost and forlorn. I pulled him into my room and folded him gently into my arms. We melted together. Then, at long last, we fell into bed. It was sweet—a relief more than anything. I wondered what it would mean in my life.

The next morning I shot the aria from *Madame Butterfly* starring the six-foot-three Cio-cio-san (me). It was a day for Hollywood lore. Cio-cio-san laments her sailor lover leaving her with her son. Cardiff thought it would be dramatic to have me sing in a shroud of mist on a Japanese mountainside.

I got myself dressed in underrobes and formal kimono, exhausted from the night before. Dipped into my *geta* (tall thong shoes) and high, formally decorated *katsura,* with white rice makeup augmenting Westmore's now superfluous condoms around my eyes, I reported to the set at the bottom of the mountainside.

Cardiff gave me my marks from which to descend the mountain as I sang "Un bel dì." What he didn't tell me was that he would have to manufacture the look of mountain mist because the weather was not going to cooperate that day.

I gingerly put my brown contact lenses in my eyes, lugged myself to the top of the mountainside, and waited for "action." Several cameras were going to roll at once. I saw a few crew members standing by at strategic points on the sloping mountainside. I thought they were for security. The playback began over the loudspeaker. I knew the lyrics to Puccini's opera by heart (I still do), so when Cardiff yelled "action" from below, I thought the scene would be a first-take breeze.

Slowly I descended the mountainside, feeling quite lovely in that beautiful setting and in my colorful kimono and thinking about the night before. I knew the music was gorgeous and all I really had to do was lip-synch the lyrics properly. That's when I spotted the first crew member light a huge match. He threw it onto pile of green wood and leaves. Then the second crew member followed suit. Jack Cardiff was going to get his effect of mist by lighting smoking fires all the way down the mountain.

I began to choke, thereby having trouble with the lip-synching. My eyes were tearing so profusely that my brown contact lenses swam out of the corners of my eyes and down my cheeks. Once the fires began they couldn't be put out. I tried my best. I lip-synched my heart out, hoping the close-ups would be usable, but it was hopeless. The long shot ended up in the picture, which meant Jimmy Stewart could have played Cio-cio-san and no one would have known the difference. We were lucky the mountain didn't burn down.

That evening, when Steve returned from Tokyo to rejoin us in Nara, I brought up my relationship with Montand. We were sitting in our hotel suite, Montand having discreetly excused himself for dinner.

"Do you notice that we are becoming very close?" I asked. Steve didn't flinch. "Yes," he said, "I noticed. And it's awful to watch."

I could hardly form the words, but I knew I had to be honest with him.

"I want you to know," I said, "that I'm not sure where this is going and I wish you had been around more. I know we have an understanding that each of us is free, but I really like him."

Steve flicked his tongue back and forth against his upper lip.

"You know," he said, "Montand flaunted his relationship with Monroe when Arthur Miller was around."

"No," I said, "I don't know that. I think they both felt an attraction and didn't mean to hurt anyone with it. You know how it is in the business."

Steve lit a cigarette and poured himself a drink from our hotel bar.

"Well," he said, "there's something you should know."

"What's that?" I asked, realizing the next few minutes would be crucial in determining my relationship with both Steve and Montand.

"Montand bet me at the beginning of this picture that he could make you fall in love with him," said Steve.

I couldn't speak.

"He what?" I asked, stalling for time.

"Yes," said Steve. "He told me that he had accomplished that with Marilyn Monroe and he was going to do the same with you. I guess he won, eh?"

My mind flashed to all I had heard about Montand and Monroe during *Let's Make Love*. I remembered how interested Steve had been in observing Simone's handling of the situation after the scandal hit Europe. I remembered that he and our screenwriter, Norman Krasna, thought Montand would be good for our picture because he had a European-lover image now.

But would he really have seduced Marilyn on purpose without regard for the feelings of everyone else involved? Yes, Montand had been cavalier in his assessment of Marilyn's schoolgirl crush on him, but that didn't mean he had been a manipulative lothario, endeavoring to carve one more notch on his belt.

"He really said that?" I asked Steve. "He purposely set out to prove he could chalk me up as one more of his conquered women?"

Steve nodded as though he didn't really want to bring such news to my attention, yet for my own good he thought I should know.

I turned away and went to bed. We spoke no more about it.

The next day I confronted Montand. I told him what Steve had said about him, word for word. Then I watched for his response.

He looked stunned, hurt, frightened, and trapped all at the same time. His expression was full of so many reactions that I couldn't read anything clearly. I waited. He said nothing. I expected him to defend himself—to say "that's ridiculous" or "he's lying" or "do you believe that shit?" Perhaps he felt that to defend himself would be too demeaning. I wanted him to say something. Anything. But he didn't say a word. Yet his silence wasn't an admission. In fact, I saw it as a survival mechanism. It was as though he acknowledged the trouble he had caused because of his affair with Monroe. He knew he had been insensitive in his public reaction to her ongoing adoration of him. He knew he had placed Simone Signoret in an untenable position in France. Her pride was hurt, yet she still loved him. His conduct had exposed her to a lot of gossip, even regarding her own sexual preferences. Because of all the women who seemed to continually inhabit Montand's life, people questioned why Simone never objected enough to take a strong stand.

In that moment when I confronted him, he seemed to process what was happening and realize that his future in movieland was at stake. Steve Parker was the producer in whom Paramount had placed their money and trust, and Montand knew it. If Montand was regarded as a gigolo seducer of the wives of Hollywood men, his name would be mud, whether it was true or not. He knew that too. Montand understood in a flashing instant that he was playing in a field of what could be conniving, insidious Hollywood cutthroats who could ruin him because of his ways with their women. His street smarts rose to his defense and he clammed up. He knew he couldn't verbally rebuke Steve without its escalating into yet another scandal. He knew he couldn't admit Steve's accusation for the same reason. On behalf of his own survival, he elected to say nothing.

A few days later as the cast and crew celebrated the final days of our shoot, I rose and made a toast to Steve, thanking him for all he had made possible and declaring him to be the love of my life.

After dinner, Montand took me aside and sadly remarked, ''That wasn't really necessary.'' It wasn't, but the relationship between Montand and me was over.

Sometime later, I learned that Steve had been having an affair himself during the filming of *My Geisha*. That was the basic reason he wasn't around much. I didn't understand at the time what this woman meant to him or the reason he was so determined that I shouldn't leave him. There were a great many things about Steve I didn't yet understand.

•    •    •

I SAW MONTAND SEVERAL TIMES AFTER OUR TIME TO-
gether in Japan. He still called me "Bird," although he
reduced it to "Little Bird" instead of "Big Bird."

He said he was through with Hollywood and its values. He'd rather have "real" food, "real" love, and
"real" conflicts. He said playing both sides of the ocean
confused him and others.

And so whenever I'd play in France with my live
show, I'd receive flowers and a telegram from Montand.
He was becoming an elder statesman for the entertainment industry there.

Soon his power and influence began to impact on the
political system in France also. The bluntness of his language, his "man of the people" attitude inspired the
public to embrace him as their spokesman. They knew
and understood his commitment to communism because
of his background of poverty.

Then Montand did a 180-degree turn. He took to the
airways, publicly denouncing the repressive system in the
Soviet Union and criticizing the socialist leaders who still
spoke favorably of Stalin. He astonished and ignited the
French public by his reversal, provoking stinging rebukes
from the press there.

My reflections on Montand deepened. Why did I or
anyone else expect that people should remain consistent,
their values entrenched? Why shouldn't they grow and
change?

More than anything, I found myself wondering what
effect Hollywood had had on Montand. Not from the
point of view of wealth, fame, or creativity, but more in
terms of how he'd come to assess personal truth. In
Hollywood, the truth has many masters, and lying is
considered creative thinking. Montand and Steve had
played the creative-thinking game. It worked well for
them both. It came from a need, I believe, to avoid

poverty and loneliness . . . a need to succeed at being acknowledged.

Maybe that was the great American Dream—say anything to enhance, stimulate, or close a deal. So you can be somebody.

# 14

# SAY ANYTHING

*P*erhaps manipulation in Hollywood began around the poker tables in Palm Springs, years ago, with the attendance of Jack Warner (Warner Brothers), Samuel Goldwyn (Samuel Goldwyn Productions), Harry Cohn (Columbia), Barney Balaban (Paramount), Joe Schenck (20th Century Fox), Darryl Zanuck (Fox), and Louis B. Mayer (MGM).

These men lived, breathed, ate, and dreamed the picture business. They were imaginative pirates who were close, competitive friends, navigating the rocky terrain of moviemaking capitalism. They traded information and lied to each other in ways that were more rococo and colorful than the pictures they dreamed up. They controlled Hollywood. Their land of dreams was easily governable because they not only desired to manipulate each other, they desired to manipulate the public. In the main they were of Eastern European descent and wished to create the reality of the New World as they wanted it to be. If white picket fences and twin beds in the bedrooms was the image they had of life, then their films would reflect that . . . hence so would America.

I remember the old-fashioned attitudes regarding love scenes when I first began in movies. The beds had to be twin, and if a couple touched each other, one foot had to be on the floor. It was necessary for a bathrobe or nightgown to be visible on the bed in case one of the partners rose from it. I remember a love scene in *Ask Any Girl* that was impossible to stage because I couldn't do it with one of my feet on the floor.

Most of these rules were dictated by the Hayes Office (the censorship board), but I don't think the old moguls really objected. The rules reflected their own conservative attitudes toward such matters.

Later on, with the demise of the old moguls, the style of sexual expression became more and more loose and free, until we have what occurs today.

There was honor among the old-time pirates, who had their own code. They played fast and loose with the truth, and somehow it was acceptable. This modus operandi exists today and I have had the treat of observing many escapades over the years. For example: A producer friend of mine wanted Marlon Brando and Jack Nicholson for a movie. They were to play friendly adversaries. The one who got killed in the third act would elicit greater audience sympathy.

The producer gave Marlon a script where *he* got killed. Then he gave Jack a script where *he* got killed. The conflict wasn't resolved until each compared notes on the set—well into principal photography. As penance, Marlon forced this producer to live in his trailer on a hot, dry, dusty location without benefit of room service, shower facilities, or television. The producer's usual style was to put a picture together, get paid, then leave, letting the creative people work out their problems any way they could. Marlon blocked his exit this time. The producer had to face the music of his own making, which I, and others who knew him, enjoyed.

I once sat with Mike Todd in his office as he worked the phone. In between amorous phone calls to Elizabeth Taylor, he was attempting to put together *War and Peace*. He knew that Paramount had a script of their own and wanted to make the same picture. But Mike wanted some of Paramount's actors, so he called one star and claimed another had already signed. Then he called the unsigned one and pulled the same trick. The "I've got so-and-so, and I want you to join him" ploy is the basis for most variations on a theme in "creative thinking" circles. It is common practice—somehow they never think we actors will talk to each other.

A producer telephoned Dean Martin and said he was doing a TV show with Frank and that Frank had requested Dean specially. He did the same thing with Frank. Somewhere deep in their hearts stars know that they're being used to create product for profit; nevertheless, they love to believe they are in demand. And just on the off chance that the other star truly asked for them, they want to be there. Stars will do most anything for each other. Because the producers, studio heads, and press are natural enemies and users, it's a kind of unspoken rule that even competing actors and actresses stick together. The truth is usually exposed at screenings, dinner parties, and even chance meetings on the street.

Stars, particularly women stars, are more honest with each other than with anyone else. Being exploited creates a camaraderie that is tacitly understood. We regard people who pit us against one another as ruthless and untrustworthy and not respectful of our talent or our time. We delight in comparing notes, even if we are competing. We use what we hear and wonder if it is even true. Whenever a producer or studio head sees stars powwowing in a corner, their eyes glint with curiosity—they're longing to know what our conversation is about. They know there is a "Maginot Line" of protection we draw around ourselves. We know we are the ones the public basically comes to see, yet we know we need the producers to give us jobs. So, united we stand, divided we fall.

The directors are another story. They are creative. They think and feel as we do. They basically play *all* the parts. They suffer emotionally the way we do, they are frightened of their artistic judgment as we are. They operate from their hearts as we do. The producers and studio heads operate from their minds and of course their pocketbooks. The directors put their lives into a project and do one project at a time. The producers put their time and money into a project, and do more than one at a time. Actors and actresses identify with their counterparts, who put their whole beings on the line and risk the terror of the worst feeling of all—humiliation.

Actors and actresses play their "creative thinking" games too, of course. Because we can disguise our voices, we can be anyone we want to be on the telephone and elicit whatever information we need by posing as someone else. Information is the fuel that makes the town run. It doesn't matter if it is true or false. Sometimes false info is even more useful.

A female-star friend of mine turned down a picture. The producer found out that she had lost another picture to a friend of hers. The producer called her again and claimed that her friend was interested in the part. She believed him and ended up doing the film in case her judgment might have been faulty in turning it down.

Actors who want a scene rewritten can easily sabotage its original content by purposely playing it wrong.

A big male star was under contract to Jack Warner. He was miserable and wanted out. Warner refused. The star knew that more than anything Warner hated to be considered a bad guy in the press. The star went on a three-month crusade denigrating Jack Warner to the press every chance he got, even if it meant fabricating lies. Warner hated it and let the star go.

Marilyn Monroe was unhappy with her agency, MCA, during the time of her relationship with Bobby Kennedy. She went to Kennedy and complained. He commenced proceedings that culminated in the breakup of the most powerful talent agency in town.

A famous comedian used to claim that he was black-balled by the TV networks because of his acerbic material against the Kennedys. Dean Martin asked him to come on his show, proving that NBC was not blackballing him. The comedian turned the offer down, saying he would have no more comedy material if Dean proved he wasn't being blackballed.

The personal interplay between people that occurs while filming sometimes makes far better material than the script being shot.

I made a film where the wife of the well-respected executive producer was so obnoxious that the director, the writer, and the cast told her to stay away from the set. When an added scene was requested by the producer, the writer purposely wrote a terrible scene just to aggravate the wife. The picture fell apart because of the personal animosity.

I worked with a director who was so despised by the cast that we banded together and took direction only from each other. During a press junket later, each cast member promised the others we'd reveal what we really felt. The director never did get it. He thought we were just ungrateful.

On a film where the husband and wife were very influential, I began to see that they both hated the director. The wife was a sexy star who couldn't act. Her husband was her manager, who had nothing to do with the film. There was dialogue that the husband despised. On behalf of his actress wife, he pulled a knife, walked up to the director, and threatened to slit the director's throat if he forced his wife to say the lines. Not being trained in guerrilla combat, the director cut the dialogue. He also quit the picture (or was fired, I'm not sure which).

The film shut down for a few weeks while another director was brought in. However, it wasn't long before the same thing happened again. The manager husband objected to a scene his wife was scripted to play; the scene was fine with her. In order to flex his power, the husband threatened to beat his wife up so that she would be unphotographable. He drove to the producer's home and explained in detail what sort of grave bodily harm he would inflict upon his wife's face and body. The producer banned the husband from the lot and the scene stayed.

The wife had to make her own peace with the maniac she was married to. If ever she snuck a piece of chocolate or took a bite of someone else's dessert, he chastised her publicly and unmercifully. More often than not, she'd leave the set or the dinner table in tears. Yet she was addicted to the power and control her husband exerted over her. He had been a pornographic filmmaker in his younger days, and when he met her she was only fourteen years old. Her age notwithstanding, he recruited her for his films, not only as an actress, but as a makeup artist who was to learn the professional tricks of the business by applying makeup to genital parts, which was rubbed off during the sexual activity of the scene. She spoke of her past with her husband in humorous, reverential tones. She believed everything he said and everything he did. I wondered which planet *I* was living on.

Machiavellian strokes of dishonesty are as common in Hollywood as garden-variety lying is elsewhere. A person whom I respect and know very well wanted to hire a director for his picture. The director wanted to do another picture with a topflight female star. My friend brought the female star to his screening room, ran a particularly bad film by the director in question, and after the lights came up proceeded to downgrade the director so unmercifully that the female star decided to walk away from the director. My friend then hired the director the next day because he was "free."

People in our business are more than susceptible to what other people think. Everyone's opinion is valuable. That's because we never know what films might make a hundred million dollars. Even if a picture is completed and everyone hates it, they're not really positive it won't be a hit. The gift of persuasion (true or false) is highly honed. So not only can you never be sure whether people are telling you the truth, but more important, if they *are* telling you the truth, you must find out *why*.

I learned from the movie business that the truth is relative, as it is, of course, in life.

# 15

# MOVIE SETS THEN VS. NOW

When I saw the movie *Sunset Boulevard,* I wondered whether I was seeing aspects of my own future. Gloria Swanson had done the part of Norma Desmond when she was forty-nine, and she was playing a has-been! When she returned to Paramount and "Mr. DeMille" and relived her memories of being part of the moviemaking family, I identified completely. I can still remember crew members who knew the contours of my face better than I. I can still feel their caressing eyes as they watched the light of their handiwork play across my cheekbones. I can still feel the strain on their arms as they were asked by the cinematographer to hold a gobo against the key light at just the right angle to produce a dramatic shadow across my shoulder.

The young crew members don't know how to do that

anymore. The training grounds have disappeared. Studio personnel are transient. The masters are few and far between.

So, we of the old school sometimes long for the past, when mastery of the craft was at its height. Yet those were also the days when writers were banished after a script was completed. The studio head was the boss. Directors were basically for hire, except for the truly great ones. Even then, the head of the studio had the final cut and they could pull the plug anytime they felt like it.

Today there is more spontaneity. Writers speak up and rewrite on the spot. Actors improvise dialogue, which was not only unheard of in the old days, but would have been terrifying. We were more formal then. We okayed a script and we stuck to it. Actors knew their lines perfectly and were expected never to deviate. The man in the chair (the director) was a well-respected dictator. He was the captain of our creative ship and the master of our emotional souls. His vision was to be served. No one else's. Yet the studio head, then and now, could destroy a director's vision because he has the final cut.

Directors and the front office would fight and threaten to kill each other, but the sets were well run with a well-established pecking order and a code of behavior.

Nowadays the sets can be a free-for-all. Loss of formality, even loss of control, is simply the way it is. Stars get huge salaries yet some wander onto a set two hours late. Stars wield power more than they ever have. They can command script changes no one else agrees with. They can run the show.

The most difficult cultural change has been the influence of drugs on so much of our industry.

I never had much curiosity about drugs. I've smoked

two marijuana cigarettes in my life. The first time I
ended up staring at the test pattern on a television set
for about five hours. The second time I got so hungry I
nearly ate the furniture in the hotel room. I think I've
found coke and LSD and other drugs uninteresting because of my fear of losing control. I've always needed to
be aware of my environment and my behavior in it. So I
am at this stage in my life completely naive about the
effect and cause of so much that goes on with drugs in
our industry.

After one of my longer absences from picture making,
I noticed that everyone was younger and nobody interre-
lated much. There was a rushed urgency behind every
move as crew members seemed to go about their work
in closed bubbles of their own. The hours were much
longer. The family feeling was gone. There was no time
to interrelate. A palpable fear permeated the sets; everyone, no matter what their job, seemed expendable due
to the hundreds of unemployed waiting in the wings.
There were no stories, jokes, or reminiscing about the
days when Hollywood set the world ablaze and sometimes melted in its own heat. The young ones didn't
seem interested in what Duke Wayne was really like or
whether Elizabeth and Richard were as combustible as
their antics indicated. People didn't want to hear about
George Stevens altering the script of *Shane* in the cutting
room, or James Wong Howe's refusal to shoot the film
in the rain. (He won the cinematography Oscar for finally giving in!) And these wonderful tales were only the
recent past. The young crew members hardly knew who
Gable and Lombard were, much less that they were
adored by their own crews.

To the crews I found myself working with in the late
seventies, Bette Davis and Joan Crawford were black-
and-white stars on TV at three in the morning. I don't

know when the change came. I believe it was Vietnam. The conflict and tearing apart engendered by that war altered our fantasies of romanticism. The glamour of pre-Vietnam Hollywood might seem obscene today. The mystery created then by being aloof, a heavenly body in the rarefied firmament of Hollywood, suddenly was laughable, open to ridicule as manipulative and a sham. The crews and the public as well seemed to want us to become more real, more accessible, more like them. They knew, of course, that we belched, had wax in our ears, and put our slacks on one leg at a time just like they did. What was the big deal about our glamorous past?

Yet the crews' cynicism about life and the puncturing of Hollywood romanticism created a depression that seemed to pour through their eyes. So what did they do to help alleviate their pain? They smoked pot, snorted coke, and shoved needles in their arms. The wealthier of the crew members went to designer drugs. I felt like a matron at a street rumble. I couldn't compute what I sensed around me. There wasn't much to see. It was something I felt. The camaraderie was what was missing. People were working too fast, too intensely, too urgently to take the time for camaraderie.

In the earlier days, most of our work was done on soundstages in controlled environments. There were no traffic problems, gawking spectators, or airplane and helicopter interference. The weather, the light intensity, the sound, the emotional peace of mind, and the quiet rehearsals necessary to get the scenes right were under the control of the director and the cinematographer. The crews enjoyed observing the creative process as we found our moves, the levels of comedy and drama, and where we felt most comfortable with the camera. They saw what we were trying to do as we stumbled through our own creative risk taking. Therefore, we felt we were working together. We found what we needed in order to expose ourselves on the screen, and the crews were there to help us. Temperament was never a problem. It was expected and even enjoyed. The crews had something to tell their families when they got home at night.

Nowadays the actors are thrown out on the street in full view of whoever happens to be passing by. It is usually either too hot, too cold, too smoggy, or too noisy to have a proper rehearsal. No one really wants to work that way, but unfortunately movies have succumbed to economic realities and it is simply cheaper. For television shows, street scenes are still shot on a studio lot, but for movies, hardly ever. To build the sets on a soundstage with union costs escalating is unrealistic now. So the production manager gives a guy who owns a bar a few thousand dollars a day and instructs the director and actors to get the scene in one day because we can't afford more. Thus the urgency and the necessity of the sharp, swift thrust to just get the thing done. Drugs make the pressure bearable, I guess.

The audiences require more escape these days. More high-tech violence because they see lives saved and taken on their evening news programs. Since the supply of live information is more immediate and more intensely real than ever before, motion pictures must outdo the news. So I suppose it was inevitable that we'd be out on the streets shooting. . . . Everyone else is.

I haven't shot an entire picture in a studio since the sixties. I've shot some interior scenes in studios, but movies are usually done on location now. So, when we are offered films, one of the first questions we ask is, "Where will it be shot?" We know we'll have to be "away" for at least three months. This is hard on marriages, relationships, and children.

On the other hand, we are out among real people more than we used to be. No longer are we protected by the care-control mechanisms of the studio. No longer are we "under contract," belonging to them. We own ourselves now. Our independent companies produce the pictures for the studios. We are in control until it comes to the final cut. (Rarely will a studio give final cut to a director or an independent producer.) Therefore, there is no nurturing, no coddling, no sense of family feuding. We operate independently and fend for ourselves. We owe no allegiance to anyone and no one owes it to us. We are liberated from the stickiness of being cared for while being controlled. With the maturation of democracy in this country, Hollywood has matured also. We are free to be ourselves and have put aside childish petulance and adolescent expectations. It has been a painful transformation and we are still adjusting. But I thank our forefathers and foremothers for blazing the trail of cinematic creativity, pressing the issue of their own frustrations and discoveries at precisely the right pace so that those of us who came later could bring the case for creative freedom to fruition. The stars, the directors, and the producers who live in my memory made it possible for those of us today to advance and enhance our own expression.

Our responsibility now is to balance the financial with the creative as we attempt to mirror and reflect the culture that we seek not only to please, but to inspire.

Making films nowadays engenders more than ever the necessity for each of us to evaluate who we are and what we're doing. This evolution can be extremely painful, resulting in ruptured relationships and shattered communication. Our work is about more than what is on the page or in the image on screen. It is about *us,* our lives, our feelings. We *are* the people we portray, and the directors and production people are what the films are about.

Nowadays we understand that the films we are making are not the point. Rather, it is the *process* of what we learn from the experience; therein lies the teaching. We're beginning to stop and reflect upon why we are drawn to a certain subject in the first place. No longer is our business only about giving the people what they want. It's as much about what *we* want to say. We are beginning to comprehend the wisdom and emotional maturity of believing in something on film. If our hearts are engaged and not just our pocketbooks, the public's reaction is usually favorable. They, out there in the dark, are collectively looking for artistic leadership. They want to know what we feel. They want to *feel* what we feel. They have entrusted us with leading them into our dreams. They are willing to invest their time and money if we really believe in what we're doing. And they can always tell whether we are authentic or not. They can smell our belief system, they can intuit whether we really mean it.

The arguments over creative differences have changed from years ago. Today there is a genuine difference of artistic opinion. Of course, if we go with what we feel is right, that may have a positive impact at the box office.

Focus groups and previews are conducted today not to determine whether a picture will be a hit (although that is maddeningly important), but more to ascertain whether we have been clear in our intent. Was our communication comprehended? Did they understand the characters? Do they have suggestions relating to those characters? *Guarding Tess,* for instance, was originally intended to be a film told in flashbacks about an ex–first lady who is dead at the start of the movie. As a result, the preview audience didn't laugh. The film was recut so that Tess didn't die. The laughs were suddenly there.

Because of the impact of talk shows and the American habit of emotional venting in public, the studio bosses are trying to keep up with a country that has far outstripped the Hollywood connection. The public comprehends the contradictions of deeper human feelings more than the people making the films do. They are more acquainted with the shadows and gray areas of human nature than the men and women in charge of the scripts.

The studio bosses think *Mrs. Doubtfire* was a comedy starring Robin Williams's crazy, wonderful antics. The public knew it was also about the pain of divorce and child custody.

The studios thought *E.T.* and *Star Wars* were imaginative flights of childhood fancy. But the public, in the main, really believes we are not alone in the universe.

When *Terms of Endearment* became a classic, it was because Jim Brooks understood that cancer was ravaging many American families *and* because the comedy of imperious mothers and insecure daughters who feel they can never please their mothers reflects an endemic American feminine confusion. Thus the success of *The Joy Luck Club* and others.

The studios thought *Terminator 2* was a hit because Arnold Schwarzenegger was a funny, sardonic interplanetary action hero in high-tech competition with an even higher-tech evil wizard. To me, the picture worked because the mother had had visions of the future that were not pleasant, to say the least, and wanted to protect her family and the families of others from the end of the world.

To me, *Silence of the Lambs* worked because Hannibal Lecter gloried in showing his deranged mind, thereby satisfying our curiosity about cannibalistic instincts.

To me, *Jurassic Park* speaks to a genetic memory of a time we have all evolved from and wish to remember.

*Schindler's List* was about an unlikely man who finds enough goodness and caring in himself to take action.

*Quiz Show* marked the moment of decline in public morality in our country. *Forrest Gump* helped us to feel okay about our own personal histories and commitments in the last thirty-five years.

When we contemplate making a film, we often find that we have overlooked its true meaning. The audience is the entity that finds it for us and mirrors it back.

Our ability to see into our material is in direct proportion to our ability to see into ourselves. That's one of the reasons why so many of us are in therapy, or investigating our unrealized spiritual aspects, or questioning our backgrounds, our childhoods, our parents, our relatives, our relationship to God and to our fellow men and women.

Filmmakers and the people who finance and distribute films know that self-knowledge is the key to a healthy industry that dares to marry art and business.

We know that the investigation into the mystery of self will create fireworks. In fact, creative arguments nowadays revolve around who has shown more courage to go within and to analyze why his or her emotional reactions are what they are. Our onscreen characters are defective when we who create them are unclear.

Meetings these days are almost always peppered with such evaluations of what people want to say and whether they believe in themselves enough to say it. It's not, what do you want to ''do'' anymore—it's what do you want to ''say''?

Studio heads and financial people look to the artists for commitment and passion as a lightning rod for success. Complacency is out. Obsessive caring is in, even if the obsession is a power trip. It is about the work, about the message, about the living feelings that will implode within the filmmaker if he or she doesn't get the money necessary to realize the dream. When financial people hear the sounds of passion from artists, they write the checks. So many wish *they* had feelings that intense.

Yet in spite of that, when a really fine adult film doesn't gross what is expected, and indeed may not even break even, the studio heads run scared. They play to the broad spectrum of acceptability from the audience.

Recently, the failure of such critically acclaimed films as *Quiz Show* and *The Shawshank Redemption* to draw big numbers has intimidated the studios, blocking them from giving the green light to other adult films with superb scripts that might meet the same fate, for example, *Evening Star,* the sequel to *Terms of Endearment.* In the final analysis, the studios go for grosses and put art on hold.

So the dance of feeling, humanity, money, and control goes on. And as the years pass and we come closer to the turn of not only a century, but a millennium, one can feel the attempt to balance the ledger between talent and responsibility. Everyone is doing his best really. No one (with a few exceptions) is purposefully malevolent or freakish in the need to control. The lies, the manipulation, the seductions, the tears, the subjugation of one's very soul are usually done in the name of being true and authentic to one's purpose and art. It is a colossal paradox: to be true to one's authentic vision sometimes requires the basest of fakery, disinformation, duplicity, hypocrisy, distortion, spuriousness, and unctuous deception!

That is why Hollywood is referred to as the Big Knife. That is why civilians are fascinated by how we conduct our ''reality.'' We do things in Hollywood in the name of entertainment that most governments do in the name of espionage.

Money, power, sex, and talent are the checkers on

our board. The honored ingredients necessary to achieving the shiniest American Dream of all.

In the nineties, we sense that we are coming to a point where we must resolve the greed and longing for those checkers. Are we giving back as much as we receive? How low will we stoop to titillate the basic instincts of our audiences just to make money?

We are coming to a point where spiritually and sociologically we need to accept the responsibility of the First Amendment. We have not yet evolved into loving and maturely aware people in this land of unbridled freedom and democracy. Too often we are like cruel, self-involved children whose very survival depends upon material protection and territorial imperatives. If our excuse in Hollywood is that we are simply reflecting the culture when we tell our stories, then it is time to demonstrate our creative leadership and tell stories that contribute to the culture we would *like* to reflect.

These illusions we spin, these dreams we weave, are important. They can even be life altering.

And as we seem to be spinning out of control while plunging into a new age, I and many others are finding that we need to establish a dominion over ourselves rather than imposing domination on others. We can do something about *who* we are. We can really do nothing about anyone else.

Our films, our art, our books help us to see who we are as well as who we might aspire to be.

I hope for a time when the exercise of and approaches to self-knowledge will no longer be ridiculed. When the sharing of human experience can be freely expressed without the accusation of sentimentality or of washing one's linen in public. I hope for an environment where the investigation of self will not be looked upon as self-indulgent and self-centered, but rather as self-centering.

If we are not centered in self, how can we be centered in our work and our expression of human life?

To make a film that works, each of us involved has had to look long and deeply into ourselves—where we came from, where we've been, and where we wish to go—before we can even begin to know and understand the characters we wish to paint upon the Big Screen. When we look honestly within ourselves, it is clear that our view of the world changes. We are not victims of the world we see, we are victims of the way we see the world.

We in Hollywood make and sculpt and fashion unusual pictures of the world we live in, in accordance with how we see ourselves. It is easy to commit millions of dollars to violent pictures if we feel violent within ourselves. Altering our perspective of the world will only come from alterations within ourselves. To me, that is our challenge in Hollywood as we head into the year 2000. Even nature seems to be saying "a balance comes from within. Begin now before it is too late."

# 16

# AAAAARGHH!

## Acting With Aging, Anxiety, Anger, and Accomplishment

*I*t's no fun becoming old, but it can be fun for an actress because it's a nice feeling to command the respect that comes with age, wisdom, and experience. Older actors become a kind of royalty. When we were young, it was obvious what we didn't know. With age we are a mystery. When we were young, people wanted to know us from the outside in. With age they want to know us from the inside out. In youth people wanted to know us in bed. In age they simply want to know us. Our interior gold attracts many "minors."

When I was twenty years old and did my first picture, the seriousness of becoming a long-distance runner never occurred to me. I was flippant about my talent and early success, presuming that the magic would always be there. I didn't know enough about the perils of success to worry about its impermanence. It didn't occur to me to police myself or take care that I wasn't robbed of my due or worry that someone else might possibly be gaining on me. I had an interesting life, was making lots of money, had a husband who seemed to emotionally support and believe in me. I simply felt driven to express myself. When I look back at how supremely naive I was, I don't know how I lasted. On the other hand, perhaps my attitude was what sustained me. I *expected* that success was and always would be my choice.

The lessons of failure and aging would come later as my life and my work unfolded, and they were directly related to what I learned from the characters I played. My young parts, when I was in my twenties, were wide-eyed, curious, and openhearted. Something like me. I trusted in people as I found them, walked into the face of danger because it was an adventure, fell in love at the drop of a good love scene, and never stopped to consider the consequences of much of anything. I didn't analyze my characters much, never had pages of notes and suggestions for the director, and rarely studied my lines the night before. Frankly, I winged it. . . . Something like the characters I was playing.

Yes, my characters were usually what I would call "pixilated." They were so pixilated, people called me "kooky" for many years. Perhaps I drew characters to me that helped me analyze myself in an entertaining way. The girls I played in *The Trouble with Harry* and *Artists and Models* were zany, droll, chirpy characters who got away with being outrageous. I remember giving an interview during those years in which I claimed to be designing an image for myself that would enable me to get away with anything.

My character as Princess Aouda in *Around the World in Eighty Days* was my plea to be authentic in playing any nationality. *Eighty Days* was also the commencement of my love for travel.

Japan was my first location, and from then on my life became a travelogue, which remains true to this day. I found that I was either playing parts that exemplified what I longed to do, or I continued in my life what I had begun on the screen.

I couldn't happily make Westerns or pictures on location outside in the sun because I had hypersensitive blue eyes. I devoured Vitamin A just to keep my eyes open. I didn't care much for dusty cowboy towns or horses anyway, and I felt silly playing Glenn Ford's girlfriend in *The Sheepman,* trying to make peace between cattle ranchers and farmers, neither of whom I knew anything about or even cared about.

And when I worked with Shirley Booth in *The Matchmaker* and *Hot Spell* (she was my idol at the time), it never occurred to me that I would one day be her age (forty-five!!). But I was learning through these scripts the emotional tone difference between playing comedy and drama.

Then came *Some Came Running,* which changed my acting life. It enabled me to combine comedy and drama. Smiling through tears became my specialty.

The process of fashioning the acting magic is an exercise no one else in the world can comprehend unless they've tried it.

I personally need to know the physical characteristics and body movement of the person I'm playing. From there I work inward.

When I arrived on the set of the location for *Some Came Running,* I had no idea how I would play the part until I stepped off the bus in the first scene with Frank Sinatra. I looked down and my toes were turned inward. I realized then that Ginny Moorehead wanted to walk pigeon-toed. She wanted to stumble and be slightly un-coordinated, just as she was in her life. She wanted to lurch through life lovingly, putting other people's welfare before her own.

When I was sure of her body movement, I knew what she chose to put on her body. The dresses were her misguided idea of sexy; so tight that her bra strap always showed. I knew she wasn't fastidious and never even noticed that her black roots showed beneath her dyed red hair. Because she was so unconcerned with herself, she elicited a feeling of warmth and pity from the audience. When Dean and Frank chimed, "Hell, even she knows she's a pig," it made a cruel sense.

Ginny was one of my favorite characters because I didn't have to search for her. She revealed herself to me immediately. She was a definable character.

Probably I have been a character actress from the beginning. I like eccentricity and contradiction in a character. I adore unpredictability that surprises even me. I love going to the edge of characters and never going over. From the beginning I loved the risk. Then again, sometimes the character didn't demand such audacity.

Fran Kubelik in *The Apartment* was one of those. I could not articulate anything definite about her. In fact, I was never really sure who she was. That was precisely how she was . . . unformed, a victim of circumstance who didn't have an evident self-profile to fall back upon. She *reacted* to everyone else around her. I, therefore, had to react, not act, in that picture. It was finer and more subtle writing than I was used to.

Billy Wilder and Izzy Diamond were so brilliant in their observations about life that often Jack Lemmon and I would interact in the commissary over lunch without ever knowing that we were enacting a scene that was missing. A day or two later, what we had said would appear as script pages.

Dean and Frank were teaching me to play gin rummy at the time we were shooting *The Apartment*. I would play gin in between setups. That's how the gin game ended up in the movie. I used to hold up four fingers when my mouth said three, just for fun. That's in the movie too.

During the scene where my brother comes to rescue me and there is a physical scuffle, I had a hard time reacting with panic and concern, so Billy got a huge piece of wood and cracked it in two in front of my face below the camera. I was properly shocked.

During the scene where Fran is left alone on Christmas Eve, something went wrong with the sound. When the picture was over, I went in to "loop" (dub in my voice) with crying. The soundtrack during that crying scene came from a bottle of menthol I inhaled. It made me blubber into the microphone. . . . It's hard for me to think it's necessary to really work up the tears when the same effect can be achieved with a little well-used Hollywood technology.

I don't mean to belittle real feelings translated to the screen, and I won't. But it is true that an audience always reacts more to what you hold back as an actor than what you express. Think of Bette Davis dying in *Dark Victory*. Audiences can identify with that withholding feeling.

The same goes for playing drunk. As Jack Nicholson told me, you play trying *not* to be drunk. Again, that's what the audience identifies with, because they always try *not* to be drunk when they are.

A director can't really help an actor with those internal mechanisms. He can be helpful by being kind and patient or he can think he's being helpful by challenging you to do it or else.

When Billy Wilder approached Jack Lemmon and me to do *Irma La Douce,* I was thrilled that I would be doing a musical, which was its original incarnation in Europe and on Broadway. But Billy decided against the music. Perhaps that was because he had never done one. Many good directors feel that musicals with a good script are just that—a good story with music. But a musical picture is a different language altogether. The structure of the plot, by necessity, has to be different, because it is continually interrupted by musical numbers. A scene can't provide all the information in a musical. The lyrics of a song have to extend the flow of information in a scene, otherwise the song is redundant and the audience feels bored by the repetition.

I didn't particularly like the plot of *Irma.* I thought it was caricaturish and hard to believe. The music took it into the realm of fantasy, and that's what made it work for me. Without the French music, I had a problem.

But Billy was right, for himself, not to make it a musical. He said he didn't know how. So he made a kind of Feydeau farce instead. But I felt the movie was slightly crude, clumsy. I didn't understand why I got nominated for an Oscar, and would have been really nonplussed had I won. I knew I wouldn't, but had that happened, I was ready to make a speech for the legalization of the oldest profession in the world.

The biggest disappointment to me in my early career was William Wyler's remake of his own film *These Three,* retitled *The Children's Hour.* It was adapted quite faithfully by John Michael Hayes from Lillian Hellman's play, only in the earlier film version two women were in love with the same man. This time Willy intended to do it right: a man (Jim Garner) and a woman (me) were in love with the same woman (Audrey Hepburn).

I, therefore, conceived Martha's character (as per the script) to lovingly build her adoration and emotional involvement with the character of Karen so that the audience would realize early on what was going on. In fact, Martha was unaware of her feelings being in any way inappropriate until the little girl exaggerated Martha's behavior into a lie. Within that lie was the ounce of truth.

Audrey and I became very close working together. She was, and remained until her death, one of my favorite people. Audrey trusted Willy and on many occasions would turn to me, sigh, and remark with confidence how wonderful it was to work with someone to whom you could entrust your artistic integrity.

But after the shoot was completed, Willy got cold feet about the lesbian subject. He cut out all the scenes that portrayed Martha falling in love with Karen. Scenes where I (Martha) lovingly pressed Karen's clothes, or brushed her hair, or baked her cookies ended up on the cutting-room floor. The *audience* was supposed to be aware of the growing love Martha developed for Karen, which is what gave the film tension, because Karen was not aware either. In eliminating those scenes, Willy gutted the intention of the film.

Thus, in the end, he was not faithful to Lillian Hellman's play and the result was a disaster with the critics. One called it a "cultural antique." Another led his review with "The les-bian said the better."

I was crushed. So was Willy. But he hadn't been willing to take the chance and go all the way.

•     •     •

SOMEWHERE ALONG THE LINE, AS THE YEARS PASSED, I realized that I had carved a career out of playing victims. I hadn't been aware of this until I analyzed my parts.

*Ask Any Girl* with David Niven was a comedy in which a small-town girl was victimized by the big city. *Career* was the drama of a party girl victimized by her own behavior. Fran Kubelik in *The Apartment* was the victim of a married man's insensitive guilt and the male power structure in the business where she worked. Finally, as her life became too much for her, she tried to kill herself.

In *The Children's Hour,* my character, Martha, was the victim of a child's lie.

In *Can-Can,* although my character was strong and funny, she was a victim of the whims of Frank Sinatra.

In *Two for the Seesaw,* Gittel Mosca was the prize victim of Greenwich Village . . . street-wise, dancer-wise, Mitchum-wise, marriage-wise, life-wise.

In *Irma La Douce,* the title character worked hard so her pimp could continue to live the lifestyle to which he was accustomed.

In *Yellow Rolls-Royce,* I was a gangster's moll trying to make the best of things. In *Woman Times Seven,* all seven women were victims of their circumstances told in endearingly Vittorio De Sica terms.

In *What a Way to Go,* each of my character's husbands died, leaving me with millions of dollars—and no life.

The ultimate musical victim without parallel was *Sweet Charity* Hope Valentine. She was just like her name—sweet, full of hope, believed she was a valentine, and gave everybody her charity. Of course, Charity should have been a hard-bitten little whore who was basically only serious about the money she kept in her coffee can.

It was time to do something else. I had learned all I needed to learn about the various forms of victimization.

I graduated to roles involving women's relationships to work and family, but not before going through the first phase of discovering what it meant to be unwanted and out of work.

THE YEAR WAS 1976 AND I WAS FORTY-TWO YEARS OLD.

I had given up a year and a half to work for George McGovern in 1972, done two films that were unsuccessful, *Desperate Characters* and *The Possession of Joel Delaney,* and made my foray into television with a series, *Shirley's World,* that was so bad I made certain I was unavailable to watch it every Wednesday night at 9:30.

Suddenly I realized the meaning of the word "has-been." It seemed to be happening to me. I had been away from Hollywood because of my political work, and when I did return to pictures, my choices were dreadful. There were no parts for me. I never felt I was blacklisted because of my opposition to Nixon (although most of Hollywood supported him). The reason I couldn't get work was because I was unbankable. The days of being the new quirky girl in town were long past. I was middle-aged and gaining—not only in my life, but my body.

I became depressed and felt underutilized. I was a racehorse with some Thoroughbred blood in my veins and I couldn't find a racetrack.

I was living in New York, enjoying life to a certain extent, but aware that with every day that passed I was becoming more and more estranged from my real home—Hollywood. For the first time, my future was murky, undependable. I began to worry about myself. Gone were the work-crammed younger days of adoration and flippancy. I was feeling the ravages of time and the stark wisdom of reality.

I made a decision to return to my beginnings. I went back to dancing class, put myself on a strict diet, lost thirty pounds, and returned to the stage. At least I could rely on my training from childhood. If it worked I would be guaranteed a place to express myself and a form of income.

I knew when I opened at the MGM Grand that I was a has-been movie star with a club act as a backup because I had nowhere else to go. I drove my body unmercifully to look thin and taut. I lived at the gym and ate nothing. And I was terrified to face an audience.

One of the individuals who was most responsible for giving me the courage to proceed was the composer Cy Coleman. He had written the music for *Sweet Charity* and I loved his talent and generosity. He was willing to help me put my act together, which of course featured many of his songs. That was fine with me. Most of his work was for actors and dancers who sang anyway.

So there I was, a movie star who couldn't get work, opening in Vegas and hopefully stints beyond. Thank God, the show was a hit. I was thrilled. I went from Vegas to Europe and finally to New York, where we played the Palace, and I was a hit there too. I had a new career, which I felt I could depend upon as long as I could draw audiences. But a confusion in the audiences' perception of me soon became evident, which prevails to this day. Audiences who frequent live concert performances are not really sure what to expect from me. Are they going to see a movie star, a political activist, a person who will lecture about metaphysical matters, or a singer/dancer who sometimes does musicals? They are not sure.

This is especially true with audiences in the United States (except on the two coasts). To American audiences, I belonged on the screen; Hollywood was my base—my real home. It was the town where I would find acknowledgment. This has produced an anxiety in me to somehow remain on the screen, because the screen is my natural medium of expression, my life's blood bank. Yet with every successful picture I am lucky enough to be a part of, comes confusion relating to my stage work. Am I a character actress or a performer? And the older I play on film, the more confused the audiences become on stage. How can a gray-haired (even though they're wigs) eccentric character actress do a glamorous act of songs and dances?

My original persona was that of a movie star and I suppose that is how I will be perceived for the rest of my life, whether I continue to work in films or not.

In any case, my live show saved my life during the middle seventies, and when I finally got a good offer in pictures again, it was *The Turning Point* for Herb Ross.

*The Turning Point* became my *first* comeback picture! I played middle-aged, which was my first subtle entry into character acting, and I realized that I was beginning a new phase of learning about mother-daughter relationships through my characters. This subject seemed popular on the screen because so many mothers and daughters were having problems with each other. I felt useful again. I could say something about the complexity of women, young and old, changing values within families, and how age brought wisdom if one allowed it.

So *The Turning Point* heralded a turning point in the kinds of parts I played. Dee Dee had trained all of her young life to become a fine ballet dancer, only to make the decision, on the brink of stardom, to give it up for marriage and a family. Through Dee Dee I examined how I would have dealt with such a decision. The answer? I would never have given up my work for marriage, family, or anybody—to me it would be like telling a B-47 it shouldn't fly but should instead have a satisfying time secure in the hangar.

Work was necessary to me, which led me to understand that regardless of what happened in my life, I *needed* to be acknowledged; therefore, I would *need* to survive in a business that was notorious for making people, particularly *actresses,* disposable.

I had started as a dancer, and coming full circle again, here I was, in a picture I badly needed and was grateful for, surrounded by the world of my beginnings—ballet!

Herbert Ross, the director, was in his element with Arthur Laurents's script. Herbert had been in ballet himself as a dancer and choreographer, which was really novel because he is way over six feet tall. He saw to it that his wife, Nora Kaye, one of the greatest ballerinas who ever lived, functioned as associate producer and all-around overseer. They were brilliant as a creative team, and the footage reflected that. *The Turning Point* garnered eleven Academy Award nominations, including one for me, and was a big hit, because of their vision of and homage to the world of ballet.

It was Mikhail Baryshnikov's first feature film. He was hardworking and diligent. I liked and enjoyed him so much. We often talked in between setups about what ballet does *for* and *to* your mind, body, and spirit. He found acting exhausting because of the need to hold the emotional level all day long. Often he'd come to me at the end of a day's shooting and say it was easier to do a full ballet than to sustain emotionality during the waiting hours.

I loved being around accomplished ballet dancers again. I had never been good enough to become a soloist. Quatre ballet was about all I could handle. I was too tall (5′7″) and I didn't have beautifully constructed feet (high arches, high insteps). My extension on my left leg was pretty good, but my feet wouldn't point with the curve that suggests the ultimate in beauty. My real forte

was jumps, especially grand jetés, and hopping on
pointe.

I loved watching ballerinas on the set try to act and
dance at the same time. Many of them couldn't. So focused were they on the movement, they couldn't form
words in their mouths. They could spontaneously talk
and dance at the same time in real life, but found it
difficult to remember lines while they were executing
steps.

We shot the last scene in the film first, in an upper
foyer of a theater across the street from the Palace Theater. I had just closed my one-woman show at the Palace
and the marquee with my name on it was still up.

I looked down at it and remembered all the years of
ballet pain. I was now playing the part of a woman who
had said enough is enough. I wondered when I would
come to that conclusion. I also wondered what my life
would have been like had I never gone to ballet class at
all. Dancing meant the appreciation of form, art, and
beauty—discipline was a given. It meant punctuality,
junk food, no sleep, noisy trains, and rising above adversity. It also meant struggle and triumph of the spiritual
over the physical. In the end, when all of those things
came together, the feeling of soaring with the body into
forms of exquisite geometry made the experience of being alive a heavenly state of being.

Even though *The Turning Point* was a big hit for me
and everyone involved, it was dismissed by some as a
"women's picture." Still, I was encouraged because I
had found a way back into Hollywood.

The glare of the white soundstages at high noon, the
early calls and clogged freeways in the mornings, the
desire and anxiety to please the front office entered my
life again. So too did the camaraderie of a film set, the

expression of human emotion, and the feeling of once again being appreciated.

What would I do, I thought, if it should all go away for good? What else was there as important in my life? I had a long-distance marriage that had become platonic and unsatisfying, a daughter who had her own life, a passport that had stamps on it from nearly every country in the world, a relationship that was winding down, and an uncertain view of my future.

I began to seriously question the meaning of my life, my purpose and divinity, my reason for being alive, where I was going, and where I might have come from.

This was when spirituality and metaphysics became important to me. I began to ask so many spiritual questions. I read everything I could find, including the Bible, the Koran, and most every book written on reincarnation, the laws of Karma, and extraterrestrials. My investigations took me to remote areas of the globe and soon I found an entirely new circle of friends.

As I learned the metaphysical axioms for reality which concluded that the reality of our lives was basically our own personal creation in order to learn, and that indeed life itself is an illusion or dream that deeply affects us because of its lessons, I began to perceive Hollywood's reality differently. The parallels were so similar. We in the movie business created illusions for other people to believe in as real, while we were doing the same thing with ourselves in our own lives. In other words, we were each responsible for creating everything that happened to us. Therefore, we were empowered to uncreate as well, if we so desired.

I wanted to uncreate what was happening in Hollywood relating to women's parts.

The parts being written for women in Hollywood reflected confusion. It was almost as though the men who wrote them were trying to figure out who *they* were, not who the women were.

I received two scripts that were essentially the same, on the subject of open marriage (*Loving Couples* and *A Change of Seasons*). I couldn't decide between them so I did both, figuring one would work. *Both* were awful. Neither the female nor the male characters were real as each attempted to deal with monogamy, infidelity, and finally communication in marriage. Once again I was on the outside looking in.

The writers debated at length on the problem, as did the directors and producers. In the meantime, women were essentially excluded from the mainstream of movie-making. They became also-rans, dutifully fulfilling the expectations of the leading male character, or vociferously opposing the leading male character. Or more than likely, women couldn't get parts in the movies at all because the leading male characters were costarring with each other. Buddy pictures became the mode of the day. I went back to metaphysics, where I could create my own reality, which seemed to be the newly developing human art form anyway.

Once more I found myself, as did many others, wondering if there would ever be good parts for women again.

Enter Jim Brooks and *Terms of Endearment* and my *second* comeback picture. He understood the contradictions, the nooks and crannies, and the magnificent "magnanimosity" of women.

The picture changed the Hollywood landscape where women were concerned. But no one could come up with a follow-through. Jim stood alone in his consummate understanding of contradictions in human beings; of men *and* women. He was also brilliant about aging.

During the making of *Terms,* I was so glad to find myself comfortable with the aging aspects of Aurora.

I remember Jim being so sensitively concerned about my vanity as he suggested using my own gray roots as an insignia of Aurora's decline in physical pride and appearance. Not only did I not mind, I found a comforting pleasure in seeing that my future could lie in playing older roles successfully. At least I would continue to work and maybe I could even say some important things through my acting. However, I remember the day we shot a test of Aurora's decline. The cameraman had to leave early. He forgot to put a filter in the lens.

The entire company saw the film the next day. The wrinkles embedded in my face were much more startling on film than what met the naked eye. I was mortified. In that moment I knew I was old, and I was not yet fifty. Hollywood has a way of forcing you to look into the future, and what I saw was not mirthmaking.

After *Terms of Endearment,* there was nothing out there. I decided to do *Cannonball Run II.* The critic from *USA Today* said Dean Martin and I should fire our agent.

I spent the next few years writing and shooting the five-hour miniseries of my book *Out on a Limb,* determining with my cowriter and friend Colin Higgins, who was also involved with his own spiritual search, what was palatable to a huge audience and what wasn't.

The show was not as highly rated as we expected, even though it won its time period on the second night.

One thing fascinated me in terms of our competition. *Mafia Wife* beat us out the first night. Two women battled in the arena of public taste. One on a spiritual search, the other on a power trip. The Mob won. Enough said.

My character in *Steel Magnolias* became a pathway for my own increasingly irascible expression. The lines by

Robert Harling ("I've been in a bad mood for forty years.") spurred me to take a sarcastically witty course of action in my own life when I found that with age I could no longer suffer fools gladly.

I adored working with no makeup, a gray, disheveled wig, and a wardrobe that would put a bag lady to shame. I felt free to be older and funnier and ignore social decorum. In fact, I could imagine myself some years from now, being similar to Ouiser Boudreaux. Rich, flamboyantly sarcastic, and more than happy to be alone.

In that respect I have extracted what I considered the best from characters and used whatever gave me fun and pleasure.

By the time I got to *Madame Sousatzka,* I had come through the fire: I knew I was into the last period of my life. Sousatzka was my tribute to every teacher I had ever had, including my parents. I wanted to play her even older than I could get away with. I seemed to empathize with the bittersweet loneliness of teaching others because my time was now measured. I know my portrayal was shocking, but aging *is* shocking, and I wanted to paint my impressions with broad strokes.

With *Madame Sousatzka* I came closest to living a part. Experimenting, I decided to employ a metaphysical technique. The director, John Schlesinger, and I conceived how Sousatzka dressed, moved, talked, and felt about herself and her piano students. I then threw her up to the universe, got out of my own way, and allowed Sousatzka to play herself through me! Acting is a metaphysical exercise anyway in that we actors create a reality we then proceed to believe is real. So taking Sousatzka one step further seemed inevitable to me because I could trust Schlesinger's taste.

Sousatzka would "come in" right before the cameras

rolled in the morning and leave after the last scene every night.

When we shot the final scene of the picture, she left for good, and within five minutes my throat seized up, I had a fever, and came down with the flu. I don't know why that happened. Metaphysicians would say it was due to the change of energy. I was proud of that performance, even though only about twelve people in the world saw the picture. It also launched me into character acting once and for all. Producers were no longer intimidated to send me scripts of older women for fear I'd be insulted. In fact, they became so liberated from their fear that some of the suggestions I got were astonishing, *Driving Miss Daisy* being one of them. I very much respected Dick and Lili Zanuck, but I felt that I had not yet graduated to Jessica Tandy's roles.

When Mike Nichols and Carrie Fisher asked me to do *Postcards from the Edge,* it felt like old times again. A big-budgeted movie with stars (Meryl Streep, Dennis Quaid, and Gene Hackman); a sumptuous catering table all day long (food was becoming more and more important to me); a musical number to sing, rewritten by Stephen Sondheim; a great director, a superb costar, a witty and dramatic script, and the best part I had had in a long time.

But the audience had changed. They weren't that interested in yet another examination of mother-daughter conflicts. *Postcards* was another modest hit, and once again, studio heads muttered that "women's pictures" were risky.

The same thing happened with *Used People.* The people didn't care that much for family problems on the screen. The culture did not want to look at itself. Times were hard enough, I guess. They wanted to escape. Yet I kept looking for stories with intelligent meaning. *Wres-*

*tling Ernest Hemingway* didn't work because it took itself
too seriously. It had *too much* self-conscious meaning.
But by now I just wanted to work with people I respected and I didn't much care about box office.

I had become a respected matron of many meanings in
Hollywood.

Many was the script that crossed my desk calling for
me to play a woman of seventy-five and older.

When *Guarding Tess* arrived, I read the description of
the character: Tess Carlisle, seventy-five, widow of the
former president. I elected not to be insulted, read the
script, loved it, decided to do it, and made essentially
only one change in the script. Where it said Tess Carlisle, seventy-five, I simply reversed the numbers to say
Tess Carlisle, fifty-seven. Nobody said anything and no
one knew the difference.

When *Guarding Tess* became a modest success—number one at the box office until *Naked Gun 33¹/₃*
opened—I felt the old twinge of excitement at being a
box-office hit again. People were glad to see me at parties and social gatherings. They were most deferential
regarding my life and body of work. But it made me
chuckle too. I remembered how it was when nobody
cared. There was polite acknowledgment of my presence, but nobody spent much of their precious time
locked in conversation with me in the corner of the
room. Yes, how fleeting, and in the long-term, meaning-
less fame and success really were. Critical and box-office
success means something if it contributes to the knowledge of who I am, and that knowledge comes from the
experience of failure as well as success.

I used to be concerned with what other people might
think of me. Now I'm concerned with what *I* think of
other people. That goes for the audience too. I have
opinions of them now just as they have opinions of me.

And sometimes my opinion of them is not overly respectful. I don't much care anymore what they think because I'm not sure they do think.

I care about acting now, acting and performing. I do it for myself. I have come to have a deep respect for my profession and what it takes to last. I'm not sure an audience's opinion has anything to do with it.

Probably my biggest acting challenge now will be the recreation of Aurora Greenway in *Evening Star*. She is twenty years older and coping not only with aging and the trials and tribulations of her grandchildren, but also with her colorful and irrepressible sexuality. She goes to a psychiatrist to cope with the grandchildren. He is twenty-five years younger. She promptly seduces him. He succumbs willingly, and for once we see a woman of sixty on the screen who still has the juice and passions that I and many other women of age possess in real life. We are not willing to go gently into that good night, retiring quietly. We have much to contribute to a relationship—wisdom and experience and a better understanding of human nature. We want to continue to be acknowledged. And as Jim Brooks proved, life that is worth living comes from contradictions we are trying to resolve. Life is better after you've lived it awhile.

I thank each character I've tried to portray. I've learned to feel more through them. They have helped me know more about myself. They have helped me to be less judgmental as to what is right and what is wrong where human behavior is concerned. They have helped me celebrate the defects in life with more gusto.

I still think of myself as an enthusiastic adventurer willing to try anything new. When people approach me on the street with "my goodness, you're still here?" it gives me pause. How many of them were three months old when their parents first saw me? It is somehow inconceivable to me that I am not thirty anymore. What happened and why so fast?

Yet, in the stark night of being alone and sometimes unwanted, there is a small voice that still resides wisely and comfortably in my heart which whispers, "You ain't seen nothing yet."

# 17
# THE ANSWER

s I have wandered around in time, through my recollections and reflections, I wonder what is the connective tissue that makes me remember the people and events in the particular order that I do.

There is an invisible harmony underlying my life and there always has been, as I believe there is in all lives. Our task is to sense it and be true to it. "There is a divinity that shapes our ends—rough hew them how we will," said Hamlet.

I believe there is something unknowable yet certain about why we are compelled to our individual positions in the universe that is often reflected in the most unlikely places and with the most duplicitous people.

Such was the case with the most meaningful person in my life . . . my husband.

There are basic personal and fundamental reasons why I believe in some of the practices and truths I have come to know in metaphysics.

I came to a crossroads in my life one day and my spiritual beliefs saved me.

For those who do not share my beliefs, I can only say that what I am about to describe is inexplicable, even to me. I therefore offer no explanation. It is the truth and it happened.

I had had many spiritual channeling sessions because of my interest in metaphysics. Channeling is a process by which a disembodied spiritual teacher or guide (some would say an angel) uses the body and mind of a chan- neler to impart information and teachings. Sometimes the information is correct, sometimes only partially cor- rect, sometimes not at all correct.

During one particular channeling session, I discussed my private life, especially my growing concerns regard- ing Steve and our marriage. The channeler stopped talk- ing. I wondered what was wrong. Then he spoke again as though he was about to make a difficult but necessary presentation.

"Your husband," he said, "is not what he says he is.

"He never lived in Japan with his father. In fact, the first time he was in Japan was as part of a USO enter- tainment group after the Second World War. His father was not a diplomat. He was a poor cobbler who was illiterate. His mother did not die when Steve was young, she left her family because life with them was too diffi- cult.

"Steve never served in the armed forces as he claims. He was a private first class who never left his base. He was obviously not one of the first troops into Hiroshima and he never adopted a Japanese child he called Sachiko. He is living now with a woman in Japan whom you are already aware of. What you are not aware of is that he has transferred most of the money you hold in your joint account to this woman's account. All the investments he has controlled over the years have been made in her name. He has been building a legal case for his style of living which in the event of a divorce, a judge in a court of law would claim you willingly endorsed. This has been the reason for desiring that your daughter live in Japan. The woman is there, his office is there, his life is there, so it was easier for him to manipulate the money away from you.

"He has more than tolerated your relationships with other men. In fact, he welcomed such possibilities as long as you didn't leave him.

"Your parents tried to warn you on several occasions, as did your daughter in her own way. I believe you received a letter to that effect which you disregarded because you knew your parents were prejudiced against Steve from the beginning.

"But when you presented your parents with a trip around the world and they found themselves in Japan, they asked questions of people closely associated with your husband. They summarily wrote you that there were too many parties, too much liquor, too many geishas, and too much reckless immorality. You did not wish to register this information because you knew they didn't like him.

"What they didn't understand was that it was worse than they perceived. Your husband betrayed you for material gain, and you will find if you investigate your finances that you are bankrupt."

I couldn't process what I heard. It was too shocking, but the next day I hired a detective and an attorney. I closed the bank accounts and waited.

I didn't hear from Steve.

A few weeks later I was apprised of the detective's findings, which verified *everything* the channeler had said, in graphic detail, fact by fact.

I called Steve in Japan. I told him what I had found out. There was a long pause. Then he said, "And you believe these things about me?"

I was surprised at how strongly I answered him. "Yes, I do," I said. "I'm shocked and really hurt, but yes, I think that you are not what you have led me to believe, in almost every way."

Another long pause. "Well," he answered finally, "I find this extremely sad."

I waited for an explanation. Then he said, "I'll come to LA right away. I'm very busy but we obviously need to talk."

For a moment I thought everything would be all right. Perhaps there was an underside to his story that I didn't know about. Then he said, "Will you send me some money?"

"No," I answered so firmly it shocked me.

There was another pause.

"Well," he said, "I guess I won't be living in the style to which I'm accustomed anymore."

"I guess not," I replied.

He said he would cable me his flight arrival information.

I waited. Nothing came. I called his office in Tokyo. He wasn't in the country. I continued to call his secretary. Finally she cabled me his flight arrival time. I was relieved.

I met the plane but he wasn't on it.

He cabled me his regrets and apologies and said he would contact me later. He never did.

The next time we met was during our divorce proceedings.

He looked at me sheepishly across the table. Then he shrugged. Point by point Steve's and my attorneys questioned him about his fabrications and his handling of the money I had earned over the years we were married. He admitted everything. When I asked him if the mob-kidnapping story in Vegas was true, he answered evasively. "It was better for Sachi to be in Japan." When I questioned him about Yves Montand's bet with him, he said he couldn't remember.

I sat looking at him, this stranger who had been my best friend for twenty-five years, this person whom I had believed and trusted and loved. I had been living a lie that had plummeted me into a jolting reality. And I was bankrupt. He had squandered millions and transferred the rest. I had to start all over and I was in my middle forties.

I had joined the ranks of successful female stars who had been betrayed and bilked out of a fortune by a husband who seemed to have played the role of understanding best friend/protector.

Steve was the best actor I had ever "worked" with and Hollywood had taught me to believe in illusion if I wanted to survive.

But Hollywood had also taught me something else: whenever a dreadful experience occurred, I could deal with it by asking myself, How did I contribute to this reality?

If I had the power to create or allow unhappiness and misery, I also had the power to uncreate it.

What Steve did was obvious; what I did was more subtle and took some searching. I decided to go through a course of past-life regressions, because I couldn't understand why I had drawn this to myself. I wanted to determine what Steve and I had perhaps meant to each other in some other time and place. I know how this must sound to people who have been through bitter divorces of their own, but since all reality in life is what you perceive it to be, this was and is mine.

As I lay on the table using the Chinese acupuncture technique of psychic regression, with an experienced facilitator, the truth I longed to understand came up in my mind like pictures. I saw that Steve and I had loved each other through aeons. That was why I loved and trusted him so much this time around. I saw that he had interrupted his own journey to the light to act as a teacher of discernment for me. Yes, he was a con man; yes, he was dishonest; yes, he was a cheat; but these traits were traits he chose to express during this lifetime so that he could serve others, namely me. Our meeting and loving was meant to be, and even today I feel he has been the most important person and teacher in my life. I think I drew him into my life to do just exactly what he did in order for me to learn. I am equally responsible as he for what happened. I didn't pay attention; I chose to remain blind, and in fact I aided and abetted his behavior by being so willing to avoid the stark truth.

As a matter of fact, during our divorce, the "mandatory settlement" judge not only allowed the money Steve had taken, he also claimed community property laws dictated that Steve was entitled to half of everything I'd ever make in the future because I had allowed and encouraged him to live the way he was living with no complaint. At first I was enraged and vowed to take our divorce to the Supreme Court if I had to.

Then something happened that was almost beyond my control. We were meeting in the judge's chambers. I began to sob from a place so deep I frightened the judge and Steve's lawyers as well as my own. I hardly knew what I was thinking. I heard myself say, "Give Steve whatever he wants now and in the future."

My attorney took my arm and tried to restrain me.

"What are you doing?" he pleaded. "Fight him. You know he doesn't deserve any more from you. He's bled you enough."

"It's worth it," I sobbed. I turned to Steve's attorneys and said, "Tell him he can have whatever he wants."

They left the chambers, presumably to call Steve.

"Why are you doing this?" asked my attorney.

"I don't know," I answered. "But I know it's right."

Steve's lawyers returned.

"Steve only wants a hundred and fifty thousand dollars spread out over ten years," said one of the attorneys.

My attorney nearly fainted. "This is how you win a divorce settlement?" he asked in confusion.

"I guess so," I answered. "Maybe there are other kinds of laws operating here."

He blinked. I left the judge's chambers.

Steve and I have never talked since. He and I both know in our own way what we meant to each other. We will meet again in some other time and place, of that I am sure. I wonder what we will remember? Another thing I am sure of: we will recognize each other and there will be love there.

I believe that each of us human beings serves ourselves and each other as we try to understand our soul's journey through time.

I believe that the people in our lives who hurt us the most are true servants to our learning. I believe it is time to get off the wheel of victimization and pay tribute to those who open our eyes, regardless of how harsh their methods might be. They are masters in their own way. They stimulate us to know ourselves.

Steve has been a master for me if for no other reason than because of him I became free of blinding dependence upon a man.

# Afterword
# JUST "DESSERTS"

*O*nce you've tasted the pungent, sweet-sour banquet of Hollywood and its lessons, you can't walk away from the table. It is with you forever. It rumbles inside you as an undigested feast, reminding you that you gobbled too much, too fast, with too rapid a relish, motivated by an urge to indulge yourself because it all could be taken from you.

Many of us like to say our real lives are conducted elsewhere, away from the sticky, seductive fame-and-fortune mongering that force us to confront how greedy and profane and corrupt we are all capable of being. In the real world, we feel that we "like" ourselves better. But that's because the real world doesn't challenge us the way Hollywood does.

Nowhere else in the world are we afforded the opportunity of seeing just how far we'll go to fulfill our fantasies. Since the fulfillment of visions, dreams, and desires becomes possible in Hollywood, what becomes more possible is the genial talent we have for sabotaging our emotional fulfillment as we achieve our longings.

I don't know many really happy people in Hollywood. There is always that *look* lurking behind the eyes of the accomplished. It's the look of "lostness." There is little "foundness" in the faces of the rich and famous who have achieved their champagne wishes and caviar dreams. Any one of them would be nostalgic for the days of struggle, when relationships seemed more meaningful, days more filled with passion and outrageous ideas, surroundings more precious because there was a deeper awareness of work and value. Struggle was how we identified ourselves, then as well as now, and without it we can feel bereft.

Hollywood is a land where the talented, accomplished, and wealthy live in two emotional territories simultaneously. We are not secure that we deserve what we have in a world that is suffering and predominately poor; yet we will do almost anything to ensure that we are never again part of that other world. We long for the meaning of the past, yet we never want it back again.

So where are we? We have not *found* the place in ourselves that is ready to embrace the abundant creativity we render for payment. It is somehow not all right that we love what we do and get paid outrageously for it. We find it hard to accept. We find we always need to do more to earn such a state of being. Our identification with struggle is so inbred and so profound that we can't let it go. We are not willing to esteem our dreams and allow ourselves to surrender to the accomplishment of them. Somehow we feel we need to struggle more, need to compete more, need to connive and strategize and manipulate in order to stay in the race. We presuppose that there *is* a continual race. Yet, we feel the race is never over. That it is neither won nor lost. It slows down, it speeds up. There is always someone gaining on us, so we fretfully look over our shoulders to calculate their oncoming speed—and meanwhile trip over a hole in front of us. Yet we discover that when we surrender to loss, the town often finds us again. Yet we can't establish an MO because the rules keep changing. Prediction is impossible. The only constancy is change.

And so we attend the succulent Hollywood banquet school with wide-eyed gluttony. We take what we can because if we don't, we feel somebody else will. We sometimes watch our fellow artists behave as though they were hungry monsters from an alien planet. We know there are impulses of those monsters in ourselves, and as we observe a loving and civilized friend behave like a crazed, enraged animal because his or her hidden buttons are pushed somewhere under the table of the sweet-and-sour feast, we see ourselves and we are afraid.

As we see some of our friends turned away from the table and can't determine why, or how we can help them, we wonder when and if it will happen to us. We always feel there are dictatorial hosts presiding over the banquet, handing down judgment on our talent, bequeathing or denying the prizes of rich and just "desserts."

We see relatives and children of our feted favorites scorned and needled into positions bestowed by nepotism, which is a guarantee of starvation, and we wonder if we would do the same.

We know that rejection is our fundamental fear, yet we place ourselves daily in situations that ensure it. Then bravely we adjust and go on. Is this foolish? When we are praised, applauded, and rewarded, we cry. Why? Out of relief at finally being loved and acknowledged?

Would any of us attend this mouthwatering feast if we had been loved enough as children? Are we here in this soul-shaking place because we were never noticed enough? Did we inherently understand that Hollywood was our golden key light so that attention would be paid?

If we traced each of our routes to this land of illusion, would we find similar baggage strewn along the road?

And we know we can never go back again. Once you're part of Hollywood, it is your home. The home of the heart of your dreams and your created reality, where the most evolved emotion is the sensitivity to have your feelings hurt without retaliating. You don't want to become a successful well-functioning unfeeling thing. You want to live a life behind your eyes without feeling lost, yet admitting there is so much to find, and you want to continually remind yourself that to retain the capacity to have your feelings hurt is proof that you are still learning.

This Hollywood cosmic school is internal and external. It is as big and as deep, or as limited and superficial as we wish to make it. It leads out that which is within us. It is our vision without end. It is our Alpha and our Omega. When we arrived, we had stars in our eyes, and when we lucky stars leave, it will be because the scenario has been decreed from above. Because no one ever really leaves Hollywood. No one really leaves unless they are called away by God. Even then, the impulse would be to come back again and make a movie about the experience.

# About the Author

SHIRLEY MACLAINE's accounts of her professional and personal journeys have all been national and international bestsellers, beginning with the publication of *"Don't Fall Off the Mountain"* in 1970. Six additional autobiographical works have followed: *You Can Get There from Here, Out on a Limb, Dancing in the Light, It's All in the Playing, Going Within,* and most recently, *Dance While You Can.*

*Explore the world of*

# Shirley MacLaine

---

## "DON'T FALL OFF THE MOUNTAIN"
___27438-4   $6.99/$8.99 in Canada

## YOU CAN GET THERE FROM HERE
___26173-8   $6.99/$8.99

## DANCE WHILE YOU CAN
___29786-4   $6.99/$8.99

## OUT ON A LIMB
___27370-1   $6.99/$8.99

## DANCING IN THE LIGHT
___27557-7   $6.99/$8.99

## IT'S ALL IN THE PLAYING
___27299-3   $6.99/$8.99

## GOING WITHIN
___28331-6   $6.99/$8.99

- - - - - - - - - - - - - - - - - - - - - - - - - - - - - - -

Ask for these books at your local bookstore or use this page to order.

Please send me the books I have checked above. I am enclosing $____ (add $2.50 to cover postage and handling). Send check or money order, no cash or C.O.D.'s, please.

Name _____

Address _____

City/State/Zip _____

Send order to: Bantam Books, Dept. NFB 40, 2451 S. Wolf Rd., Des Plaines, IL 60018
Allow four to six weeks for delivery.
Prices and availability subject to change without notice.          NFB 40 6/96